THE WORLD RESHAPED
Volume 1: Fifty Years after the War

From the same publishers

Richard Cobbold (*editor*)
THE WORLD RESHAPED
Volume 2: Fifty Years after the War in Asia

The World Reshaped

Volume 1: Fifty Years after the War in Europe

Edited by

Richard Cobbold
Director
Royal United Services Institute for Defence Studies

Foreword by

H.R.H. The Prince of Wales

First published in Great Britain 1996 by
MACMILLAN PRESS LTD
Houndmills, Basingstoke, Hampshire RG21 6XS
and London
Companies and representatives
throughout the world

A catalogue record for this book is available
from the British Library.

ISBN 0–333–65452–8 hardcover
ISBN 0–333–65453–6 paperback

First published in the United States of America 1996 by
ST. MARTIN'S PRESS, INC.,
Scholarly and Reference Division,
175 Fifth Avenue,
New York, N.Y. 10010

ISBN 0–312–16020–8

Library of Congress Cataloging-in-Publication Data
The World reshaped : volume 1: fifty years after the war in Europe / edited by
Richard Cobbold : foreword by HRH the Prince of Wales.
p.   cm. — (RUSI defence studies series)
Includes bibliographical references and index.
ISBN 0–312–16020–8
1. History, Modern—1945–   I. Cobbold, Richard.   II. Series.
D840.W68   1996
940.55—dc20   95–53536
                                                                                      CIP

© Royal United Services Institute for Defence Studies 1996

All rights reserved. No reproduction, copy or transmission of
this publication may be made without written permission.

No paragraph of this publication may be reproduced, copied or
transmitted save with written permission or in accordance with
the provisions of the Copyright, Designs and Patents Act 1988,
or under the terms of any licence permitting limited copying
issued by the Copyright Licensing Agency, 90 Tottenham Court
Road, London W1P 9HE.

Any person who does any unauthorised act in relation to this
publication may be liable to criminal prosecution and civil
claims for damages.

10   9   8   7   6   5   4   3   2   1
05   04   03   02   01   00   99   98   97   96

Printed in Great Britain by
Ipswich Book Co Ltd, Ipswich, Suffolk

Contents

Notes on the Contributors   vii

Foreword by HRH The Prince of Wales   xi

Introduction by Rear Admiral Richard Cobbold   xii

1 Europe: Past, Present and Future
   Geoffrey Till   1

2 The Liberation of Europe: Safeguarding the Legacy
   The Rt. Hon. Lord Carrington   15

3 The End of the War in Europe and of National-Socialist Tyranny
   President Richard von Weizsäcker   29

4 Don't Forget the Sea
   Admiral of the Fleet the Lord Lewin   43

5 An Address to the Council of Europe
   Tadeusz Mazowiecki   70

6 The North Atlantic Alliance: Yesterday, Today and Tomorrow
   Field Marshal Sir Richard Vincent   78

7 Why We Are Here: The New NATO and Its Vision of a New Europe
   General George A Joulwan   95

8 Thanks For The Memory
   Wing Commander Andrew Brookes   107

9 European Security
   Major Nicaise   119

10 Out of the Past Grows the Future
    Major Ralf Jung   126

11 Repression to Rejuvenation: Eastern Europe
    in a New Continent
    His Majesty King Michael of Romania   133

12 Brute Force and Genius: The View From The Soviet Union
    Dr Christopher Bellamy   146

13 Resistance and the Re-emergence of German Democracy
    Manfred Rommel   172

14 France in the Aftermath of War: 182

    France in 1945
    Pierre Miquel   182

    France and Germany Reconciled
    Jean Guitton   185

    The Construction of Europe 1945-1950
    Elisabeth du Réau   187

15 Sweden's Neutrality – A Debatable Balancing Act
    Lars Hjörne   194

16 Compendium of Articles From The RUSI Journal 1945-1989   204

    Index   242

Notes on the Contributors

Dr Christopher Bellamy has been Defence Correspondent of the *Independent* newspaper since April 1990. He has reported from recent wars in the Gulf in 1991, in Bosnia from 1992-94 and, most recently, from Chechnya in January 1995, where he was able to combine his background as a Russian military specialist with front-line reporting. Prior to joining the *Independent*, he was senior research analyst in the Centre for Defence Studies, University of Edinburgh, where he completed his PhD on the Russian and Soviet View of Future War under the supervision of Professor John Erickson. He was also consultant editor on the Soviet-German war for *The Times Atlas of the Second World War* (1989). Educated at the Royal Military Academy, Sandhurst and the Universities of Oxford, London, Westminster and Edinburgh, he interspersed service in the Army and Civil Service with his academic career before entering journalism.

Wing Commander Andrew Brookes was educated at Leeds and Cambridge Universities. After completing pilot training, he served on five Victor, Canberra and Vulcan squadrons. He has published eight books on aviation history and is a former RUSI Trench Gascoigne prize winner. He is currently a Group Director at the RAF Staff College. Andrew Brookes was born shortly before VE Day. He gives a *very personal* view of the development of post-war Europe before looking ahead to the future.

Rear Admiral Richard Cobbold CB FRAeS left the Royal Navy in 1994 after 33 years, having specialised in naval aviation and commanded three ships, most recently Second Frigate Squadron. In the late 1980s he held senior appointments at the MoD, including Director Defence Concepts, Assistant Chief of the Defence Staff (Joint Systems) 1992 to 1993 and ACDS Operational Requirements for Sea Systems to 1994. He was appointed Director of the Royal United Services Institute for Defence Studies in 1994.

The Rt. Hon. Lord Carrington has held several senior government posts including Secretary of State for Defence and Secretary of State for Foreign and Commonwealth Affairs. He was Secretary General of NATO from 1984 to 1988 and Chairman of the EC Conference on Yugoslavia from 1991 to 1992. He is currently a Director of Christie's International plc and The Telegraph plc.

Jean Guitton is a member of the Académie Française.

Lars Hjörne has recently retired as Editor-in-Chief of *Göteborgs-Posten*, Sweden's second largest morning daily (Liberal). He in now chairman of the Board and has handed editorial responsibility to his son, Peter. Shortly after the British government closed its Consulate General in Gothenburg – as part of a cost-cutting exercise – Lars Hjörne was appointed Honourary Consul General, a post in which he is still serving.

General George A Joulwan has held a variety of command and staff posts in four tours in Europe, two combat tours in Vietnam and several in Washington DC. He commanded US Southern Command in Panama before being appointed Supreme Allied Commander Europe in 1992.

Major Ralf Jung is an Officer in the Armoured Reconnaisance Group of the *Bundeswehr* and took part in the 36th Army General Staff course at the Leadership Academy of the *Bundeswehr* in Hamburg.

Admiral of the Fleet the Lord Lewin KG GCB LVO DSC has had a distinguished career in the Navy and Ministry of Defence, culminating in his appointment as Chief of the Defence Staff from 1979 to 1982.

Tadeusz Mazowiecki was a prominent member of Solidarity in the 1980s and Prime Minister of the first Solidarity government formed in 1989. He was Special Reporter on Human Rights in the Former Yugoslavia for the United Nations until his protest resignation in the Summer of 1995, following the fall of Srebrenica. He is a leading member of the Polish Parliament in the Freedom Union political party.

His Majesty King Michael of Romania, since his enforced exile in 1947, has been actively engaged in his country's affairs and lectures widely on the problems of transformation of Communist societies in Eastern Europe.

Notes on the Contributors

Major Nicaise serves in the French Army and has been a student at the College Interarmées de Défense from 1994 to 1995.

Elisabeth du Réau is a Professor at the Sorbonne-Paris III.

Manfred Rommel completed his Abitur in 1947 and went on to train as a lawyer at Tübingen University, working in regional government administration in Baden-Württemberg. He was first elected Mayor of Stuttgart in 1975, a post he continues to hold today, while continuing active involvement in regional and city politics as a member of the Christian Democratic Union (CDU). He is the recipient of a number of International Orders, including the French Knight of the Legion of Honour and a CBE from the United Kingdom.

Professor Geoffrey Till is Professor of History at the Department of History and International Affairs, Royal Naval College, Greenwich.

Field Marshal Sir Richard Vincent GBE KCB DSO is Chairman of the North Atlantic Military Committee at NATO Headquarters in Belgium.

President Richard von Weizsäcker trained as a lawyer at Oxford, Grenoble and Göttingen after serving in the Army during the War. He joined the CDU in 1950 and had a successful international business career. A keen Protestant churchman, Dr von Weizsäcker was Assembly President of the German Evangelical Church from 1964 to 1970. In 1969 he first entered the *Bundestag* and was CDU/CSU Floor Leader until 1981, when he became Vice-President of the *Bundestag*. In 1979 he became a member of the Berlin House of Representatives, from 1981 to 1984 serving as Governing Mayor of Berlin. From 1984 to 1994 he was President of the Federal Republic of Germany.

ST. JAMES'S PALACE

The 50th Anniversary of VE Day is one of those important occasions that should move us all to look back and remember, but also, if we are wise, to look forward from the present, armed with our knowledge of the past.

In commemorating the victory in Europe, our first duty is to recall the debt we owe to all those who fought to gain that victory, and to the many who gave their lives for us. We should remember the victims of war who died, dragged down by the horrors of Nazism in their own countries. But we should also recollect the huge sense of relief that greeted the end of the war in Europe; a relief felt not only by people in Britain, but also by our Allies and those liberated in the last months and days of the war. Moreover, there is little doubt that many people amongst our former enemies shared a sense of gratitude as they realised the nightmare was over.

The euphoria of VE Day, which we have all seen so vividly on the newsreels of the time, was soon to be dissipated in the difficult years that followed. The rebuilding of Europe, driven forward initially by the generosity of the United States, soon became enmeshed in the confrontation of the Cold War. But much of Europe was rebuilt and the achievements of the first four decades which followed the Second World War were remarkable. Now, the disintegration of the Soviet Union has given us a further opportunity for peace and prosperity throughout Europe. Already we can look forward to a future when a war between the countries of Western Europe is inconceivable. And we have the substantial task to extend the same sense of optimism to Central and Eastern Europe.

The end of the Cold War has left the world a more uncertain and unstable place, where those who seek progress and a better life for the people of our continent must be ready to apply fresh thinking to these new challenges. In this volume, the contributors look back, each from his own perspective, to show how the present has been fashioned out of the horrors of war and the rebuilding and confrontation which followed. They then look forward to a future when a lasting reconciliation may be achieved if we can continue to build on the foundations of mutual understanding and co-operation laid in Europe over the last fifty years.

Charles

Introduction

Rear Admiral Richard Cobbold

VE Day in 1945, certainly in Britain, belonged to Winston Churchill, and everyone from the King downwards shared in the celebrations. In his diaries, Field Marshal Sir Alan Brooke, the CIGS, described 8 May 1945 as 'a day disorganized by victory. A form of disorganization that I can put up with.' He goes on to describe his difficulty in getting to Buckingham Palace because of the impenetrable crowd outside...but he arrived in good time. 'The Prime Minister', Brooke noted with gentle irritation 'was very late and insisted on coming in an open car.'

But while Churchill was certainly prepared to revel in the public adulation on 8 May, five days later he was thinking ahead, warning against complacency after victory and the dangers of 'falling back into the rut of inertia, the confusion of aims and the craven fear of being great'. He saw the trials lying ahead for the United Nations as the Conference on International Organization began to do its work in San Francisco; perhaps he thought back to the time before the United States entered the war, to the Conference in August 1941 in *USS Augusta* and *HMS Prince of Wales*, to his first meeting with President Franklin D Roosevelt, and to the Atlantic Charter from which the United Nations grew, and arguably eight years later, NATO did also. Churchill saw the hard times ahead, and using his most purple prose exhorted the country 'Forward, unflinchingly, unswervingly, indomitable, till the whole task is done and the whole world is safe and clean.' And if we are optimistic, as we must be, we may consider we are still going forward.

Not many months later, in March 1946, Churchill reflected in Fulton Missouri on the outcome of Yalta :'From Stettin in the Baltic to Trieste in the Adriatic an Iron Curtain has descended across the Continent.' Stalin, most American newspapers and many Labour MPs denounced the speech, but the idea was to run and run in popular consciousness for more than four decades. Later in 1953, in cosily crafted phrases, he described the emerging strategy of deterrence as 'Indeed I have sometimes the odd thought that the annihilating character of these agencies may bring an utterly unforeseeable security of mankind', and more famously 'Safety will be the sturdy child of terror and survival the twin brother of annihilation'. Again in 1955, adumbrating the weakness of a 'Trip-Wire' he said: 'The policy of the deterrent cannot rest on nuclear weapons alone. We must, together with our NATO allies, maintain the defensive shield in Western Europe. Unless the NATO Powers had effective forces there on the ground and could make a front, there would be nothing to prevent piecemeal advance and encroachment by the Communists in this time of so called peace.'

Six months after postulating the Iron Curtain, Churchill addressed the subject of the future of Europe, in Zurich, with the same blend of vivid images and perceptive insights: '...over wide areas, a vast quivering mass of tormented, hungry, careworn and bewildered human beings gape at the ruins of their cities and homes, and scan the dark horizon for the approach of some new peril, tyranny and terror...we must build a kind of United States of Europe...the first step in the recreation of the European family must be a partnership between Britain and France.' If Churchill seemed almost awesomely prescient, the other futurologists of the class of '45 did not do uniformly well: if they made a fair attempt at the implication of nuclear weapons, they underestimated the pervasiveness of computer and information technologies; if they foresaw difficult times for the war's victors, they overlooked the prospects for a vigorous economic rejuvenation of the vanquished (though this was to be of far-reaching importance); if many expected the British Empire to suffer a sea-change into something new and strange, and Churchill's crystal ball seemed rather murky on this subject, they did not expect the Soviet empire to crumble and implode in the late 1980s. The emergence of the United States as the sole military Superpower of the mid-nineties merely restores the reality of 1945, but the Utopian dream enjoyed by many, more in hope than in good judgement, has broken up into multipolar instability, with glimpses of a demonic chaos thrust onto our unwilling consciousness by media images. The collapse of the Soviet Union, like that of Nazism, has not provided the 'end of history', but the need for effective international security organizations is as acute in the mid-1990s as it was in the late 1940s.

Needing is one thing, obtaining is different. Nationalism, tribalism, and religious extremism are but a few of the factors that will inhibit the more constructive drivers of vision, enlightened self-interest, generosity and pragmatism that should generate hope and confidence for the future. The problems and circumstances of today may be different from fifty years ago, but human aims may not have changed significantly.

The purpose of this book is to make connections between the Second World War and today, and to project into the future: to show how the difficulties and opportunities that we face now, have their roots in both the wartime and the Cold War periods. We have asked a number of writers, each with their own distinction and perspective, to write from their experiences, and where they can, to look ahead. We have complemented these essays with the texts of some outstandingly relevant speeches of recent years, with the thoughts of three middle-ranking officers from Britain, France and Germany, and, with a compilation drawn from the *RUSI Journal* over the past fifty years. The result is not comprehensive, nor is it intended to be, but like the accumulation of circumstantial evidence, the elements can be put in place and a picture emerges that is not tidy (but then nor is the world) but has colour and substance.

Perhaps the seminal essay is Geoffrey Till's, for it provides a framework into which the other essayists can place their work. A number of his themes are picked up by others, sometimes starting from different positions and reaching different conclusions. Geoffrey Till's historian's eye dominates, noting the similarities between the bounds of the European Coal and Steel Community and those of Charlemagne's Empire and the perennial European security dilemma of how to cope with the power of a united Germany. The answer, not least in the mind of Robert Schuman has been, since the end of the war, economic integration. The war split Europe into two, and the commonalities enjoyed by the western countries made it much easier to conceive of the area's integration; but Till also contends that the dissolution of the Soviet Union and the clear wishes of the central and eastern European states for links with the west, raises again the question of who the Europeans are. Till also writes that in this larger Europe, enlightened self interest has not yet outgrown rampant nationalism as events in Moldova, Chechnya and the former Yugoslavia show. He sees a stark choice on the future of Europe: whether all the sacrifices of the Second World War can be made worthwhile, or whether the advent of another such conflagration is just a matter of time. By implication, at least, he does not see a middle way. Finally and challengingly, he sees the European Community as likely, eventually to replace NATO at the heart of the European security system.

Lord Carrington touches on many of the same points; from his mildly ironic beginnings as a poorly armed leader of a defence-in-waiting on Britain's beaches in the summer of 1940, he writes with the immense authority of his experience, seeing the need for an expeditious NATO expansion to include East European countries, and the permanent need to maintain the Transatlantic relationship. He writes of safeguarding the legacy from the war, and asks particularly if the West has done well since the fall of the Soviet Union: he returns an open verdict, judging that Governments have not yet done enough to build strong, new, international security structures.

We reproduce a speech by President Richard von Weizsäcker, who sees VE day as a day of remembrance. In a most powerful, moving and frank speech, he acknowledges the enormity of the genocide of the Jews, and charges the older generation of Germans to be honest in their remembrance so that there may be reconciliation. He charges the young never again to be forced into the enmity and hatred of other people:

> 'Let us honour freedom.
> Let us work for peace.
> Let us respect the rule of law.
> Let us be true to our conception of justice.
> On this 8 May, let us face up as well as we can to the truth'.

Lord Lewin takes a look, over a much longer timescale, at Britain's maritime heritage. Rightly he sees the naval war of 1939 to 1945 as just one episode in a continuum when changes of technology and circumstance have not changed the core value of the use and control of the sea to Britain. Having traced the golden thread through the centuries, he sees potential dangers in the future if we are tempted to make further false economies in maintaining our maritime capability.

We then reproduce a speech by Tadeusz Mazowiecki, the former Prime Minister of Poland, to the Council of Europe in Strasbourg in 1990 on the occasion of Poland's accession to the Council of Europe. He talks of the aspiration of the states of Central and Eastern Europe, 'the rebirth of the Europe that virtually ceased to exist after Yalta'; and of the shared heritage, the unparalleled opportunities and the accompanying risks. Although he describes the quickening pace of events and the advances being made in so many areas, what he has to say remains entirely relevant today, so perhaps progress made only opens up new vistas of advances yet to be achieved. He ends by quoting Pope John Paul II on the peoples of West, Central and Eastern Europe: 'I feel I share the desire of millions of men and women who know they are linked by a common history and who hope for a destiny of unity and solidarity on the scale of this whole continent'. One is, nevertheless, tempted to hark back to Geoffrey Till's question of who these people are who seek to be pan-Europeans; is there real coherence, or are we destined to be divergent peoples struggling in a net of linkages that emphasizes the friction as much as the common?

And so to the military perspective and NATO. The contributions of Field Marshal Vincent and General Joulwan both, from different viewpoints, make clear that NATO is the uniquely successful security organization of our era, that it can adapt and has adapted, proactively. The story of NATO is central to the theme of the book, for the Alliance grew out of the Second World War, was the western bastion during the Cold War, and now faces a future in which doubters are vociferous, but for which it has potentially great strengths. Unsurprisingly those nations, particularly in Central Europe, who least take their security for granted, are most pressing in their desire to join a vigorous NATO. Although Field Marshal Vincent as Chairman of the Military Committee and General Joulwan as Supreme Allied Commander Europe each occupy a high central appointment within the Alliance, the alignment of their views is instructive since one is a European and the other American.

Three pieces from middle-ranking British, French and German officers follow. Half a generation on from today, their contemporaries may be at the top of the military tree in their respective countries having to sort out the problems left by the decisions that are taken today. Inevitably it is the problems that concern them, for the successes and the opportunities will be taken for granted. And thus middle-ranking officers are today training, teaching and influencing their successors half a generation removed again. It is, however, not so much a matter of passing on a torch, more a process of professional osmosis, a process moreover that should develop not only along the axis of time but also between allies, and most importantly between these three leading military countries in Europe.

The next part of the book contains five national perspectives from Romania, Russia, Germany, France and Sweden.

First in this section, King Michael of Romania looks at his country's transition from the devastation of war to the country's dolorous experience under Communism and how Romania emerged less well equipped and less appropriately led then other countries similarly placed, to take advantage of opportunities arising from the removal of the Ceausescus. He argues strongly against the introduction of a two-tiered approach to integration into Europe and NATO since this would be both self-perpetuating and dangerous. It is a remarkable essay from a leader in exile, part disinterested, part committed, illuminating brightly the concerns and ambitions of one country amongst the renewed Central European democracies. Democracy looks to be a fragile flower in Romania and King Michael sees the need for a new start, hopefully after the 1996 elections.

Christopher Bellamy writes on the Soviet Union following the dominant but conflicting traits of brute force and genius. Perhaps the key interlinked points are the enormous human sacrifices made by Russia in the Second World War, far more than the conventional figure of 20 million dead, and the ruthless will to win overwhelmingly. This was carried through to the unremitting continuation of the struggle after the war with little consideration for the chronic suffering of the Russian people. In this lay the roots of a military Superpower eventually unsustainable by the sterile economy. The Soviet Union for some years after the war did not look on atomic weapons as anything more than a powerful tactical tool, and saw their ability to absorb nuclear strikes as part of their military capability. Bellamy also traces the expansionist tendency of the Soviet Union, and the development of the Soviet Navy, which again brought unsustainable success. Now Russia again faces enormous challenges, not least to rebuild the state. Sometimes it is tempting to wonder if the right things have been remembered, and the wrong things forgotten. Russia remains as Churchill remarked: 'a riddle wrapped in a mystery inside an enigma'. But Churchill continued: 'but perhaps there is a key. That key is Russian national interest.' The problem for the West is to identify what that interest is at any particular time, and whether the Russians think the same.

Looking back to the turbulent times of the War, Manfred Rommel traces the path of the Treaty of Versailles through the often hidden paths of the German resistance. For all the attempts, the resistance did not succeed and Rommel recognizes how the generosity of the settlement of the Second World War by the United States, Britain and France allowed democracy to flourish in the German republic in a way it could not after 1919. Democracy, he concludes, must be nurtured, and the people must be well informed and vigilant.

To cover the perspective from France, we have produced three short pieces from distinguished academics. Pierre Miquel of the Sorbonne looks at the state of France in the immediate aftermath of the war – devastated, demoralised, fragmented – and how de Gaulle gave back the spirit to his country, centralizing power, and napoleonically opposing party activists. But the Fourth Republic adapted to the post-war world without him and in January 1946 de Gaulle retired grumpily to Colombey-les-Deux-Eglises to await his recall. Next Jean Guitton, of the Académie Français, provides a personal impression of the deeply rooted mutual dependence of France and Germany. Finally, Elisabeth de Réau, also from the Sorbonne, traces the construction of Europe from 1945 to 1950, describing the beginning of the European idea.

Last in this section, Lars Hjörne looks back at Sweden's involvement in the Second World War, blending a journalist's scepticism with his own youthful experiences. He highlights the spectrum of opinions and doubts that were prevalent at the time in Sweden, and exemplifies how much that was done was good, and how some things should have been done better. But it is difficult not to conclude that Sweden's prolonged affair with neutrality and non-alignment is becoming more difficult to sustain, and that her future lies in security integration, as well as economic integration, with Europe.

Finally, we have tracked through fifty years of the *RUSI Journal* and put together a compendium from the collected wisdom of the Institute and its visitors. Needless to say, in the harsh security of hindsight, some of the wisdom has aged better than other parts, and some of the predictions may be judged more percipient than others. But I think that our survey does show that the Institute has consistently been trying to address the relevant issues, and we must continue to do this, and attempt to do it well.

And at the end of it all, there is the question: so what? Clearly we cannot deduce a systematic prescription, but I hope that we might be able to see some of our problems with the extra dimension that the different perspectives give. Perhaps we should go back to 1945. President Roosevelt died less than a month before VE day and the 50th anniversary of his death was sparingly marked in London: this was the American to whom Britain owes a debt greater than to any other. In an undelivered address for Jefferson Day, the day after he died, Roosevelt would have described this vision: 'The work my friend is peace. More than an end to this war – an end to the beginnings of all wars.' Churchill, to whom Roosevelt cabled: 'It is fun to be in the same decade as you', was closely attuned to the views of his old friend, but rather more sceptical: '...the day may dawn when love of one's fellow-man, respect for justice and freedom, will enable tormented generations to march forth serene and triumphant from the hideous epoch in which we have to dwell. Meanwhile never flinch, never weary, never despair.' At a time when the roles of the military are changing and when there seems to be a widening gap between military realities and public and media perceptions, perhaps the last word should go to Field Marshal Sir Alan Brooke, who wrote prosaically on VE Day; 'I do feel it is time the country was educated as to how wars are run and strategy constructed.' That may not be a full answer to the 'So What?' question, but it goes some of the way, in an important direction.

1 Europe: Past, Present and Future

Geoffrey Till

INTRODUCTION

For many centuries European history has been moulded by the desire of some of its leaders to create some sort of unity out of diversity, in order to create the conditions needed for peace and prosperity. Their aim was to produce a system that deterred aggression, insulated by-standers from the effects of unrest and turmoil in particularly difficult parts of the continent and which, in a general way, encouraged political, social and economic convergence. These were certainly the aims of the Congress and Conference systems of early 19th Century Europe. At that time, five of Europe's leading powers preserved the *status quo*, contained internal instability and deterred inter-state conflict. Because they could not agree on the rules for intervention, the focus of the system returned about mid-century to an alternative reliance on the striking of beneficial balances of power between the independent states of Europe. The disproportionate growth of German power opened the way for the United States to participate in the system too.

Because many thought the balance of power caused the First World War, there was a revival afterwards of the earlier concept of European community. The idea petered out in the 1930s under the pressure of what seemed to be so much more dramatic ways of uniting great areas of Europe – by force. The result of that was the Second World War. But will the human catastrophe of the Second World War prove to be the decisive event changing the historic structure of Europe into permanently more benign forms?

THE REBIRTH OF THE EUROPEAN IDEA

Surveying the wreckage of post-war Europe in November 1945, Winston Churchill described what he saw as '...a charnel house, a rubble heap, a breeding ground for pestilence and war.' Yet until then, Europe had been the effective centre of the world. What had brought this proud continent to such a state? Significantly, people who had distinguished themselves in the resistance movements of occupied Europe were amongst those who most strongly argued that Europe had a common identity which was not recognised by its existing institutions. Its main troubles arose from a failure to recognise this simple fact and so were essentially self-inflicted. In effect, the Second World War in Europe was a civil war. The problem arose from the Europeans' tendency to identify themselves with the nation states in which they happened to be living, and therefore not to realise that these nation states were a comparatively recent aberration in the broad historical sweep of European events. The nation state was not the rule, it was the exception. For evidence of this, the more historically minded pointed to the determining influence across the centuries of the great European empires and were apt to point, for example, to the unnerving similarities between the borders of the European Coal and Steel Community and those of Charlemagne's empire. What was needed to avert further disaster was a conscious campaign to remind the Europeans of everything they had in common, and a political programme to defend and extend it.

In the immediate post-war period, there seemed plenty of evidence to support the notion that there were indeed common patterns of interest and behaviour across the continent. Between 1945 and 1950 for example, most countries of Europe experienced a swing to the left in the composition of their governments. Social democrats, socialists and communists joined forces in a campaign to reconstruct their shattered economies and to create lands fit for heroes to live in. Only in Germany, with the arrival of Konrad Adenauer, was there a significant exception to this leftward trend, but even he was clearly to the left of his predecessor. But in the early 1950s, the pendulum seemed to swing the other way, with the arrival of conservative consolidators like Britain's Harold Macmillan or France's General de Gaulle. The left-wing parties of the earlier decade likewise shifted towards the centre. Perhaps the reward for this in the 1960s was their return to government in Britain, Germany and elsewhere. Left-wing radicalism however also re-appeared and played a significant part in the dethronement of General de Gaulle and led to a wave of student protest across the continent that affected Amsterdam, Berlin, Paris, even London. Ethnic groups operating below the level of the traditional nation state (the Celts, Walloons, Flemings, Basques, Bretons and so on) also seemed to threaten existing institutions.

Good and bad, all these common currents seemed to underline the point that Europe did indeed have a great deal in common. This was particularly true in the economic field. In the immediate aftermath of war, Europe was devastated, with 60 million refugees and homeless, with national bankruptcy threatening the victors as well as the vanquished, and with revolution in the air. Plainly, ordinary methods and orthodox assumptions could not cope with such a shambles. In the war, the British, Russians, Americans and eventually the Germans had shown what a national, governmental, approach to industrial mobilisation could achieve. Perhaps the same could be true for the post-war reconstruction of Europe? The tremendous expansion of the French economy owed much to Jean Monnet's Commissariat General, and exemplified the extension of the state's role in the economy that held true across Europe. But the 'Europeans' like Monnet and Robert Schuman went further, and argued that it was not enough for the nations to run their own economies. These would only work properly if Europe were treated as an economic unit, transcending political boundaries. This was the origin of the Schuman Plan – an amazingly ambitious attempt to rationalise the iron, coal and steel industries of the European heartland. The resultant treaty to set up the European Coal and Steel Community was signed in April 1951. Symbolically, the treaty was printed in France, using German ink on Dutch vellum. The Belgians provided the parchment for the cover, the Italians the ribbon and Luxembourg the glue to stick it all together.

The ECSC was undoubtedly an economic success. It also provided valuable experience of harmonisation and encouraged further ventures along the road to integration. Thus, in June 1955 at Messina, the establishment of both EURATOM and the European Economic community was discussed. The Treaty of Rome followed two years later. The EEC also proved an economic success and in due course provided strong incentives for countries reluctant, or unable, to join in 1957 eventually to do so.

It had always been at the back of Schuman's mind that economic integration could also solve one of the great problems of European security, namely the over-mighty power of a united Germany. The division of Germany after the Second World War had perhaps ameliorated the problem, but few thought it a permanent solution. Plans to de-industrialise the whole country – to turn it into a kind of central European cabbage patch – foundered on the simple fact that Germany's economic recovery was essential to Europe's well-being as well as to the future good neighbourliness of the German people. Schuman's Coal and Steel Community, however, went a long way towards solving the problem since integrating the Ruhr into the rest of the region by this means should make war not only unthinkable but materially impossible. The EEC should do the same, but on a grander scale, especially if it were to develop a political identity.

The result of all this was a process that increasingly encouraged the erstwhile adversaries of the Second World War to think of themselves as Europeans. In some cases, this tendency was encouraged by another historic development that derived in large measure from the experience of the Second World War, namely the abandonment of Empire.

The extent to which countries felt 'European' seemed to be inversely related to how much real estate they occupied outside Europe. Certainly, the remaining Imperial powers of 1945, namely the French, British and Portuguese, were amongst the most suspicious of the notion of an integrated Europe. But a rising tide of anti-colonialism, the demonstrated weaknesses of the Europeans, especially in the Far East between 1941-5, and pressing economic, social and strategic problems at home, led inexorably to the dissolution of their empires – at a rate far faster than almost anyone had anticipated. Accordingly, there was a shift in their political and strategic interests back towards Europe, that mirrored the parallel regionalisation of their economic activity.

EUROPE AND THE COLD WAR

Far from ushering in an era of peace and reconciliation, the Second World War seemed instead simply to plunge Europe into another long period of conflict and danger. Even before the end of the Second World War, the United States and the Soviet Union were beginning to think of themselves as adversaries rather than as continuing allies, with Europe as the new battleground. The United States was alarmed at Russia's apparent expansionism in Eastern Europe, the continued hostility of her ideology, the oppressive nature of her Stalinist regime and her reluctance to run down her armed forces from high wartime levels.

For its part, the Soviet government claimed that the West had been implacably hostile to the Revolution since its very inception, and that the Americans were now using their monopoly in nuclear weapons to interfere in the various self-defence arrangements in Eastern Europe, which bitter experience had shown it was necessary for the Russian people to make.

During the late 1940s, both Superpowers consolidated their own halves of Europe. The Soviet Union took much of Eastern Europe into its own sphere and sought to turn it into a political, economic and military collectivity. The United States committed itself to the political and economic security of Western Europe through the Marshall Aid programme and the Truman doctrine of 1947/8. Lastly, Soviet expansionism was 'contained' militarily by a structure of security alliances culminating in the signing of the NATO treaty in 1949.

The polarisation between East and West was completed in the summer of 1950 with the Korean war. Since Europe was thought to be probably the main constituent of the global power balance, it inevitably became the epicentre of the Cold War, although the reverberations of this struggle spread across the world.

In defence of their positions, both Superpowers in effect adopted a policy of Massive Retaliation in the 1950s. Conventional forces were thought to be much less important to the resolution of future conflicts, and in fact were significantly reduced by both sides. Instead, everyone expected the threatened or actual use of nuclear weapons to be a key element in the resolution of every major dispute between the great powers, not least in Europe.

Against this sombre background, the world lurched from one crisis to another. In 1956, the Suez operation divided the West at a time when the Russians were brutally suppressing the Hungarian uprising. In 1957, the launch of the Sputnik shattered America's military self-confidence, inspiring alarmist fears of a Soviet lead in nuclear weaponry. Then there was the second and third round of the long-drawn out Berlin crisis. In 1960 relations were further embittered by the U-2 spy-plane affair, the consequent collapse of the Paris Peace Conference and Berlin Wall crisis. In June 1963, President Kennedy told the enraptured crowds 'Ich bin ein Berliner.' Literally this translates as 'I am a doughnut!' but everybody knew what he meant. It was quite a dangerous time.

In several of these crises, politicians at least considered the use of nuclear weapons to respond to situations impossible to resolve by other means. The more common and powerful nuclear weapons became, however, the less credible this kind of 'extended deterrence' was thought to be. With both Superpowers (but with the United States in a marked lead) in the 1960s and 1970s moving away from the apparent strategic simplicities of the 1950s towards the greater reliance on conventional forces and tactical and theatre nuclear weapons that was the hall mark of strategies of 'Flexible Response', Europe became, with this, even more of an armed camp.

Despite the success of related attempts to control the dangers inherent in nuclear weaponry, all was not, however, harmony and light. In Europe, there was considerable shock when the Soviet Union felt it necessary in 1968 to suppress division within the ranks of the Warsaw Pact by invading Czechoslovakia. Nevertheless, NATO pursued the double-barrelled 'Harmel Doctrine' of offering the Soviet Union a resolute defence on the one hand, but actively attempting to improve relations on the other, especially through the arms control process. Through the 1970s, relations between the two sides slowly improved.

Relations between the two sides became rather more tense in the early 1980s, although they never approached the levels of tension common in the 1950s and although they were by now much less focused on Europe than they had been. Reacting to such technological and strategic challenges as the American Strategic Defence Initiative and the Maritime Strategy put tremendous strain on the Soviet military-industrial complex, and played a large role in persuading Mr Gorbachev to seek improved relations with the West and to reduce the burden that military expenditure was putting on an economy that was clearly failing anyway. With that, he ushered in a process that quite unexpectedly led to the collapse of Communism and the Soviet Union, the end of the Cold War, the fall of the Berlin Wall and the end of the 40 year old division of Europe on the one hand, and between the old allies of the Second World War on the other.

As far as the political shape of Europe was concerned, the strategic competition between the two Superpowers during the Cold War era had two main consequences. Firstly, their rivalry drew a line through Europe, splitting the continent into halves. The Western half had a good deal more in common with itself than the whole of Europe would have had, and it therefore became much easier than it otherwise would have been to conceive of the areas integration. Even more importantly, the US Marshall Aid programme of 1947-50 (designed to 'permit the emergence of political and social conditions in which free institutions can exist') provided much needed capital, but on condition that its recipients collaborated in its sensible use. Stalin saw this as dollar imperialism and rejected it (thereby confirming the division of Europe) but Western Europe eagerly grasped and developed the opportunity such largesse represented and set up the Organisation for European Economic Cooperation to administer it. The OEEC pioneered the way for the Coal and Steel and the European Economic Communities of the next decade, thereby considerably accelerating progress towards integration. Moreover, as part of the 'Grand Design' of an Atlantic Alliance between the United States and Europe, American leaders often went out of their way to encourage the Europeans to cooperate with each other, if only to reduce the burden the United States would otherwise have to bear in their common defence.

With the end of the Cold War, however, new consequences for European togetherness seem to be emerging. On one hand, the likelihood of a consequently reduced American military and diplomatic presence in the area would automatically 'Europeanise' its political and security structures. On the other, the dissolution of the old Soviet empire and the clear interest of the new national leaders of the region in political and economic linkages with their Western neighbours raised in its acutest form, the age old question of who the Europeans are. This question is likely to dominate the European agenda for the next few years.

INTEGRATION: COUNTERVAILING PRESSURES

Nationalism, a comparatively ancient impulse, was not interred alongside its victims in 1945. It remained, and indeed remains, a significant force in modern Europe, acting as a continuing constraint on the progress towards European integration that so many resistance fighters had wanted to see. If Europe were indeed to take on new forms it would only be able to do so to the extent and in the areas that nationalist considerations permitted.

In the early days, the influences of nationalism revolved around the tense relations between Britain, Germany and France. The initially difficult relationship between the French and the Germans over such issues as the strategic potential of the Ruhr were solved by the Coal and Steel Community as already described. But the defence of Western Europe against the Bolshevik hordes in the East plainly required the re-armament of Germany in a form acceptable to France and other countries that had only recently been occupied by the *Wehrmacht*.

The initial scheme to solve the problem, through the creation of a European Defence Community, foundered in 1954 on the opposition of Britain and France to the consequent loss of their strategic independence and this created something of a crisis in confidence between the Europeans and the Americans. The creation of the Western European Union in the same year, together with treaty arrangements leading to the stationing of substantial British forces in West Germany, solved the problem and facilitated German admission to NATO in 1955. Since then, Franco-

German relations have become much better than ever they had been before the Second World War, and from the late 1960s, leaders of the two countries in fact became amongst the staunchest advocates of further steps towards integration.

The traditional rivalry between France and Britain, while less virulent, was not so easily managed. It reached its post-war apogee in the time of General de Gaulle, whose public view that the British were too Atlanticist and insufficiently European, caused him to veto their belated application to join the European Community. Infuriating though this was to a British political establishment that had come to the reluctant conclusion that its economic future lay in Europe, de Gaulle's rejection was privately regarded with some equanimity by many federalists. While the European Community managed to survive the Gaullism of the French, it may not have done if confronting the Gaullism of the British as well. The British had perforce to regard their continental commitment as being expressed largely through their leading role in NATO, a habit of thought persisting long after their eventual entry into the Community in 1973.

As far as the rest of Europe was concerned, the traumatic experience of war and/or brutal occupation during the Second World War showed the limits and the dangers of basing one's security on illusory ideas of sovereignty and national independence. Typically, the smaller countries of Europe (most obviously the Benelux countries) were at the forefront of this new realism and in many ways urged on the progress towards integration. In the eastern half of the Continent the destructive forces of local nationalism, which had played so signal a part in twice plunging Europe into catastrophic war, were brutally suppressed by the Soviet Union. Whatever this did for the democratic values of the East Europeans, at least it provided 40 years of stability in the region.

All this shows that nationalism was still a significant factor in shaping the fortunes of post-war Europe, but that it, perhaps unexpectedly, took forms, or was dealt with in ways, that were broadly helpful to the cause of European integration. But in more recent times, and especially with the ending of the Cold War, there have been many signs of a revival in European nationalism, as a political force within the political systems of many leading West European states, or as forces that have created turmoil, war or its prospect, in much of Eastern Europe. The comforting notion that enlightened economic self-interest would consign old-fashioned nationalism to the dustbin of history has been shown to be an illusion, at least in places like Moldova, Chechenya and the former Yugoslavia. Even in Western Europe, domestic politics have taken a noticeably more nationalistic, though not necessarily malignant, turn. In all its forms, however, nationalism will remain a severe brake on progress towards European integration.

This might also be the effect of events and developments within the domestic political environments of the leading states of Europe. The politicians making the decisions about the present and future evolution of Europe were, and remain, the representatives of electorates who elected them largely for domestic rather than European reasons. As it happened, though, domestic events in the main European states in the first few post-war decades tended to produce leaders who eventually became good Europeans. This was always true for the smaller countries and for Germany, and became true for France with the departure of General de Gaulle in 1969. However in Britains' case, for nearly the first 30 years, domestic politics produced leaders who kept the British out of Europe – but that perhaps also helped the cause of European integration, for the reasons already discussed.

Nonetheless, more recently, in the unexpectedly slow and painful process of ratifying the Treaty of Maastricht for example, there has been much evidence that the peoples of Europe have far more parochial concerns and preoccupations than the visionaries might have expected 40 years after the signing of the Treaty of Rome. Others would put a different gloss on the matter. It is remarkable how much progress has been made in the past 40 years given the historic strength of nationalism and national or sectoral concerns generally. The Union's problems over the past several years have nonetheless been an emphatic reminder of the persisting strength of the nationalistic and domestic constraints on integration.

THE FUTURE OF EUROPE

So what is likely to be the future of Europe? Will it be one which will be seen to have made the sacrifice of the Second World War all worthwhile, or will it be one that may make another such conflagration merely a matter of time ?

As far as challenges to the future security of the region is concerned, in NATO, the WEU, the European Union and the OSCE, Europe certainly has a diversity of means by which it can respond. These organizations are all leading elements in Europe's new security system. They are all intended to build collective security, manage disorder and encourage convergence, especially in the general social, economic and political sense. They all have something distinctive to offer.

We therefore seem to be moving into a period dominated not by a balance of power but by a balance of institutions, in which all these organizations will find a place in a new European security system. The question is the relationship between them, and their relative importance. Which will be at the centre, around which the others revolve ?

The European Union is an obvious contender. Its advocates argue that this is an ancient idea whose time has finally come. Only when the Europeans integrate will they finally be able to put the seal on the long tragic experience that culminated in the Second World War. It would create a healthy balanced security relationship with the United States and with the new Russia. It would also finally solve 'the German problem.' The advocates of union also emphasise the irresistible economic momentum propelling the Europeans together, whether many of them like it or not.

To them, the security conclusion seems inescapable. Europe will develop a security identity dimension and many Europeans would see it supplanting NATO at some stage. The Franco-German Corps of May 1992 can be seen as a second attempt to begin to achieve what the European Defence Community of the 1950s so signally failed in doing. In the shorter term, however, the *economic* thrust of European policy would appear to be exactly what is needed on Europe's geographic margins to the east and the south. In the future, the security agenda will also be affected, and perhaps even dominated, by broader issues such as human rights, environmental degradation and resource depletion. In the past,

NATO's scientific committee has in fact produced specialist reports in surprising areas – 'The Preservation of the Coliseum (against car-related pollutants)' was one – 'The Disposal of Municipal Sludge' another. But the EC will surely be a much more natural forum for such issues than NATO. For all of these reasons, the EC is likely eventually to replace NATO at the heart of the European security system.

There are nonetheless reasons to be cautious about the speed of this development, even if its eventual likelihood is conceded. The Union's fragilities have been displayed at every stage in the negotiation and ratification of the Maastricht agreement. While nearly all Europeans would emphasise the need for reconciliation after the experience of the Second World War and the Cold War, very many would deny that increased togetherness necessarily implies integration. Nor would they necessarily accept that growing economic interdependence is a phenomenon that can be restricted to Europe. For some Europeans, therefore, Maastricht goes too far; for others it does not go far enough. The Europeans are also divided in the extent of their sensitivity to the Atlantic connection. While all, or nearly all, are anxious not to exclude the Americans from European affairs, some are more willing to take risks on this point than others. This does not make it easy to achieve consensus in the construction of new security frameworks for Europe.

But, with the inclusion of more parts of Europe, the widening of political and economic cooperation is likely to be at the expense of the deepening of existing relations, since it will make economic convergence and political consensus more difficult to achieve. While economic interdependence will inexorably encourage federation, there remain acute concerns for the political and cultural identities of the region's constituent populations. These feelings may not make economic sense, but they are nonetheless deeply felt. The ambitions of the federalists are also likely to be frustrated by the domestic, economic and political particularities faced by the national leaders. There will always be sensitive forthcoming elections, ongoing crises and preoccupations at home, specific local economic problems that encourage prevarication and delay. 'Give me perfect harmonisation, Oh Lord', such leaders might say, echoing St Augustin, 'but not yet.'

Despite all this, the Pan-Europeans are likely to be right in the long run. The structural reform of the Common Agricultural Policy shows that substantial reforms *are* possible. Moreover, over the 1980s we have seen a coalescence on foreign and defence policy (for example in the Gulf in the 1980s) which, while still a long way short of unanimity, has reached a level that most Europeans of the 1960s would have regarded as extraordinary. A return to the level of regional fragmentation and tension characteristic of the first half of the Twentieth Century now seems inconceivable.

Even so, it will clearly be a very long time before the EC is able to assume the leading role in the European security order.

The Western European Union has always been a mechanism for the solution of problems of European integration, rather than an actor in its own right, and this seems unlikely to change. It does have, and has recently displayed, a defence competence. As a means of demonstrating the capacity for military cooperation it compares well to most other regional security organisations, even if it does not yet pretend to the cohesion of NATO. It could certainly be a convenient mechanism by which European collaboration is extended outside Europe, or even, conceivably inside it. The recent assigning of forces like the Franco-German Corps and the UK/NL Amphibious Group gives it more *gravitas,* but is carefully designed to avoid threatening NATO's interests.

The Organisation for Security and Cooperation in Europe comprises 53 countries and has recently changed its name and produced a number of permanent institutions constructively distributed around the capitals of eastern and central Europe. Its principle of unanimity, its breathtaking diversity and its lack of a military or an economic structure must inhibit its prospects as the centrepiece of the new European order. Its achievements either in the August coup or in the former Yugoslavia have not been encouraging. Its main achievement, the CFE agreement, now looks to many to be an irrelevance. While it will certainly encourage convergence, it has not so far been impressive as a collective security organisation, and it is hard to conceive of its ever being able to take over from NATO.

NATO itself will certainly change and be revised. It will probably remain at the centre of the new European order at least into the next century. It has an impressive track record in inhibiting political dispute between the Europeans, and in facilitating the military cooperation between them that their individually constrained defence budgets require. It keeps the United States in Europe, and its military institutions have so far proved surprisingly resilient and robust. For these reasons, NATO has been able to develop mutually beneficial relations with the other institutions of Western security, enveloping the WEU and striking a mutually beneficial relationship with the OESC and with central and eastern Europe, through the North Atlantic Cooperation Council and Partnership for Peace.

For all these reasons, NATO has been adapted to meet the change in its circumstances, a process starting with the London declaration of July 1990. The emphasis is now on positive multilateral cooperation against the common enemies, now not rogue states, but general conflict and instability. Whatever its long-term future and centrality to European security, the fact that it now comprises, in a variable but nonetheless effective and regional form, all the erstwhile adversaries of the Second World War, including the United States and Russia, strengthens the claim of what might be called 'the NATO system' to be regarded as the chief mechanism for European post-war and post-Cold War reconciliation as we approach the end of the Twentieth Century.

2 The Liberation of Europe: Safeguarding the Legacy

The Rt. Hon. Lord Carrington

We now seem to be in a period of reminiscence, accompanied I suppose, with a dash of nostalgia for lost youth, though not going so far as to wish for a repeat performance of the Second World War. But perhaps at any rate for those of my generation who are fast disappearing, there are some lessons to be learned from our experience before and during the Second World War.

LESSONS OF THE PAST

We all of us learned some lessons from those days and sometimes learned them rather painfully and at first hand. Clearly, the first one was that of unpreparedness.

I joined the Army 56 years ago, or 58 years ago, if you count Sandhurst as the army – and as a University of Life it was not a university and not much of a life. I remember being struck, even at the age of 19 on joining my Regiment, at the curiously leisurely and lethargic way in which we all seemed to be preparing for the inevitability of a Second World War, astonished not least at the lack of equipment. Three months before the outbreak of war, we were, in exercises using flags instead of Bren guns, and broomsticks instead of anti-tank rifles. In the event, broomsticks were just as effective as the Boyes anti-tank rifle!

But oddly enough, morale in the Services was enormously high and even after the debacle of Dunkirk, which we have somehow managed to almost transform into a victory, it never occurred to many of us that there was any possibility of losing the war.

I remember in the Summer of 1940, guarding three and a half miles of beach between Hythe and Folkestone, with 48 Guardsmen, 46 rifles, two Bren Guns and my pistol and reflecting with great sympathy on the appalling fate of any German division which landed on my beach.

We were, of course, very naive and no doubt stupid, but morale and leadership plays an enormous part in our attitudes, and nobody who was alive at the time can ever forget the effect of Winston Churchill – his presence, his manner, his speeches, his determination and his courage, and what a decisive effect it had on all of us.

I find the revisionism of some of those who are writing today repellent – most of them were not around at the time and those who write about Winston Churchill, such as that loyal patriot Mr Ponting, reveal more about themselves and their motives than they do about that great man. So, preparedness and morale and leadership were two of the lessons which came out of the war. There was another one, curiously enough, which hasn't much to do with defence but quite a lot to do with what happened domestically and politically after the war. All of us, from the most diverse backgrounds, were thrown together in a way which would have been inconceivable in peacetime.

Of my tank crew of five including myself, we all slept in a hole underneath our tank, cooked together and ate together from our 14-man pack. Incidentally, only the military could have devised a 14-man pack to be divided for use between five people – and we each learnt something from the other. Three of my tank crew had been unemployed in the 1930s, and had almost certainly joined the army because they were frustrated and hungry. I could not have found better or more splendid and robust companions. I learned something from that.

DESTRUCTION

Misfortune is not usually self-inflicted. Whilst Germans believed from their inter-war experience that inflation was the cause of their political problems, we in Britain of my generation felt that the greatest social evil was unemployment.

Towards the end of the war, we saw the devastation and misery and homelessness of the German towns and German people, the hundreds of thousands of displaced persons wrenched from their homeland. Our main reaction was of the horror and the senselessness of it all. Not of the cause for which we were fighting – if we wished to retain our way of life, it was necessary to defeat the evils of the Nazis – but the human folly of Western civilised people so conducting their affairs. I remember very vividly the appalling destruction of Hamburg and Cologne, where, in that city of one million or so people, there remained only around one hundred houses not damaged.

THE END OF WAR?

Many of my generation were determined to see that such a catastrophe should never happen again. We did not want to see that happening to our children and to our grandchildren. Of course, there was a feeling of relief, a feeling that we had come through it all and won, but equally an awareness that we had an obligation to try to prevent another world catastrophe.

Russia and 'Uncle Joe'

There are those who sit comfortably in their studies writing books cataloguing the mistakes that the Americans and British made at the end of the war. For example, not to tackle the Russians, once and for all. That is gravely to misunderstand the mood of the country in 1945. In the first place, we were extremely tired, and I doubt whether it would have been very easy to galvanise the British and Americans into fighting another bloody war against the victorious and very powerful Soviet Union.

But, more importantly, the Russians were great heroes, as indeed they deserved to be for the stupendous efforts they made on the Eastern front. 'Uncle Joe', as he was called in the British newspapers, was an enormously popular figure. There was no way that public opinion could have been mobilised against the Soviet Union.

It was only after the political conquest of Eastern Europe, the iron hand of communism descending upon those countries, which had once been part of Europe, and now 50 years later, once again part of it, that public opinion began to be aware of the dangers of the Soviet expansion.

Leadership

Until very recently, those who fought in the Second World War and our predecessors who had experienced the First World War, have been responsible for the direction of our policies: Schmidt, Mitterand, Bush, Heath, Callaghan, and before them, Eisenhower, Macmillan, De Gaulle, Adenauer, all framed Western policies. It is in a very large sense due to their experience that we managed, in the post-war period, to devise a system of security which has averted a Third World War in these last nearly 50 years – a Security Policy based on preparedness, no appeasement and firm leadership.

A NEW DEFENCE POLICY – NATO

The need for a new defence policy arose as a result of the immediate post-war actions of the Soviet Union – the domination of Eastern Europe, the Berlin Airlift and the threat of a totally Marxist Europe under Soviet control. Great credit should be given to the Labour Government of 1945 and in particular to Mr Bevin, not only for their realization of that danger but their uncompromising stand against Soviet Communism at a period when the Soviet Union was still regarded by many in this country as an important ally.

From this confused situation arose the conception of NATO and containment, which over the last 45 years has been successful in preventing a Third World War and a nuclear catastrophe. At the same time came Mr Monnet's vision of a united Europe. He rightly believed that the rivalries of the Western European countries had led directly to the wars of the 19th and 20th Centuries, and that the removal of those enmities by a real effort of collaboration and unity would transform the international scene.

These two things – the birth of NATO and the European Community – have been the two most significant factors arising from the Second World War. It is a truism to say that all of us have for the last 45 years lived under the umbrella of NATO, always mindful of the possibility of a nuclear war, resigned to the vast expense of maintaining our armed forces at a suitable level to ensure deterrence, reminded constantly of the dangers that faced us.

At regular intervals we were jolted and reminded of our danger by Soviet aggression – Hungary, Czechoslovakia, Afghanistan, and parts of Africa. We got used to it. We knew we had to do certain things, however unpalatable and expensive they were, and the great majority of those in the United States and Western Europe were content to go along with it. Indeed, they believed – and I think that they were right – that they had little option if they wished to preserve their way of life and Western values.

Nuclear strategy – Russia and NATO

It would be idle to pretend that nuclear weaponry did not play a most significant part in NATO's success. First of all, the sole possession by the Americans of a nuclear capability ensured, in the light of the Nagasaki and Hiroshima bombs, that the Soviet Union would not seek, nor risk, a Third World War.

Later, when the Russians acquired the technology, American superiority made the prospect of a conflict remote. Even when nuclear parity was achieved, the prospect of a nuclear war with the terrifying consequences to the world as a whole made a full-scale war unlikely, except by mistake. The risk of mutual self-destruction was too great. Those who campaigned against nuclear weapons never really understood that, nor that it was the nuclear weapons that were instrumental in saving us from disaster.

It has to be said that in the face of considerable political difficulties, almost all the Western Governments stood firm in supporting a nuclear strategy and at a time of great difficulty, even supported the deployment of medium range nuclear missiles in Europe. We should not underestimate the effect these decisions had upon the eventual collapse of the Soviet

Union and its demise as a Superpower, achieved in spite of, and not because of nuclear disarmament.

NATO AND THE BREAK UP OF THE SOVIET UNION

I remember when I was appointed Secretary General of NATO having some misgivings about the consensus rule – in other words, that no decisions could be taken up until all 16 members of the Alliance agreed. But there was never really very much difficulty since the objective of the Alliance was supported wholeheartedly by all its members. They were as a rule prepared to subordinate their national interest for the greater good of the security of the whole rather unlike the Community if I dare say so.

So for 45 years we got used to living in an expensive and dangerous but certain world, in which we could identify a potential enemy, who, from time to time, reminded us of his unpredictability. There is nothing which cements an alliance so firmly as fear and danger. It is when that danger is removed or is apparently removed that the problems begin.

Five years ago, we found ourselves in a situation which most of us never believed could or would happen, and which opened up all sorts of possibilities which none of us had dreamed about. If you look back on what was said at the time of the collapse of the Soviet Union, you may find it understandable but rather curious that no one seemed to foresee the problems that were bound to arise.

For each of the four major countries in NATO, the break up of the Soviet Union had a special impact.

For the Americans, the collapse of the only other Superpower removed one danger but posed important questions. Should the US continue to be the world's policeman? Was the effort and expense justified? Was it politically acceptable in America? Why should the US act globally unless its vital interests were involved? These questions are as yet unanswered. For the French – who have always viewed with misgiving the American domination of NATO – cultivated a relationship with the Soviet Union which gave them a special role in the Western Alliance, a sea change occurred over night.

For the British, who believed that they had a vital bridging role between the Americans and Continental Europe, that special role disappeared.

For the Germans, the dream of the unification of Germany became achievable and with it came the revival of traditional interests in the newly liberated Central Europe. And all this coincided with a change of generation of leadership in almost all the countries of the Western world, a leadership much more of the Vietnam generation than that of the Second World War.

International problems

After the initial phase of euphoria, when everyone seemed to think that the millennium had arrived, we were brought down to earth with a big bump – the invasion of Kuwait, the break up of Yugoslavia, to name but two of the most serious international problems. It is ironic to reflect that if Mr Brezhnev and the Cold War had still been alive, and the Soviet Union still in being, neither the Gulf War nor the break up of Yugoslavia would have happened.

Saddam Hussein would have been far too frightened of the Russians, and the consequences of what the Russians and the Americans might do, ever to have invaded Kuwait.

And the six republics of Yugoslavia, in spite of the death of Tito, would have been far too nervous of Soviet ambitions in their country to contemplate a break up of the Federation. And indeed, if the Soviet Empire had still existed and the break up had taken place, the Americans would very swiftly have moved in to ensure that vital strategic ports in the Adriatic did not fall into Soviet hands. Yugoslavia and Kuwait will not be the last of the international problems. Trouble looms in the countries of the former Soviet Union and elsewhere.

Security Council – Speed of response

This brings me to the first of our many disappointments and disillusionments. We had hoped that the inability of the Security Council to act firmly and swiftly because of the Superpowers' rivalry would disappear, and that a more amenable Russia would join the United States and the other members of the Security Council in creating a Security Council capable of being the world's policeman and of taking action in all parts of the world to prevent or stop disputes which could lead to war or famine.

This has not happened. Not because of Russian intransigence, but because the Security Council is not really capable of doing the job. It becomes clearer every day that, unless it gets a very firm lead from the United States, nothing much is going to happen. We saw that in the Gulf, in Somalia and elsewhere. This is an unpleasant truth for the United States, but it is something that we and they have to face. The United Nations has no troops of its own, and is not very well organised to deal with any even if it had. Sir Brian Urquhart, for whom I have a great admiration and who was for many years a most distinguished Deputy Secretary General, advocates a UN fire fighting force under its own command. I find it difficult to see how that would work in such a diffuse organisation – nor who would be the contributors. And, though the UN has struggled manfully in a number of places to assert its authority, no one can truthfully say it has been very successful. Its authority has been flouted, from Yugoslavia to Somalia to Haiti.

US leadership

Much, therefore, depends upon the leadership given by the United States and there are signs – and perhaps understandable signs – that the new Administration is not prepared to get involved in situations in which American interests are not closely involved. I was in the United States at the time when the 12 US servicemen were killed in Somalia. The question asked and asked trenchantly, was 'what American interests did those 12 servicemen die for?'

And the resounding answer by public and press was 'none'. I don't think it is going to be easy to convince the United States, whether by itself or in conjunction with others, that it should intervene in areas in which it has little interest. Moreover, the new Administration's eyes are firmly set on US economic problems, domestic and international.

The future of NATO

The second question which concerns us is the future of NATO. It seems to me a perfectly legitimate question to ask 'what is NATO now for?' The potential enemy has, at any rate temporarily, disappeared. The focus and the purpose of the organization is less clear. The wise course is to keep the Alliance in being, in case of the unexpected, whether it be the resurgence of Russia or something unforeseen. But it is not easy to maintain an organization with so nebulous a purpose and certainly not at the level of expenditure which we have incurred over these last 40 years. What then should we do? Should we, as some suggest, include all Europe and Russia and the ex-Soviet Union states in the organization? But what is the purpose of a defence organization of that kind? Against whom would it be defending itself?

The size of the organization would be such as to render it in practice so diffuse as to be almost militarily and politically useless and become, as the Russians seem to want it to be, the military arm of the CSCE. Would it be better then to include only those countries of Eastern Europe recently liberated and now democratic. The reactions in Russia would no doubt be hostile, since it would be perceived that the Alliance was directed against them. It could be argued too that, at this particular moment, to make life more difficult for the moderates in Russia would not be a sensible policy.

There is no doubt that the military are dissatisfied and there are many Russians who feel that the recreation of the Soviet Union should be their primary objective. But again, should the Russians be given a veto over what we consider to be our best interests? In any event, I am inclined to doubt whether anything that the West does or does not do will greatly influence the political outcome in Russia. The Russians will decide for themselves, either democratically, or by some coup, who is to govern them in future.

We have, it seems to me, two options:

- firstly, to accept the Eastern Europeans as full members of NATO, whilst at the same time offering Partnership for Peace to the Russians;
- secondly, Partnership for Peace for both Eastern Europe and Russia, but at the same time making a clear statement that the independence of the East Europe countries is a vital interest to NATO.

I prefer the first alternative for there is considerable anxiety in Poland and the Czech Republic over NATO's obvious hesitation.

Europe and the US – Working together

There are some who do not rate highly the chances of the American forces sitting in Europe very long. I am one of those who believes very strongly in the importance of the European/North Atlantic relationship, for it has clearly been a key factor in the prevention of global war. We have to accept, however, that in the American mind, Europe is a great deal less important than it was four years ago. It was the place in which the war would start, and its prevention is clearly and rightly a US priority.

A US presence in Europe was, therefore, absolutely vital. That is not so now. The Americans are preoccupied with their relationship in the Pacific– Japan and increasingly China whose economic growth is phenomenal. The new generation of leaders and politicians have no personal experience or memories of the Second World War, the friendships, the shared dangers or the problems which confronted Western Europe in the aftermath of the War.

Equally in Europe, the removal of the immediate threat is for some, evidence that America and the nuclear umbrella is to them no longer as important as it was and the close ties to the last 45 years are no longer so necessary. The tendency for national self-interest to take precedence over international cooperation is hard at work. I believe the worst thing that could happen is a serious erosion of the transatlantic relationship. The friendship and collaboration that has existed between both sides of the Atlantic has maintained stability and order in an unstable and disordered world. We would be very foolish to throw that away.

THE FUTURE OF THE EUROPEAN UNION

Lastly, the collapse of the Soviet Union has made even more difficult the future development of the European Union. Mr Monnet, I think, would be pleased at the progress that we have made, and it is a mistake to underestimate the achievements so far. It is inconceivable that any member of the 12 can have any quarrel with any one of the others which would lead to war. It is much better to quarrel about 'mad cow disease' than to resort to machine guns in Flanders. But it would be foolish to say that we have not got our difficulties. It was to be hoped that a more united Europe would be able to play a greater and more positive role in world affairs, not in competition with the United States, but as a more equal partner capable of influencing events by its political cohesion and its economic prosperity. That has not happened.

The Fall of the Berlin Wall underlined one of these complications – for a united Germany will, with its population of 80 million, be the dominant European power.

The French who, understandably after three bloody wars with the Germans, are anxious to maintain a special Franco-German relationship, have been distinctly nervous that a united Germany would once more turn its attention to central Europe where it has long been a dominant power, and away from Western Europe and the Communities.

It has therefore been the French policy to cement the relationship of Germany to the Community in such a way that they find it essential and advantageous to stay a member of the Western European Club. This policy has been encouraged by Chancellor Kohl, who perhaps feels that the successor generation of German politicians are not as committed as he is to German integration in Western Europe.

The Maastricht Treaty

The consequence was the Maastricht Treaty, whose main purpose was to advance the unity of Europe in such a way that the Germans were irrevocably committed. That Treaty, though its intentions were understandable, went much too far and much too quickly. I don't believe that the 12 disparate nations – soon to be 16 – of the Community, with their different traditions, different political systems, different economic levels and the different ideologies of their governments, are ready to accept in full what was demanded of them in the Maastricht Treaty.

I speak as a European firmly committed to British membership. It would be folly, economic and political, for Britain to divorce itself from Europe. All considerations – geographical, military and every other – show that we are and must be a part of Europe. But the growth of the Community must be organic and not as a result of a series of artificial dates by which certain things have got to happen. Probably, most of the things in the Maastricht Treaty will one day come about. But they will come about because everybody in the Community wants them to. I believe that this more pragmatic approach is gaining ground.

The French are clearly having second thoughts about a Europe in which they are not the sole arbiters. The days in which the French could dominate the Germans have gone. The new generation of Germans have no guilt about the Second World War and occupation of France, and as a united country nearly twice as large as any other in the Community, are flexing their muscles. The Germans on the other hand, are clearly nervous about losing the Mark, the symbol of their resurgence, in a common currency.

The Danes had much the same problems with Maastricht as we did. Of course, there are those who want to go ahead faster – probably the smaller countries of Europe who have nothing much to lose. But realism seems to be gaining ground.

But over and above all that, we are faced with the problems of the East European countries who badly want once again, to become accepted members of a Europe to which they once belonged. This poses a dilemma. If we do not in some way accommodate the Eastern European countries, there will be widespread disillusion. When the colonial master disappears, there is a natural tendency to believe that all problems will now be solved. They never are. Indeed in some instances, they get much worse. The countries of Eastern Europe are in much the same position as were the erstwhile colonial countries. Disillusion can be very dangerous indeed. If we do not allow them to export their goods to us and manage trade between us to their disadvantage, there will be real trouble.

But, if we accept them as members of the Community, together with those members of EFTA, such as Sweden, Norway, Austria and Finland who may want to join, we shall create problems in the running of the Community. Foreign Affairs and Defence for one thing, difficult now, will be doubly difficult and we can all think of many other examples in a Community consisting of 20 countries as opposed to 12.

One thing is, to me at any rate, absolutely clear. You cannot widen and deepen the Community at the same time, and those who believe it possible are deceiving themselves.

I believe that the gradual approach is the best. Let us start the process of membership of the Community for the Eastern Europeans, particularly in the economic field. Let us accept, as indeed we should, the Swedes and Finns and Norwegians and Austrians, if they still wish to join. Let us sensibly pursue greater collaboration in Defence and Foreign Affairs and, if we can achieve a common Foreign Policy, so much the better. But it will not be easy.

CONCLUSION

How then could one sum up the record of the Western world in the five years since the disintegration of the Soviet Union? Have we done well? I think if I were the jury, I would return an open verdict. We have not yet come to terms with the changed situation. We have not thrown away the essentials, but we have not yet translated them into the new circumstances. We are too anxious to cash in on what we call the peace dividend. The planned reductions in all the armed forces of ourselves and our allies are going a long way – perhaps too long a way. The Government must beware of the effect on morale of drastic cutting. The post-war excellence of the British Services in a difficult social climate has been outstanding. Be careful not to throw it away and let us remember the lessons of the Second World War of morale and leadership. The European Community will, at any rate in 1996, be discussing openly, and no doubt at times querulously, its future. The future developments in Russia leave us filled with uncertainty, and we have yet to come to terms with the phenomenal growth in China and the possible economic explosion in the Pacific. We have not yet decided on the future of Western Defence and Governments are not yet prepared to act together or in the UN with the necessary determination. We had better get on with it.

3 The End of the War in Europe and of National-Socialist Tyranny

President Richard von Weizsäcker

Many nations are today commemorating the date on which the Second World War ended in Europe. Every nation is doing so with different feelings, depending on its fate. Be it victory or defeat, liberation from injustice and alien rule or transition to new dependence, division, new alliances, vast shifts of power – 8 May 1945 is a date of decisive historical importance for Europe.

We Germans are commemorating that date amongst ourselves, as is indeed necessary. We must find our own standards. We are not assisted in this task if we or others spare our feelings. We need and we have the strength to look truth straight in the eye – without embellishment and without distortion.

For us, 8 May is above all a date to remember what people had to suffer. It is also a date to reflect on the course taken by our history. The greater honesty we show in commemorating this day, the freer we are able to face the consequences with due responsibility. For us Germans, 8 May is not a day of celebration. Those who actually witnessed that day in 1945 think back on highly personal and hence highly different experiences. Some returned home, others lost their homes. Some were liberated, whilst for others it was the start of captivity. Many were simply grateful that the bombing at night and fear had passed and that they had survived. Others felt first and foremost grief at the complete defeat suffered by their country. Some Germans felt bitterness about their shattered illusions, whilst other were grateful for the gift of a new start.

This chapter is based on a speech to the Bundestag given by President Weizsäcker on 8 May 1985 during the ceremony commemorating the 40th anniversary of the end of the war in Europe.

It was difficult to find one's bearings straight away. Uncertainty prevailed throughout the country. The military capitulation was unconditional, placing our destiny in the hands of our enemies. The past had been terrible, especially for many of those enemies, too. Would they not make us pay many times over for what we had done to them? Most Germans had believed that they were fighting and suffering for the good of their country. And now it turned out that their efforts were not only in vain and futile, but had served the inhuman goals of a criminal regime. The feelings of most people were those of exhaustion, despair and new anxiety. Had one's next of kin survived? Did a new start from those ruins make sense at all? Looking back, they saw the dark abyss of the past and, looking forward, they saw an uncertain, dark future.

Yet with every day something became clearer, and this must be stated on behalf of all of us today: 8 May was a day of liberation. It liberated all of us from the inhumanity and tyranny of the National-Socialist regime.

Nobody will, because of that liberation, forget the grave suffering that only started for many people on 8 May. But we must not regard the end of the war as the cause of flight, expulsion and deprivation of freedom. The cause goes back to the start of the tyranny that brought about war. We must not separate 8 May 1945 from 30 January 1933.

There is truly no reason for us today to participate in victory celebrations. But there is every reason for us to perceive 8 May 1945 as the end of an aberration in German history, an end bearing seeds of hope for a better future.

II

8 May is a day of remembrance. Remembering means recalling an occurrence honestly and undistortedly so that it becomes a part of our very beings. This places high demands on our truthfulness.

Today we mourn all the dead of the war and the tyranny. In particular we commemorate the six million Jews who were murdered in German concentration camps. We commemorate all nations who suffered in the war, especially the countless citizens of the Soviet Union and Poland who lost their lives. As Germans, we mourn our own compatriots who perished as soldiers, during air raids at home, in captivity or during expulsion. We commemorate the Sinti and Romany gypsies, the homosexuals and the mentally ill who were killed, as well as the people who had to die for their religious or political beliefs. We commemorate the hostages who were executed. We recall the victims of the resistance movements in all the countries occupied by us. As Germans, we pay homage to the victims of the German resistance – among the public, the military, the churches, the workers and trade unions, and the communists. We commemorate those who did not actively resist, but preferred to die rather than violate their consciences.

Alongside the endless army of the dead mountains of human suffering arise – grief at the dead, suffering from injury or crippling or barbarous compulsory sterilization, suffering during the air raids, during flight and expulsion, suffering because of rape and pillage, forced labour, injustice and torture, hunger and hardship, suffering because of fear of arrest and death, grief at the loss of everything which one had wrongly believed in and worked for. Today we sorrowfully recall all this human suffering.

Perhaps the greatest burden was borne by the women of all nations. Their suffering, renunciation and silent strength are all too easily forgotten by history. Filled with fear, they worked, bore human life and protected it. They mourned their fallen fathers and sons, husbands, brothers and friends. In the years of darkness, they ensured that the light of humanity was not extinguished. After the war, with no prospect of a secure future, women everywhere were the first to set about building homes again, the 'rubble women' in Berlin and elsewhere. When the men who had survived returned, women had to take a back seat again. Because of the war, many women were left alone and spent their lives in solitude. Yet it is first and foremost thanks to the women that nations did not disintegrate spiritually on account of the destruction, devastation, atrocities and inhumanity and that they gradually regained their foothold after the war.

III

At the root of the tyranny was Hitler's immeasurable hatred against our Jewish compatriots. Hitler had never concealed this hatred from the public, but made the entire nation a tool of it. Only a day before his death, on 30 April 1945, he concluded his so-called will with the words: 'Above all, I call upon the leaders of the nation and their followers to observe painstakingly the race laws and to oppose ruthlessly the poisoners of all nations: international Jewry.' Hardly any country has in its history always remained free from blame for war or violence. The genocide of the Jews is, however, unparalleled in history.

The perpetration of this crime was in the hands of a few people. It was concealed from the eyes of the public, but every German was able to experience what his Jewish compatriots had to suffer, ranging from plain apathy and hidden intolerance to outright hatred. Who could remain unsuspecting after the burning of the synagogues, the plundering, the stigmatization with the Star of David, the deprivation of rights, the ceaseless violation of human dignity? Whoever opened his eyes and ears and sought information could not fail to notice that Jews were being deported. The nature and scope of the destruction may have exceeded human imagination, but in reality there was, apart from the crime itself, an attempt by too many people, including those of my generation, who were young and were not involved in planning the events and carrying them out, not to take note of what was happening. There were many ways of not burdening one's conscience, of shunning responsibility, looking away, keeping mum. When the unspeakable truth of the Holocaust then became known at the end of the war, all too many of us claimed that they had not known anything about it or even suspected anything.

There is no such thing as guilt or innocence of an entire nation. Guilt is, like innocence, not collective, but personal. There is discovered or concealed individual guilt. There is guilt which people acknowledge or deny. Everyone who directly experienced that era should today quietly ask himself about his involvement then.

The vast majority of today's population were either children then or had not been born. They cannot profess a guilt of their own for crimes that they did not commit. No discerning person can expect them to wear a penitential robe simply because they are Germans. But their forefathers have left them a grave legacy. All of us, whether guilty or not, whether old or young, must accept the past. We are all affected by its consequences and liable for it. The young and old generations must and can help each other to understand why it is vital to keep the memories alive. It is not a case of coming to terms with the past. That is not possible, it cannot be subsequently modified or undone. However, anyone who closes his eyes to the past is blind to the present. Whoever refuses to remember the inhumanity is prone to new risks of infection.

The Jewish nation remembers and will always remember. We seek reconciliation. Precisely for this reason we must understand that there can be no reconciliation without remembrance. The experience of millionfold death is part of the very being of every Jew in the world, not only because people cannot forget such atrocities, but also because remembrance is part of the Jewish faith.

'Seeking to forget makes exile all the longer; the secret of redemption lies in remembrance.' This oft quoted Jewish adage surely expresses the idea that faith in God is faith in the work of God in history. Remembrance is experience of the work of God in history. It is the source of faith in redemption. This experience creates hope, creates faith in redemption, in reunification of the divided, in reconciliation. Whoever forgets this experience loses his faith.

If we for our part sought to forget what has occurred, instead of remembering it, this would not only be inhuman. We would also impinge upon the faith of the Jews who survived and destroy the basis of reconciliation. We must erect a memorial to thoughts and feelings in our own hearts.

IV

8 May marks a deep cut not only in German history, but in the history of Europe as a whole. The European civil war had come to an end, the old world of Europe lay in ruins. 'Europe had fought itself to a stand-still'

(M. Stürmer). The meeting of American and Soviet Russian soldiers on the Elbe became a symbol for the temporary end of a European era.

True, all this was deeply rooted in history. For a century Europe had suffered under the clash of extreme nationalistic aspirations. At the end of the First World War peace treaties were signed but they lacked the power to foster peace. Once more nationalistic passions flared up and were fanned by the distress of the people at that time.

Along the road to disaster Hitler became the driving force. He whipped up and exploited mass hysteria. A weak democracy was incapable of stopping him. And even the powers of Western Europe – in Churchill's judgement unsuspecting but not without guilt – contributed through their weakness to this fateful trend. After the First World War America had withdrawn and in the thirties had no influence on Europe.

Hitler wanted to dominate Europe and to do so through war. He looked for and found an excuse in Poland. On 23 May 1939 he told the German generals: 'No further successes can be gained without bloodshed... Danzig is not the objective. Our aim is to extend our *Lebensraum* in the East and safeguard food supplies... so there is no question of sparing Poland; and there remains the decision to attack Poland at the first suitable opportunity....The object is to deliver the enemy a blow, or the annihilating blow, at the start. In this, law, injustice or treaties do not matter.'

On 23 August 1939 Germany and the Soviet Union signed a non-aggression pact. The secret supplementary protocol made provision for the impending partition of Poland. That pact was made to give Hitler an opportunity to invade Poland. The Soviet leaders at the time were fully aware of this. And all who understood politics realized that the implications of the German-Soviet pact were Hitler's invasion of Poland and hence the Second World War.

That does not mitigate Germany's responsibility for the outbreak of the Second World War. The Soviet Union was prepared to allow other nations to fight one another so that it could have a share of the spoils. The initiative for the war, however, came from Germany, not from the Soviet Union. It was Hitler who resorted to the use of force. The outbreak of the Second World War remains linked with the name of Germany.

In the course of that war the Nazi regime tormented and defiled many nations. At the end of it all only one nation remained to be tormented, enslaved and defiled: the German nation. Time and again Hitler had declared that if the German nation was not capable of winning the war it should be left to perish. The other nations first became victims of a war started by Germany before we became the victims of our own war.

The division of Germany into zones began on 8 May. In the meantime the Soviet Union had taken control in all countries of Eastern and Southeastern Europe that had been occupied by Germany during the war. All of them, with the exception of Greece, became socialist states. The division of Europe into two different political systems took its course. True, it was the post-war development which cemented that division, but without the war started by Hitler it would not have happened at all. That is what first comes to the minds of the nations concerned when they recall the war unleashed by the German leaders. And we think of that too when we ponder the division of our own country and the loss of huge sections of German territory. In a sermon in East Berlin commemorating 8 May, Cardinal Meißner said: 'The pathetic result of sin is always division.'

V

The arbitrariness of destruction continued to be felt in the arbitrary distribution of burdens. There were innocent people who were persecuted and guilty ones who got away. Some were lucky to be able to begin life all over again at home in familiar surroundings. Others were expelled from the lands of their fathers. We in what was to become the Federal Republic of Germany were given the priceless opportunity to live in freedom. Many millions of our countrymen have been denied the opportunity to this day.

Learning to accept mentally this arbitrary allocation of fate was the first task, alongside the material task of rebuilding the country. That is the test of the human spirit: to recognise the burdens of others, to help bear them over time, not to forget them. It had to be the test of our ability to work for peace, of our willingness to foster the spirit of reconciliation both at home and in our external relations, an ability and a readiness which not only others expected of us, but which we most of all demanded of ourselves.

We cannot commemorate 8 May without being conscious of the great effort required on the part of our former enemies to set out on the road of reconciliation with us. Can we really place ourselves in the position of the relatives of the victims of the Warsaw ghetto or of the Lidice massacre? And how hard must it have been for the citizens of Rotterdam or London to support the rebuilding of our country from where the bombs came which not long before had been dropped on their cities? To be able to do so they had gradually to gain the assurance that the Germans would not again try to make good their defeat by use of force.

In our country the biggest sacrifice was demanded of those who had been driven out of their homeland. They were to experience suffering and injustice long after 8 May. Those of us who were born here often do not have the imagination or the open heart with which to grasp the real meaning of their harsh fate.

But soon there were great signs of readiness to help. Many millions of refugees and expellees were taken in who over the years were able to strike new roots. Their children and grandchildren have in many different ways formed a loving attachment to the culture and the homeland of their ancestors. That is a great treasure in their lives. But they themselves have found a new home where they are growing up and integrating with the local people of the same age, sharing their dialect and their customs. Their young life is proof of their ability to be at peace with themselves. Their grandparents or parents were once driven out; they themselves, however, are now at home.

Very soon and in exemplary fashion the expellees identified themselves with the renunciation of force. That was no passing declaration in the early stages of helplessness but a commitment which has retained its validity. Renouncing the use of force means allowing trust to grow on all sides; it means that a Germany that has regained its strength remains bound by it. The expellees' own homeland has, meanwhile, become a homeland for others. In many of the old cemeteries in Eastern Europe you will today find more Polish than German graves. The compulsory migration of millions of Germans to the West was followed by the migration of millions of Poles and, in their wake, millions of Russians. These are all people who were not asked, people who suffered injustice, people who became defenceless objects of political events and to whom no compensation for those injustices and no offsetting of claims can make up for what has been done to them.

Renouncing force today means giving them lasting security, unchallenged on political grounds, for their future in the place where fate drove them after 8 May and where they have been living in the decades since. It means placing the dictate of understanding above conflicting legal claims. That is the true, the human contribution to a peaceful order in Europe which we can provide.

The new beginning in Europe after 1945 has brought both victory and defeat for the notion of freedom and self-determination. Our aim is to seize the opportunity to draw a line under a long period of European history in which to every country peace seemed conceivable and safe only as a result of its own supremacy, and in which peace meant a period of preparation for the next war.

The nations of Europe love their homeland. The Germans are no different. Who could trust in a nation's love of peace if it were capable of forgetting its homeland? No, love of peace manifests itself precisely in the fact that one does not forget one's homeland and is for that very reason resolved to do everything in one's power to live together in lasting peace. An expellee's love for his homeland is in no way revanchism.

VI

The last war has aroused a stronger desire for peace in the hearts of men than in times past. The work of the churches in promoting reconciliation met with a tremendous response. The '*Aktion Sühnezeichen*', a campaign in which young people carry out atonement activity in Poland and Israel, is one example of such practical efforts to promote understanding. Recently, the town of Kleve on the lower Rhine received loaves of bread from Polish towns as a token of reconciliation and fellowship. The town council sent one of those loaves to a teacher in England because he had discarded his anonymity and written to say that as member of a bomber crew during the war he had destroyed the church and houses in Kleve and wanted to take part in some gesture of reconciliation. In seeking peace it is a tremendous help if, instead of waiting for the other to come to us, we go towards him, as this man did.

VII

In the wake of the war, old enemies were brought closer together. As early as 1946, the American Secretary of State, James F. Byrnes, called in his memorable Stuttgart address for understanding in Europe and for assistance to the German nation on its way to a free and peaceable future. Innumerable Americans assisted us Germans, who had lost the war, with their own private means so as to heal the wounds of war. Thanks to the vision of the Frenchmen Jean Monnet and Robert Schuman and their cooperation with Konrad Adenauer, the traditional enmity between the French and Germans was buried forever.

A new will and energy to reconstruct Germany surged through the country. Many an old trench was filled in, religious differences and social strains were defused. People set to work in a spirit of partnership. There was no 'zero hour', but we had the opportunity to make a fresh start. We have used this opportunity as well as we could.

We have put democratic freedom in the place of oppression. Four years after the end of the war, on 8 May 1949, the Parliamentary Council adopted our Basic Law. Transcending party differences, the democrats on the Council gave their answer to war and tyranny in Article 1 of our Constitution: 'The German people acknowledge inviolable and inalienable human rights as the basis of any community, of peace and of justice in the world.' This further significance of 8 May should also be remembered today.

The Federal Republic of Germany has become an internationally respected State. It is one of the most highly developed industrial countries in the world. It knows that its economic strength commits it to share responsibility for the struggle against hunger and need in the world and for social adjustment between nations. For 40 years we have been living in peace and freedom, to which we, through out policy in union with the free nations of the Atlantic Alliance and the European Community, have ourselves rendered a major contribution. The freedom of the individual has never received better protection in Germany than it does today. A comprehensive system of social welfare that can stand comparison with any other ensures the subsistence of the population. Whereas at the end of the war many Germans tried to hide their passports or to exchange them for another one, German nationality today is highly valued.

We certainly have no reason to be arrogant and self-righteous. But we may look back with gratitude on our development over these 40 years, if we use the memory of our own history as a guideline for our future behaviour.

- If we remember that mentally disturbed persons were put to death in the Third Reich, we will see the care of people with psychiatric disorders as our own responsibility.

- If we remember how people persecuted on grounds of race, religion and politics and threatened with certain death often stood before the closed borders with other countries, we shall not close the door today on those who are genuinely persecuted and seek protection with us.

- If we reflect on the penalties for free thinking under the dictatorship, we will protect the freedom of every idea and every criticism, however much it may be directed against ourselves.

- Whoever criticizes the situation in the Middle East should think of the fate to which Germans condemned their Jewish fellow human beings, a fate that led to the establishment of the State of Israel under conditions which continue to burden people in that region even today.

- If we think of what our Eastern neighbours had to suffer during the war, we will find it easier to understand that accommodation and peaceful neighbourly relations with these countries remain central tasks of German foreign policy. It is important that both sides remember and that both sides respect each other. Mikhail Gorbachev, General Secretary of the Soviet Communist Party, declared that it was not the intention of the Soviet leaders at the 40th anniversary of the end of the war to stir up anti-German feelings. The Soviet Union, he said, was committed to friendship between nations. Particularly if we have doubts about Soviet contributions to understanding between East and West and about respect for human rights in all parts of Europe, we must not ignore this signal from Moscow. We seek friendship with the peoples of the Soviet Union.

VIII

Forty years after the end of the war, the German nation remains divided. At a commemorative service in the Church of the Holy Cross in Dresden held in February of this year, Bishop Hempel said:

'It is a burden and a scourge that two German States have emerged with their harsh border. The very multitude of borders is a burden and a scourge. Weapons are a burden.'

The Ambassadors of both German States accepted an invitation to attend an exhibition of 'Jews in Germany' in Baltimore. The host, the President of the John Hopkins University, welcomed them together. He stated that all Germans share the same historical development. Their joint past is a bond that links them. Such a bond, he said, could be a blessing or a problem, but was always a source of hope.

We Germans are one people and one nation. We feel that we belong together because we have lived through the same past. We also experienced 8 May 1945 as part of the common fate of our nation, which unites us. We feel bound together in our desire for peace. Peace and good neighbourly relations with all countries should radiate from the German soil in both States. And no other states should let that soil become a source of danger to peace either. The people of Germany are united in desiring a peace that encompasses justice and human rights for all peoples, including our own. Reconciliation that transcends boundaries cannot be provided by a walled Europe but only by a continent that removes the divisive elements from its borders. That is the exhortation given us by the end of the Second World War. We are confident that 8 May is not the last date in the common history of all Germans.

IX

Many young people have asked themselves, and us, why such animated discussions about the past have arisen 40 years after the end of the war. Why are they more animated than after 25 or 30 years? What is the inherent necessity of this development?

It is not easy to answer such questions. But we should not seek the reasons primarily in external influences. In the lifespan of men and in the destiny of nations, 40 years play a great role. Permit me at this point to return again to the Old Testament, which contains deep insights for every person, irrespective of his own faith. There, 40 years frequently play a vital part. The Israelites were to remain in the desert for 40 years before a new stage in their history began with their arrival in the promised land. Forty years were required for a complete transfer of responsibility from the generation of the fathers.

Elsewhere, too (in the Book of Judges), it is described how often the memory of experienced assistance and rescue lasted only for 40 years. When that memory faded, tranquillity was at an end. Forty years invariably constitute a significant timespan. Man perceives them as the end of a dark age bringing hope for a new and prosperous future, or as the onset of danger that the past might be forgotten and a warning of the consequences. It is worth reflecting on both of these perceptions.

In our country, a new generation has grown up to assume political responsibility. Our young people are not responsible for what happened over forty years ago. But they are responsible for the historical consequences.

We in the older generation owe to young people not the fulfilment of dreams but honesty. We must help younger people to understand why it is vital to keep memories alive. We want them to accept historical truth soberly, not one-sidedly, without taking refuge in utopian doctrines, but also without moral arrogance. From our own history we learn what man is capable of. For that reason we must not imagine that we are quite different and have become better. There is no ultimately achievable moral perfection. We have learned as human beings, and as human beings we remain in danger. But we have the strength to overcome such danger again and again.

Hitler's constant approach was to stir up prejudices, enmity and hatred. What is asked of young people today is this: do not let yourselves be forced into enmity and hatred of other people, of Russians or Americans, Jews or Turks, of alternatives or conservatives, blacks or whites.

Let us honour freedom.
Let us work for peace.
Let us respect the rule of law.
Let us be true to our conception of justice.
On this 8 May, let us face up as well as we can to the truth.

4 Don't Forget the Sea

Admiral of the Fleet the Lord Lewin

> *He who commands the sea has command of everything.*
> Themistocles 500BC

Sixty years ago Britain was a maritime nation. There was hardly a family in the land that did not have a father, uncle, nephew or son who owed a living to the sea. Hundreds of thousands were employed in shipbuilding, the docks swarmed with stevedores, the Red Ensign Navy was the biggest in the world, the White Ensign flew in every ocean, our smaller ports teemed with fishing vessels. Those who wished to travel to other lands had no other option but to go by sea. On long voyages they adopted the routine of shipboard life, experienced the magic of the sea and prided themselves on being of a seafaring race.

All that has gone. The great shipyards are derelict, efficient container ports handle cargo with tens of men, not thousands. The British Merchant Navy is 23rd in the league of world tonnage, our fishing fleets are threatened with extinction by shortage of fish and foreign competition. Travel abroad takes only hours to any destination in soul-less identical cylinders that give no impression of the world outside. As a Nation we are in danger of forgetting the importance of the sea, how it has shaped our past and will influence our future. Our prosperity and security have always depended on the free use of the sea; while the future is impossible to predict, history can teach us lessons whose prevailing theme is so recurrent it deserves the status of an axiom.

A LONG TRADITION

With quite remarkable skill and craftsmanship our ancestors built wooden boats 3500 years ago to trade with neighbouring tribes across estuaries and across the channel. The centuries passed. The Romans came – and left – by sea. Then came the Saxons and the Danes. Under the Romans the British had lost their taste for the sea and were subjected to attack by others more warlike than themselves, early proponents of amphibious warfare. The exception was King Alfred, the first to realise the importance of the fleet in seaward defence and his people were left in peace. Alfred's lesson was soon forgotten; the pattern of assault from the sea continued until the culminating defeat by the Normans, who came by sea across the channel unopposed and by their victory at Hastings began a new era in our history.

The next two hundred and fifty years saw the consolidation of England as a nation state but with the kings holding a double position in both England and France. It was these competing claims of monarchy that led to the Hundred Years War with France, a war that was fought entirely on French soil – because England commanded the sea. Those well known victories won by English archers – Crecy, Poitiers, Agincourt – were made possible by the opening battle of the war fought at sea off Sluys when King Edward's Fleet, manned by archers and men-at-arms but sailed by seamen, defeated the French Fleet which had been assembled for invasion. Thereafter the free passage of men, horses and material to France was ensured.

While internal struggles for monarchical succession occupied the military in England, the eyes of the merchant venturers turned to the sea and the New World that was being revealed by Columbus and Vasco da Gama. Not content to look on, an expedition financed by Bristol merchants and led by the brothers Cabot, reached the mainland of North America. Seaborne trade, which hitherto had been confined to the landlocked seas the Mediterranean, the Channel, the North Sea and the Baltic, was about to become oceanic.

> *Here beginneth the Prologue of the Libel of English policie, exhorting all England to keep the sea, showing what profit commeth thereof...*
> De Politia Coservativa Maris, Anon. 1437

Spain and Portugal were leading the race for maritime supremacy in the new world which their great maritime voyagers had opened for trade and exploitation. To avoid conflict, a Papal Bull allotted to Spain all discoveries to the west and to Portugal all to the east of a line drawn down the mid-Atlantic. The Dutch and the English were undeterred by this edict and their maritime trade prospered.

Henry VII fully appreciated that a flourishing ocean trade needed a flourishing navy behind it to protect the ships from piracy and illegal seizure. He built a number of fine king's ships, the first Royal Dockyard, the first dry dock.

> *Whosoever commands the sea commands the trade, whosoever commands the trade commands the riches of the world, and consequently the world itself.*
> Sir Walter Raleigh, 1616

The importance of the sea to England's growing trade was undeniable. Trading voyages to Norway, the Baltic, Iceland, Spain and Portugal were soon followed by voyages further afield. Hawkins started trading ivory from West Africa to Brazil, Willoughby tried to reach Cathay by the North East Passage and failed, but was followed by Chancellor who reached the White Sea and opened a flourishing trade with the Russians. Hawkins then found the slave trade from Africa to the West Indies more profitable that ivory and initiated the infamous but lucrative triangular voyages – England – West Africa – Caribbean – England – with a full cargo on each leg. The monarch, statesmen and merchant venturers were eager to invest in these enterprises and great fortunes were made.

Inevitably the Spaniards resented this competition in their sphere of influence, and their resentment was aggravated by the exploits of Francis Drake, a former apprentice and later partner of Hawkins. His raids on the treasure stores in the Caribbean, his circumnavigation which challenged the Spanish monopoly in the Pacific, his amphibious attack on Cadiz all exacerbated the already bad relations with Spain. The execution of Mary Queen of Scots, King Philip's niece, was the final spur that determined Philip on the Great Enterprise, the Armada against England. The English fleet had more resourceful commanders, better ships for the task, experienced seamen and some luck with the weather and the Great Enterprise ended in disaster.

Spanish maritime power now declined and that of the Dutch and the English burgeoned. The Dutch already had a near monopoly of the coastal trade in Europe and had established trading outposts in the Spice Islands. English overseas trade developed with the founding of the great chartered companies, the East India Company and the Hudson Bay Company. Colonies were established in Virginia and New England and a trading station in Surat, followed later by others at Madras, Calcutta and Bombay. But although the merchant navy, financed by venture capital, expanded, the Navy, the King's ships, financed from the Exchequer, fell into decline as the monarch's political difficulties with Parliament increased. Pirates ranged at will in the Channel, capturing ships and burning English towns and villages, corruption percolated naval administration.

> *The trade of the world is too little for us two,*
> *therefore one must down.*
> A Dutch Sea Captain, circa 1650

In the middle of the 17th century came the inevitable climax of Dutch and English imperial and economic rivalry, the first of the three Dutch wars. Fortunately for the English, the Civil War had brought into office an administration that restored the fortunes of the Navy so that it was better prepared.

Each of these wars against the Dutch was confined to the sea, in effect a series of encounters in which a hundred warships or more on each side fought fierce gun battles at close range. It was a new form of sea warfare in which ships were shattered and casualties were appalling. The first two wars ended by mutual consent when both sides were exhausted, but without the underlying reasons for the conflict being resolved. The Dutch were finally defeated in the third war chiefly because the French, who had changed sides to ally with the English, had invaded Holland with their armies. The only English involvement on land was an amphibious operation to capture Dunkirk.

Undismayed by this reverse, only fourteen years later the Dutch Fleet of some 400 ships, led by William of Orange, sailed to invade England, a bigger and better armada than that of one hundred years before. They evaded an English Fleet of low morale and divided loyalty to their King and disembarked in Torbay, the largest and most powerful Army ever to land on British shores. It was a bloodless invasion followed by the Glorious Revolution, which set King William and Queen Mary on English thrones. King James left to seek sanctuary with the sympathetic Louis XIV and the English found themselves allied with the Dutch in a land war in the Low Countries against the French.

FRENCH RESURGENCE

While Spanish maritime power had declined and the Dutch and English had been locked in combat, the French had built up a formidable fleet. There now began a century in which the French struggled with the English to gain the supremacy at sea that they enjoyed on land. For England there were two overriding considerations: freedom to use the sea to trade with a growing colonial empire, and the danger of invasion. For both a powerful fleet was essential. Control of the sea brought the added advantage that English armies could be transported and supplied to aid Continental allies.

The first confrontation came early. The exiled King James was determined to regain his throne, with the help of Louis XIV. Ireland was his first enterprise. French troops were landed but the French Fleet failed to prevent William and his armies from crossing the Irish Sea unmolested and his sea communications were never threatened. Defeated at the Battle of the Boyne, James fled back to France and another invasion force was assembled in Brittany for an assault on England, but it needed the support of the French Fleet for the crossing. Cruising aggressively off the coast a powerful English Squadron met the French Fleet and in a series of engagements off Barfleur and La Hogue 15 French ships were destroyed. The threat of invasion evaporated and English supremacy at sea was ensured. The bells of London pealed without ceasing for three days. Three Lords took down with them £37 000 in coin to distribute among the sailors.

Valuable lessons on the importance of sea power had been learnt and were to be applied in the next war, the War of the Spanish Succession. On the death of the King of Spain, France made a bid to add Spain to her empire which England and Holland could not accept. An English Army under Marlborough was transported safely to the continent; his victory at the Battle of Ramillies ensured that the ports in the Spanish Netherlands could not be used to challenge for control of the North Sea.

The Navy's contribution to these campaigns ensured that the enemy got no reinforcements from the Mediterranean by sea and drew off and dispersed his strength by amphibious operations. Gibraltar and Barcelona were captured. An ambitious attack on the French Naval base of Toulon from land and sea was unsuccessful, but the strong French fleet was destroyed in the harbour by bombardment from the sea.

With her main fleet impotent, the French resorted to attacks on seaborne trade by privateers. There was no shortage of fast small ships or sailors from the fleet and serious losses were inflicted on shipping important for the prosecution of the war. The introduction of convoy and the provision of naval protection under the Cruisers and Convoys Act proved a satisfactory counter.

The war ended with the Treaty of Utrecht which left no doubt where victory lay. England, now united as Britain, gained valuable bases in the Mediterranean and on the Atlantic seaboard of North America and was given the monopoly of the rich slave trade with the Spanish colonies.

Sea Power, added to Marlborough's military genius, had given Britain a decisive capability of attacking her enemies at places and times of her own choosing.

> *He that commands the sea is at great liberty, and may take as much or as little of the war as he will ... whereas these that be strongest by land are nevertheless many times in great straits.*
> Francis Bacon 1597

Britain was now the predominant maritime power in the Mediterranean and the Atlantic and colonial gains bought with them new opportunities for trade. Rivalry, particularly in the Caribbean, led to an outbreak of war with Spain. In the early stages, Admiral Vernon captured Porto Bello, but a second combined operation to capture Cartagena failed because of the incompatibility of the commanders and poor direction from the government at home. Admiral Anson set out on a circumnavigation from which he returned four years later having caused alarm and despondency among the Spanish settlements on the Pacific coast of South America and with 32 wagon loads of treasure, a welcome contribution to the Exchequer.

Meanwhile, another dynastic war had broken out in Europe – the War of the Austrian Succession – and this brought France into alliance with Spain. A British Expeditionary Force led by George II was safely convoyed across the North Sea where it successfully evicted the French from Germany but failed to prevent the French occupying the Austrian Netherlands. From this springboard the French now prepared to invade across the Channel in support of Stuart challenger Bonnie Prince Charlie, who had evaded watching frigates and landed in Scotland. A waiting British Fleet and offensive raids against the invasion forces in the Channel Ports persuaded the French to abandon their plan. Powerless to intervene, they watched as the Duke of Cumberland's army was carried north by sea to defeat the Young Pretender at Culloden.

Elsewhere at sea, two decisive victories off Finisterre further weakened the French ability to attack Britain's colonies or trade. Although militarily successful on the Continent, French losses at sea and the growing threat to her colonies made her ready to agree peace. Britain, nearing the bottom of the Treasury purse, was not in a strong bargaining position, but an indecisive Treaty held little prospect of a lasting peace.

EXTENSION AND CONSOLIDATION

The spark for the next conflagration was struck in North America. The French had colonies in Canada and in New Orleans, the British had settled on the Atlantic seaboard, but were pushing westward and there were no agreed boundaries. The French started building a chain of forts to close the gap between the Ohio and Mississippi rivers, blocking the British settlers in their search for new trade. Fighting broke out. Small British reinforcements were sent and disastrously defeated. French reinforcements evaded a British intercepting squadron in fog on the Newfoundland Banks and war, which the British wished to avoid, became inevitable.

The war started badly for Britain. In the Mediterranean Admiral Byng lost the naval base of Minorca and paid with his life – whether this example encouraged his contemporaries to do better is questionable. An amphibious force sent to capture Louisberg, the strategically placed French harbour commanding the entrance to the St Lawrence, was pre-empted by the arrival of strong French reinforcements.

Concurrently, war broke out in the cockpit of Europe, a consequence of the unsatisfactory terms of the treaty that ended the previous war. France, Austria and Russia allied against Prussia which, with a Hanoverian King, Britain was bound to help. An army half British and half Hanoverian campaigned with the Prussians in Europe, but probably more welcome were financial subsidies and a series of amphibious raids on the French coast which kept the French nation in a state of consternation, and diverted tens of thousands of French troops to defend their homeland.

In 1758 the tide began to turn. In a copybook combined operation, the postponed attack on Louisberg was successful, providing the base for further operations in French Canada. Two participants are worth noting: Brigadier Wolfe, the Army second in command, and James Cook, Master and Navigator of HMS *Pembroke*.

1759 was the Year of Victories. Close cooperation between the army and the navy ensured the capture of Quebec – Wolfe now in command and Cook sounding the channel to the foot of the Heights of Abraham – and opened the door to the defeat of the French in Canada. The French planned yet another invasion of England; their Fleets at Toulon and Brest were to unite and convoy troops across. But when the Toulon Fleet was spotted passing Gibraltar, Admiral Boscawen sailed his squadron in three hours, overtook and defeated the French off Lagos. The Fleet in Brest sailed to the south to meet their comrades, but were intercepted by Admiral Hawke in Quiberon Bay and destroyed or dispersed. Once again, the threat of invasion was eliminated.

The war now became global in extent. At first the Navy's main preoccupation had been the protection of trade, particularly in the Caribbean and the Indian Ocean, but as superiority at sea was achieved French bases in the West Indies were attacked and one by one her islands were captured. In the Indian Ocean, after a number of inconclusive actions, the French squadron retired to Mauritius leaving the British in control of the sea round the Indian coast. Robert Clive, supported by the navy, concluded a campaign that ended French prospects for command in India.

In an effort to stave off defeat, the new Spanish King was persuaded to join the French – a disastrous move for Spain. A brilliantly planned amphibious operation delivered 12 000 British troops in a hundred transports before Havana, to the surprise of the Governor and his commanders who were celebrating Mass on Trinity Sunday. Havana fell after a siege, and a squadron of warships and a hundred merchant ships were captured. On the other side of the world a similar but smaller joint army-navy operation captured Manila and the Philippine Islands surrendered. The British Navy now had tight control of the Atlantic seaboard and the Mediterranean; British seaborne trade flowed freely; the French and the Spanish were ready for peace. A generous treaty returned many of the conquests to the vanquished, but having removed the threat to the American colonies, Britain retained control of Canada.

The removal of the external threat emboldened the American colonists to become increasingly critical of the heavy hand of the Westminster politicians who, without much tact, thought it only reasonable that the colonies should contribute to the cost of their own defence. Rebellion erupted in 1775, and in the desultory fighting that followed, the Royal Navy's part was confined to support of army operations, often with great initiative and ingenuity, on the lakes and rivers of the interior.

The French, having learnt the lessons of the previous war, had rebuilt and revitalised their fleet. The Royal Navy, on the other hand, had deteriorated in quality and quantity in a period notorious for political jobbery and corruption. The French seized their chance, declared an alliance with the self proclaimed United States of America and sailed a fleet to North America unopposed. While the War of Independence was fought out on land, there followed a series of inconclusive naval engagements in almost every theatre. The Spanish and the Dutch joined the French, and the British were seriously over stretched. Better administration was slowly restoring the Royal Navy's strength, but not the quality of command. The culmination of the war was the Battle of the Chesapeake, again inconclusive at sea, but catastrophic on land, a battle that changed the course of history. The fleet that should have relieved General Cornwallis, besieged in Yorktown, failed to get through and Cornwallis was forced to surrender, thus ending the war on land and confirming the independence of the United States.

There was some subsequent consolation in the defeat of the French fleet at the Battle of the Saintes, while a siege of Gibraltar, which had lasted for three and a half years, failed thanks to a spirited defence by the garrison and the final arrival of a British fleet.

REVITALIZING

The period of the two previous wars had been a golden age for British Maritime exploration. The circumnavigations of Byron and Wallis were followed by the three momentous voyages of Cook, voyages which disproved the existence of a great southern continent, accurately charted the main island groups of the Pacific and paved the way for the eventual British colonisation of Australia and New Zealand. The French, too, were exploring the Pacific, but without the same tenacity. De Surville arrived on the coast of New Zealand a few weeks after Cook. Both were blown off shore in a gale: Cook returned, de Surville did not. Bouganville, a soldier turned explorer – he had fought at Quebec – preceded Cook to Tahiti but was intimidated by the Barrier Reef and failed to sight the coast of Australia or to rediscover the Torres Strait. He did not return to the Pacific.

Cook was the forerunner of a series of great British maritime explorers, the first of which he trained. Bligh, Vancouver, Flinders, Fitzroy, Beaufort and their successors established the pre-eminent position of British hydrography. Royal Navy hydrographers charted the world and, with the help of the astronomers at the Royal Observatory, ensured that Greenwich became the Prime Meridian and the basis of international time.

The salutary lessons of the War of American Independence had been learned. The fleet was now well equipped, well manned and officered by men of considerable war experience. So when revolutionary France declared war on Britain and Holland, and threatened Britain's leading position in international trade, the fleet was not only ready but of reasonable size. So began what, until 1914, was known as 'The Great War.'

A Great Coalition was formed to attack France – at one time eight foreign armies were on French soil. But cooperation was poor, one by one the allies were defeated and the French made significant and valuable territorial gains. The British, whose main contribution was financial support to their allies, did not do well on land. Ill equipped and untrained, their efforts were frittered away on a number of diverse peripheral objectives.

The navy fared better. An early victory on the Glorious First of June raised the spirits of the nation and the morale of the sailors. Although a convoy of American grain, urgently needed to avoid a famine, reached France, the French fleet lost seven ships of the line and the ever present threat of invasion receded. There were some set backs – a temporary occupation of Toulon by French Royalists supported by the Royal Navy was ended by the arrival of the young Napoleon – but other successes followed. French and Dutch settlements in India and the Far East were captured, as was the Cape of Good Hope and French Islands in the Caribbean. A French force of 15 000 men sailed to raise rebellion in Ireland, but failed to reach their destination, while a force of 1000 landed in Pembrokeshire, deserted by their naval escort, surrendered without firing a shot.

Meanwhile, the French revolutionary armies were carrying all before them in Europe. Their successes in the Mediterranean littoral eventually denied the use of bases to the British fleet and caused their withdrawal from that sea. The Spanish and the Dutch Fleets had now fallen under French control, but the British were able to defeat each in turn. First Admiral Jervis at the Battle of St Vincent soundly defeated the Spanish, thanks in part to the initiative of Commodore Nelson, and Admiral Duncan, in a hard fought battle, defeated the Dutch at Camperdown.

Napoleon was now in supreme command of the French Revolutionary Army. Britain remained his only undefeated adversary and again he contemplated the invasion of Ireland, whose people were still ripe for rebellion, but the Royal Navy controlled the sea. He turned instead to Egypt, the gateway to the East and the possible conquest of India. Evading a powerful squadron commanded by Nelson, who had been sent to reoccupy the Mediterranean, Napoleon's army landed at Alexandria and quickly defeated the Mamelukes. Nelson was not far behind; he caught the French fleet at anchor in Aboukir Bay and only two ships escaped capture or destruction. Napoleon's communications with France were now under threat. He turned north towards Turkey but Admiral Sydney Smith captured the ships carrying his siege train and turned the guns against him in a successful defence of Acre. Thwarted, Napoleon slipped through the blockade back to France, leaving his troops in Egypt to their fate.

Napoleon's return put an end to the stirrings of revolt among the European powers. A British expedition to Holland, ill equipped and worse provisioned, was lucky to return to England across the North Sea. Outside Europe joint army-navy expeditions had better success. The marooned French army in Egypt was defeated and surrendered, Danish and Dutch Islands in the West Indies were captured, in the Mediterranean the fleet captured Minorca and Malta. In the north, the Danish fleet, threatening British access to the Baltic trade, was destroyed at anchor off Copenhagen by the ubiquitous Nelson.

Had I been master of the sea I would have been Lord of the Orient.
Napoleon Bonaparte

In 1803, after the Treaty of Americas, the British feared invasion, but the Royal Navy imposed a tight blockade of French and Spanish ports on the Atlantic seaboard and in the Mediterranean. Napoleon assembled an army of over 100 000 men near the Channel ports and thousands of flat bottomed invasion barges were prepared, but the window of opportunity when his fleet could command the narrow sea never came. In 1805 Napoleon hoped that the combined French and Spanish fleets would sweep aside opposition to enable his armada to cross, but at Trafalgar Nelson put an end to those hopes. Britain's maritime supremacy was not again seriously threatened, but Britain was powerless to stop Napoleon's progress on land.

Turning his invasion army westward, in a series of great victories – Austerlitz, Jena, Friedland – he subdued all opposition. In 1808 he occupied Portugal, Britain's oldest ally, and by heavy handed persuasion installed his brother as King of Spain. This the Spaniards could not accept and the provinces rose in rebellion. Britain helped with money and arms, and an army under Arthur Wellesly, later the Duke of Wellington, was transported to Portugal where it defeated the French at Vimerio. The French army was allowed to return to France but Napoleon could not accept this defeat and he returned in person to command a huge army to subdue the whole peninsular. Sir John Moore was now commanding the British force which lay on the French flank and Napoleon decided to deal with this threat first. Heavily outnumbered, Moore and his men had to retreat through mountainous country in mid-winter. Keeping ahead, Moore and his men stood before Corunna and fought a battle which gained just enough time for his men to embark in the ships of the waiting fleet, the largest evacuation of a British army until Dunkirk.

At sea, Napoleon, powerless to challenge Britain's naval supremacy, attempted to strike at British maritime trade. Prohibition of British cargoes in European ports was accompanied by a *guerre de course*, privateers operating against merchant shipping. Again convoy proved an outstandingly effective defence, and less than one per cent of the thousands of convoyed ships was lost.

With the withdrawal of Moore's army, Napoleon thought the Spanish rebellion was ended, and he handed over command to his Generals. But within months Wellington was back with an expeditionary force and the long Peninsular Campaign began. The French were handicapped by extended and difficult lines of communication threatened by a hostile population, the British had the sea behind them and assured continuous supply, and this advantage eventually proved decisive. The French were further disadvantaged when troops were withdrawn to reinforce Napoleon's ill-judged campaign against Russia, a campaign which ended in his defeat before Moscow, and eventually, his abdication.

*It is our maritime superiority that enables me to
maintain my army.*
The Duke of Wellington 1814

While Britain was preoccupied in the Peninsular and the fleet was busy controlling the European seaboard from the Baltic to the Dardanelles, relations with the United States deteriorated. The Americans objected to British attempts to control neutral trade, and the British, short of seamen, infuriated the Americans by seizing British seamen serving in American ships. President Madison issued an ultimatum requiring relaxation of controls, the British Government, after some delay, conceded but before this decision reached Washington, Congress had voted to declare war.

Initially the British suffered badly at the hands of powerful American frigates, and US privateers took over five hundred British merchantmen in seven months. But the end of the war in the Peninsular released the pressure on the fleet, a powerful joint force was sent to the Chesapeake, and a series of amphibious operations followed, culminating in the capture of Washington and the burning of the White House. Peace followed. An unnecessary war, for it was in the interests of both nations to trade with one another, not to fight.

PAX BRITANNICA

The century that now followed was the period of the Pax Britannica. If the army was needed to intervene, sea transport was assured and Royal navy was on hand to lend support, ashore as well as at sea. Naval landing parties made significant contributions in India during the Mutiny, in China, in West Africa and during the Boer war. Greece was helped to independence with the defeat of the Turkish fleet at Navarino. Captain Hobson RN signed the Treaty of Waitangi which added New Zealand to the British Empire.

In mid-century, the European powers were squabbling over the bones of the Turkish Empire. The Russian fleet callously destroyed a Turkish squadron in the Black Sea, inflaming French and British public opinion. Allied fleets were sent into the Black Sea and the Russians were ordered to concentrate their fleet at Sebastopol. This was too much for the Czar and the Great Powers drifted into the Crimean war.

After a long period of peace, neither the army nor the navy were in a fit state for the conflict that followed. Officers did not retire, promotion was into dead men's shoes, so the senior ranks were elderly and set in their ways. The army had forgotten the lessons of the Peninsular, and service conditions for the men were appalling, while the navy had failed to appreciate the potential of steam propulsion. The war was notable for incompetent command and shameful administration. Nevertheless, the allied navies safely transported the troops to the Crimea, assisted the operations on shore with bombardments and damaging raids behind the lines and prevented any interference from the Russian Fleet. An allied fleet, deployed to the Baltic, prevented the spread of the war to that theatre. After two years of inconclusive operations, agreement was reached on conditions for peace which among other things included the independence of Turkey.

The next half century saw dramatic developments in warship design. Steam replaced sail, iron and steel replaced wood, while the rifled gun, explosive shells and turret mountings increased destructive power. Each major development rendered all predecessors obsolescent, and the submarine became a credible warship. Changes in administration and improvements in conditions of service for officers and ratings followed, but slowly. Instead of being paid off at the end of each commission, ratings were recruited for continuous service and given training on entry. The introduction of compulsory retirement for officers and a limit on the number on each rank cleared the lists of aged senior officers and improved promotion prospects. The colourful exploits of naval brigades in China, Egypt and in South Africa earned public admiration and affection, this keen interest in the Royal Navy led to Parliamentary readiness to vote the means to keep the navy strong.

THE FIRST WORLD WAR

At the end of the century, Germany, a relatively young nation state, ambitious for a position as a world power after defeating France in the

Franco-Prussian war and eager to expand her overseas possessions, was challenging Britain's naval supremacy and fired the starting gun for a naval arms race. Britain was fortunate to have the charismatic Admiral Sir John Fisher at the helm. With ruthless efficiency he scrapped the obsolete ships – against a list of 154 ships from battleships to sloops he wrote 'scrap the lot' – and he sponsored the design of the Dreadnought, built in a year less a day, another ship that rendered all her predecessors obsolete.

The Kaiser's aspirations for a place in the sun were not to be thwarted; it needed only a spark in the Balkans to precipitate war. The next World War, the 'Great War' of modern parlance, was global in extent, but because of the advance in the power and complexity of weapons, of far greater cost, both in human life and resources.

At the outset a small expeditionary force was transported across the Channel to assist the French to defend their country against invasion. The rapid advance of the German armies was stemmed but it was a close run thing. War on the Western Front settled to a prolonged and uneasy stalemate, but in the next four years twenty million men, their guns, transport and supplies, were safely convoyed to and from France without the loss of a single man.

The British Battlefleet was superior in numbers to the German High Seas Fleet, but could not risk having its strength depleted by defeat in detail. The British Admirals hoped for a second Trafalgar, an overwhelming victory, but the opportunity of Jutland was not fully taken, although the German High Seas Fleet never put to sea again as a strategic victory was gained. The chance for a decisive battle did not recur.

Statesmen sought a relief from the impasse, the diversionary tactic that had so successfully drawn off men from the main front in many earlier wars. A number of plans were considered: a landing in the Baltic ninety miles from Berlin; seizing Heligoland; a landing in Flanders, but the chosen scheme was an operation to force the Dardanelles and drive Turkey out of the war, relieving pressure on Russia and Egypt.

A joint assault was needed – the navy would land the army to occupy the shore while the navy forced the Straits and together they would invest

Constantinople, but all the principles of combined operations had been forgotten. The army refused to provide the men – other theatres had higher priority. The navy declared that they would go it alone, a squadron of elderly battleships would force the Straits, appear before Constantinople when the Turkish Government would surrender to prevent the bombardment of their capital. The lesson of the failure of a precisely similar naval operation in 1807 was forgotten.

The Straits had been mined and the battleships could not get through. Belatedly troops were made available and a proper combined operation was planned. By this time forewarned, the Turks had built massive defences and heavy gun batteries. The enterprise became a costly and lengthy disaster.

> *The Admiral should run into an enemy's port immediately he appears before it ... and lose no time in getting the troops on shore. The General should settle his plan so that no time should be lost in idle debate when the sword should be drawn.*
> Wolfe 1758

Neither side appreciated the potential of submarines, which in the early years of the war were required by international convention to warn merchant ships before attacking. Losses of merchant ships, on which Britain and her allies depended for food and war materials, although serious, were not outstripping the rate of new build replacement.

By the end of 1916, the intensifying effect of the British blockade of Germany was making an early victory urgent for Germany. The German High Command believed that if they could break the back of Britain's mainstay shipping by an unrestricted U-boat campaign then 'we can force England to make peace in five months'. The U-boats were unleashed. By April the number of sinkings had risen alarmingly and expert assessment confirmed the German prediction that by December there would be insufficient shipping left to bring in necessities. The Imperial War Cabinet discussed the possibility of securing a reasonable peace.

Until this time the Admiralty had refused to countenance the general introduction of convoy, relying instead on the random patrolling of trade routes. The lesson of history regarding commerce warfare was ignored, although Mahan, writing only a few years before, had expressed it succinctly: 'The convoy system will have more success than hunting for individual marauders, a process which resembles looking for a needle in a haystack'.

It needed political pressure to change the policy, and even then the widespread introduction of convoys took time to implement but the results were electrifying. Losses in convoys dropped to less than one per cent, a twentieth of the previous highest loss rate of unescorted ships.

Slowly, the convoy system became more widespread and the U-boats were beaten. America entered the war, her armies ferried safely across the Atlantic, expecting to enter the line for the final defeat of the German army in 1919. But before then the British naval blockade had reduced the German people to the brink of starvation, the sailors of the High Seas Fleet mutinied when ordered to sail for a final raid on the Thames Estuary and revolution was simmering. The Kaiser abdicated, fleeing the country, and an armistice followed.

Once again this had been a war where control of the sea had been vital but, unlike earlier wars, the availability of sufficient merchant shipping had become the most significant factor. There was however a new element – the air. Of limited strike capability and considered to be more valuable for reconnaissance, the potential of aircraft was not sufficiently appreciated. It was years before operational analysts discovered that not a single ship was lost from convoys that had an air escort. In future, control of the sea would require control of the air above it.

TOTAL WAR

The Peace Treaty imposed severe conditions on Germany, particularly galling to the army who did not consider themselves to be defeated. In addition to heavy reparations, Germany was to be allowed only a small professional army, no conscripts, a small navy with no battleships, no submarines, and no military aircraft.

It was perhaps a feeling of affront to national pride in addition to a whipped up fear of communism that persuaded the German electorate to cast thirty eight million votes for Hitler as Head of State and Chancellor, and in 1933 only two million against.

Hitler's aims were not initially as grandiose as the Kaiser's, his aim was to right the perceived wrongs of the Treaty of Versailles and this he did by action rather than negotiation. France and Britain, who had espoused a regime of disarmament, were in no position to do more than object. Meanwhile Hitler's fascist colleague Mussolini had embarked on a colonial war in Abyssinia. The League of Nations, lacking membership of some of the more powerful nations, faced its stiffest task. Italian aggression was condemned and economic sanctions were imposed. The British Foreign Secretary presciently remarked that if the League failed 'the world would be faced with a period of danger and gloom'. But Britain would not support military sanctions nor the closing of the Suez Canal because the Chiefs of Staff advised that the navy was not strong enough to risk the loss of even one capital ship in a war with Italy. With free use of the sea to deliver his troops, Mussolini quickly conquered Ethiopia and proclaimed an Italian Empire. Hitler, encouraged by the inaction of the British and French, continued his expansion into the Rhineland, Austria and Czechoslovakia. His invasion of Poland was one broken Treaty too many and less than twenty one years after 'the war to end all wars', Europe was at war again.

Four divisions and the ground support for some air force squadrons were swiftly shipped to France, but nothing happened. Hitler was preoccupied with Poland and it was not part of allied strategy to invade Germany. But at sea the U-boats started where they had left off. On the day war was declared, the liner *Athenia* was sunk without warning. Unrestricted submarine warfare had started, but so had convoys – no need this time to re-learn the basic lesson. But escorts were in short supply, too much faith had been placed in submarine detection by asdic and German surface raiders were at sea. In the nine months of the 'phoney war' in Europe, 800 000 tons of merchant shipping were lost. Germany started the war with 57 operational U-boats. If the resources that had been committed to the building of the battleships *Bismarck* and *Tirpitz* had instead been devoted to the submarine programme, there would have been an additional 50 U-boats and as a consequence submarine attacks might initially been on the scale that was to come in 1940/41. Britain could then have faced defeat before the first Christmas of the war. As it was the losses were not disastrous – yet.

In April 1940, Hitler, anxious to secure his supply of iron ore and to secure advance bases for his submarines, invaded Norway. The Royal navy took the army to Norway and later brought them back. Having secured Norway, Hitler invaded Holland and Belgium. In due course, having delivered the British Expeditionary Force to France, the navy, with the help of the small ships, brought most of them back. Britain now stood alone and the Royal Air Force, fuelled by petrol every gallon of which had been brought across the oceans in tankers, won the battle of Britain, the aerial equivalent of Trafalgar. Britain once again faced invasion, but failure to command the Channel – and the sky above it – confounded Hitler's invasion plan just as it had balked Napoleon.

But Britain was not as alone as it looked; across the oceans came reinforcements from the Commonwealth – from Canada to Britain and from India, Australia, New Zealand and South Africa to East and North Africa. Mussolini had now joined Hitler and war came to the Mediterranean. To avoid losses, the convoys bringing the tanks, guns, ammunition and men needed to strengthen General Wavell's army in Egypt had to make the long voyage round the Cape.

Italian advances into Egypt were quickly repulsed. Early in 1941 Wavell's men had advanced to the gates of Tripoli and were on the brink of sweeping the Italians out of Africa when the Germans added their strength to a flagging Italian invasion of Greece. Britain was committed by treaty to assist the Greeks. National honour took precedence over strategic sense, and Wavell was ordered to divert half his army and air force to Greece, with shipping gathered to convoy them from Alexandria to Piraeus. It was a futile exploit: the Germans were too strong and the navy took the retreating army from Greece to Crete.

Hitler then ordered the invasion of Crete. Not a man came in by sea – the navy stood in the way and destroyed the hastily assembled armada of caiques; instead the Germans came by air. Defeat followed a heroic defence and once again the navy, true to tradition, took the army out of Crete, but sadly at considerable cost and many had to be left behind.

Meanwhile, back in North Africa, Hitler, dismayed by his allies' poor performance, had sent an air army to Sicily to wrest control of the central Mediterranean from the Royal Navy, and the Afrika Corps under Rommel to Tripoli to stiffen the Italians. The *Luftwaffe* soon made their presence felt and the Central Mediterranean became a dangerous place for the surface ships of the navy, while in the desert Rommel pushed Wavell's depleted forces back to the Egyptian frontier. Only Tobruk held out, but its supply by sea was a hazardous and expensive task.

There now began a logistic battle; reinforcements of men, and every form of war material for the Desert Army had to come the long way round Africa; the Afrika Corps had the short sea route from Italy, but sustained heavy losses from air, surface and submarine attack, with forces operating from Malta being a particular thorn in Rommel's side. The Island's viability was kept on the edge by the interdiction of supply convoys and heavy bombing. Fighters ferried in by air craft carriers – a total of over 700 Hurricanes and Spitfires reached Malta in this way – and anti aircraft batteries faced an even more desperate situation than in the Battle of Britain for fuel and ammunition were always short. In August 1942 an epic convoy operation brought relief just in time.

Rommel's great advance towards Cairo and the Suez Canal ran out of steam just short of Alexandria, his stocks of fuel and ammunition almost exhausted. They were never properly replenished before Montgomery, his armies re-equipped and replenished by convoys round the Cape, was ready to launch his attack at El Alamein. Rommel's logistics never caught up; in the next few days, three vital tankers were sunk and his fuel position became critical.

Less than three weeks after El Alamein, the allies landed in Morocco and Algeria at the other end of the Mediterranean, the first major amphibious operation since Gallipoli, but better prepared and entirely successful. In time all the Axis armies in North Africa were defeated and thanks to the ships, submarines and aircraft operating from Malta an axis re-run of

Dunkirk was avoided and 400 000 German and Italian troops were removed from further participation in the war.

The allies had now gained control of the Mediterranean. The invasion of Sicily followed, Malta acting as a springboard, and so on to the invasion of Italy. The tide had turned.

On the other side of the world, the Japanese had joined their axis allies in active hostilities. The carrier aircraft attack on the US Fleet in Pearl Harbour achieved complete surprise and much damage to the battle fleet, but fortunately the more important US carriers were at sea. For a time the Japanese carried all before them. The hard pressed Royal Navy sent the *Prince of Wales* and *Repulse* to reinforce the skeleton Far East Fleet but the carrier that should have accompanied them had run aground and was delayed, not that her timely arrival would have made much difference. The two capital ships, trying to prevent the invasion of Malaya and without air support, were overwhelmed by shore-based air attack. Malaya and Singapore fell, the navy was powerless to help and there was no significant evacuation of the defeated troops.

The Japanese navy now commanded the south west Pacific: the Philippines were taken after a long and desperate defence, the British were driven out of Burma. A Japanese carrier sortie into the Indian Ocean sank *Hermes*, the Eastern Fleet's only carrier, and forced the navy to retreat to bases in East Africa. Japanese amphibious landings were made on New Britain and the Solomons, and attacks were planned on New Guinea. Only the Coral Sea lay between the Japanese and Australia: here the first of the great carrier battles was fought. Although a tactical victory for the Japanese – the Americans lost one carrier and the second was damaged, while the Japanese lost only one small carrier out of three – it was both a strategic and psychological reverse, the Japanese advance southward was checked and the growing myth of Imperial invincibility was shaken.

Then followed the decisive battle of Midway. The Japanese Naval Commanders had studied Jutland, almost exactly twenty six years before, and planned to inflict a crushing defeat on the US fleet. They had forgotten that the speed and confusion of modern warfare had denied Jellicoe a second Trafalgar, neither had they learnt the lesson of the inconclusive outcome of the first carrier battle in the Coral Sea. They hoped that a major operation to seize Midway, the outpost defending the Hawaiian Islands, would enable them to achieve a decisive victory over the US Fleet, instead they were soundly beaten for the first time in their history. It was both the end of the beginning of the Pacific war and the beginning of the end. It was a long hard haul to final victory, a campaign that depended crucially on command of the sea and availability of shipping. Meanwhile the German war of attrition against shipping was going badly for Britain. Mis-named the Battle of the Atlantic, it was waged in every ocean.

As U-boat numbers increased so did merchant shipping losses. There was a slight lull when in 1941 the German High Command ordered a redeployment of submarines to the Mediterranean to counter the attacks on Rommel's supply line, but in the year from April 1942 to April 1943, the monthly sinkings averaged over half a million tons. It was 1917 over again, and the possibility of defeat could not be dismissed.

But in April 1943 the crisis passed, not this time by the simple introduction of convoys but by a number of measures which all came to fruition: the flow of additional escorts from allied building yards, ten centimetre radar which countered the U-boat tactic of night surface attack, direction finding on U-boat High Frequency transmissions, the closing of the mid-ocean air cover gap with more long range aircraft and the escort carriers which provided continuous air cover, but above all, Ultra, which revealed the position of the U-boat packs and allowed evasive routing.

By May 1943, the battle had swung in favour of the Allies. U-boat losses mounted and Dönitz withdrew them from the North Atlantic. Liberty ships were pouring out of the American shipyards as the rate of replacement surged ahead of losses. Meanwhile, the American army and air force streamed across the Atlantic to begin the build up in the United Kingdom for the second front. With their supply of fuel now assured, RAF Bomber Command and the US Air Force were able to step up the strategic raids on Germany.

Don't Forget the Sea

> *The Battle of the Atlantic was the dominating factor all through the war. Never for one moment could we forget that everything happening elsewhere, on land, at sea or in the air, depended ultimately on its outcome...*
> Winston Churchill

By May 1944 the invasion forces were poised, the specialised shipping needed for the amphibious assault had been assembled, the follow up convoys to deliver the continuous flow of ammunition, fuel and food needed to sustain the battle were ready. Across the narrow seas, which had been the scene of many invasion attempts in the centuries before, sailed the biggest invasion fleet the world had ever known.

The land battle on the second front was joined. As the lines of communication lengthened, the transport forward of the 20 000 tons of supplies required daily to maintain the momentum was critical. The capture of ports became of vital importance but higher priority was given to sustaining the advance. It faltered at Arnhem, and attention turned instead to the capture of Antwerp and the clearance of the Scheldt Estuary. This difficult riverine area required amphibious expertise and an assault from the sea on the well defended island of Walcheren. A previous British expedition 135 years before, aiming to destroy the port of Antwerp, had failed; this time, after heavy fighting, Royal Marine Commandos cleared the entrance to the estuary and shortly afterwards the first convoy sailed up the Scheldt and the supply position was dramatically improved.

The U-boats, defeated in the wide Atlantic, now shifted their operations to the waters closer to the ports of arrival. Although they had some success their losses were high and the delivery of essential cargoes was not significantly hindered. The armies and air forces were able to continue their operations with their logistic support assured. Overrun by the Allies from both east and west, Germany surrendered.

The contribution of the forces of the USSR to this defeat was critical, but the vast quantities of war material that the western allies shipped to Russia played an important part. The convoys to Murmansk and Archangel are well documented, but not so well known is the Persian Gulf route direct from the US which accounted for 75 per cent of the supplies. Both routes made heavy demands on scarce shipping.

The navy now turned to assist in the defeat of Japan. Already the Eastern Fleet, reinforced by the carriers and battleships released from the western theatre by the elimination of the German heavy ships, had made its presence felt with attacks on Japanese installations in the Indian Ocean. Now the British Fleet joined the US Fleet in the Pacific. Not designed for wide ocean warfare and with inadequate afloat support the contribution they could make was limited but nevertheless the carrier air groups, equipped almost entirely with robust American aircraft, performed well. The British and Commonwealth fleets were rightly represented when the Japanese surrender was signed in Tokyo Bay.

The logistic support of the Pacific war was an organisational miracle. Hundreds of merchant ships and tankers were engaged in a massive shuttle operation from the west coast of the United States to the forward bases. Over 75 000 tons of food alone was needed each month to sustain quarter of a million fighting men. Fortunately the Japanese had devoted the bulk of their shipbuilding effort to carriers and battleships, not submarines.

Churchill provides an apt final comment on World War II: 'All was ruled by that harsh and despotic factor, shipping'.

POST-WORLD WAR II

The Hot War turned Cold – a conflict of ideologies. The Soviet Union, a continental power with an insignificant navy that had played only a minor part in the war, now turned to the sea. First came merchant shipping as an earner of hard currency and in less that twenty years the merchant fleet of the USSR was fifth in the world. Starting almost from scratch and learning from recent history, priority in warship construction was given to submarines; by the 1980s the Soviet submarine fleet outnumbered all other navies. Equally dramatic was the growth in fishing fleets and the output from the Soviet universities of graduates in maritime disciplines. But all this required an expenditure on defence three times that of the major western powers, a rate of spending that finally broke the bank and brought about the collapse of communism. It leaves the unanswered question: what will happen to the submarines?

The policy of deterrence has been successful in preventing global war, but not regional conflicts. Britain has been involved in three of these. The first was Korea. The artificial division of the nation between North and South provoked invasion by the North on 25 June 1950. The United Nations called upon member states to render assistance to the South. The Americans took the lead and provided the command, and the British Government agreed to commit forces. The Royal Navy's Far East Fleet was close at hand, and on 3 July aircraft from the carrier *Theseus* flew their first operational sorties. The first troops to arrive – by air – were Royal Marine Commandos – the Americans urgently needed coastal raiding parties. With great reluctance the British Chiefs of Staff despatched – by sea – a Brigade, of which many of the men were recalled reservists. Apart from some pilots on exchange service with the US Air Force, the RAF contribution was a flying boat squadron.

It was another Peninsular War. Max Hastings, in his comprehensive history of the conflict, echoes Wellington; 'Without absolute command of the sea the UN campaign could scarcely have been fought since every soldier, every ton of supplies he consumed, was brought into Korea by ship'.

Virtually unchallenged at sea, the principal role of the US and Royal Navies became that of providing floating air bases and gunfire support. A total of 76 ships of the Commonwealth Navies served in the war area and Fleet Air Arm aircraft flew some 23 000 operational sorties.

Entirely different was the bizarre episode of Suez. President Nasser, piqued by western refusal to fund the construction of the Aswan Dam, nationalized the Suez Canal on 26 July 1956. After three months of political vacillation and ostensibly to halt an Israeli attack on Egypt which might close the canal. An Anglo-French Task Force intervened. The Egyptian Air Force was destroyed on the ground by air attack, a parachute, helicopter and amphibious assault on Port Said was completely successful, the troops were well on their way to securing the Canal Zone when universal political pressure brought the operation to a halt.

The services felt let down by their political masters, and their failure to state a clear objective before the operation was launched was a lesson to remember. From the military experience came the requirement for new amphibious shipping to replace the ageing wartime left-overs and the need for properly equipped Commando Carriers with troop carrying helicopters. Twenty six years later, without warning, the Argentinians invaded the Falklands. The services were faced with the war the politicians had excluded from the list of all possible scenarios, an operation without allies, without shore based air defence, against a fighter bomber attack 8000 miles from the United Kingdom base. It is not in the nature of the British Services to reject a challenge, but once again the critical factor was shipping. It needed more merchant ships than warships to provide the logistic support that could ensure success. The outcome needs no reminder. If the Argentineans, instead of buying expensive air defence destroyers and maintaining a naval air arm with a single aircraft carrier, had invested in ten submarines instead of two, the outcome might have been different.

Closest to the present is the Iraqi invasion of Kuwait, which prompted United Nations condemnation. Economic sanctions were quickly imposed, but these are slow to bite and only military action was going to drive Saddam Hussein back across the border. It took time to assemble the forces needed to ensure success: it was six months before the UN coalition was ready to act. The British, who provided only ten per cent of the land and air forces, needed to take up from trade 144 merchant ships to deliver the 5000 fighting vehicles, 11 000 lorries, 100 000 tons of ordnance, 260 000 tons of support, spares, and food to establish their units ready for action. If the Straits of Hormuz or Bab el Mandeb had been mined, if terrorists had hi-jacked a bulk carrier to block the Suez Canal, if the Iraqi navy had acquired submarines – it could have been a different story.

All this is in the past. Perhaps the most important lesson history can teach is the difficulty of foretelling the future. Would Napoleon, Kaiser Wilhelm, Hitler, Galtieri or Saddam Hussein have embarked on their respective enterprises if they could have seen just a few years ahead? But for the British there is much to be learnt from the past. For many centuries both our prosperity and our security have depended on the free use of the sea. This is a truth that will not change. Let us not forget it.

5 An Address to the Council of Europe

Tadeusz Mazowiecki

Europe is living through an exceptional period. Part of our continent torn up from its root almost half a century ago is now aspiring to return. Back to Europe! This expression is gaining currency these days in the countries of Central and Eastern Europe. Politicians and economists are speaking of a return. The same applies to members of the cultural world, although it was easier for them to feel they still belonged to Europe: Europe was felt to be their spiritual home, a community of values and traditions. Perhaps the expression 'back to Europe' is too feeble to describe the process we are experiencing One should speak rather of a European renaissance, the rebirth of the Europe which virtually ceased to exist after Yalta.

The fact that I'm speaking to the Council of Europe is a sign of this rebirth, a sign of the renascent feeling of European togetherness and solidarity which was all too often forgotten in the past. With these remarks, I also wish to call to mind all those among whom a sense of European Community and solidarity has remained alive. I am thinking of those who publicly voiced their protest against acts of violence such as the invasion of Hungary in 1956 and of Czechoslovakia in 1968. I am also thinking of all our western friends who, after the establishment of the state of emergency in 1981, afforded us both moral and material support. At various times throughout these difficult years for us, the personal contacts established in this way helped us to create a very valuable network which still exists and which now offers a priceless foundation for rebuilding the political and economic components of the true community with the other countries in our continent.

This chapter is based on a speech given by Tadeusz Mazowiecki, then Prime Minister of Poland, on the occasion of Poland's accession to the Council of Europe in Strasbourg, 30 January 1990. Source: Text issued by Polish Government.

The Polish people are acutely aware of belonging to Europe and the European heritage. As aware as the European people situated at the cultural crossroads adjacent to the Superpowers are of experiencing alternating phases of political existence and non-existence, and who therefore feel the need to strengthen their identity. In all these situations, Europe has always remained a beacon, an object of affection which the Poles felt ready to defend. The idea of being the 'Ramparts of Christendom' and, by the same token, of Europe itself has remained alive in Poland throughout three centuries. Europe is therefore present in the Polish conscience as a value which it is worth living for and sometimes, indeed worth, dying for. But at the same time, Poland has borne a grudge against Europe and this sense of reproach has remained engraved to the present day in our collective consciousness. We continue to regard Europe as an ideal, the home of liberty and the rule of law, and we continue to relate closely to it, but we also continue to feel reproachful because of Yalta, because of the division of Europe and for having been left on the other side of the Iron Curtain.

Today, however, now that the return to Europe, the renaissance of Europe as a single entity is becoming more and more of a reality, we are wondering more and more frequently what we have to offer, what our contribution can be to the European treasure house. I believe that we do have a lot to offer. Our contribution to Europe is both our strength and our weakness. We are like someone recovering from a serious illness. For years we have undergone the tremendous pressure of totalitarianism but we have stood firm. However, we are still convalescing. Our economy is still in a critical condition which we are trying to alleviate: the democratic institutions of our state are only just being resuscitated and rebuilt. But we have acquired experience which we shall not forget and we shall pass on to others.

If we managed to survive as an entity, we owe this partly to our deep attachment to certain institutions and certain values regarded as the norm in Europe. We owe it to religion and the Church, our attachment to democracy and pluralism, human rights and civil liberties and to the ideal of solidarity. Even when we were unable to give these values their full potential or put them into practice in our public life, we still held them in esteem, we clung to them and struggled for them and therefore we know them and know their value. We know the price of being European, the price of European heritage which Westerners today have inherited without even having to pay the rights of succession. We can remind them of this price. We therefore offer Europe our faith in Europe.

We are lodging an application for membership of the Council of Europe. We desire to 'achieve a greater unity between its members for the purpose of safeguarding and realising the ideals and principles which are their common heritage and facilitating their economic and social progress'. We wish to share in promoting human rights and fundamental freedoms. The Council of Europe, which has performed wonders in the defence of rights and freedoms and which is a rich fountain of European ideals and initiatives seems the right place for Poland, which itself achieved a great deal in the defence of these same rights and freedoms.

The gash across Europe symbolised until recently by the Berlin Wall can now begin to heal. This can be a fascinating process, although undoubtedly a very complex and lengthy one. And yet today, as opposed to yesterday, the principle political requirements exist, or are taking shape, which will make this process possible.

Our country is confronted with the enormous task of reconstituting the rights and institutions which characterise modern democracies and rebuilding a market economy, after an interruption of several decades. Added to this, there is a need to overcome enormous economic problems. We not only have to recreate rights and institutions but, in cases where they were non-existent we have to start from scratch. Otherwise our two European worlds will never manage to live in harmony.

Poland has already set to work. The government which I have been leading for barely five months has drafted and had enacted numerous laws which provide for a legal framework for the independence of the judiciary, for freedom of the press and freedom to organise, for freedom to found political parties and for local self-government which, with the forthcoming municipal elections, will soon become effective. We are preparing a new Constitution of the Polish Republic in which it will become a democratic State subject to the rule of law.

Since the beginning of the year, we have embarked upon a very difficult economic programme, one which aims not only to check inflation but also to establish the foundations for a modern market economy, after the fashion of the institutions which have proved their worth in the highly developed European countries. We intend to continue along this path, successively introducing new elements, among which importance will be attributed to reforming the system of ownership and introducing certain forms of state intervention and social protection within the market economy. We shall gradually develop this system to combine effective mechanisms for stimulating production with adequate protection for the social groups which require assistance within a free and competitive economy.

Furthermore, in collaboration with our partners in the CMEA (COMECOM), we have taken far-reaching steps to reform the organisation which, in our view, should be based on free consent between states which feel it is in their interest to be members and deal jointly with matters which they believe call for concerted measures and action. We have no desire to create closed associations cut off from the rest of the world, not only by frontiers but by customs barriers. We wish to avoid this so as not to create a Europe where economic walls have replaced the political ones.

We know you also favour an outward-looking policy and this is all to the good, for otherwise there would be a hidden obstacle preventing us from making the progress towards each other, despite the desire for *rapprochement* which is clearly expressed in all current appeals for an undivided Europe.

Just as the Berlin Wall not so long ago was both a symbol of the divided Europe and a physical barrier splitting Germany into two separate states, so its collapse, while offering an opportunity to unite Europe, at the same time raises problems of German unification. No people can be denied the right to live within the same state. But the division of Germany resulted from a major disaster caused by the Nazi state which destroyed tens of millions of lives. It is therefore not at all surprising today if, at a time when the prospect is emerging of a united German State, the memory of this disaster arouses anxieties which cannot be alleviated even by obviously weighty counter arguments such as the fact that today the situation is different and the Germans themselves are different. We acknowledge these arguments. But we must understand these anxieties and overcome them by settling the German question with the agreement of all the interested parties and in a manner which, from the outset, will offer a credible sense of security to all those who require it and which above all will guarantee the inviolability of the Western frontier of Poland.

The upheavals in Central Europe and the Soviet Union are creating unparalleled opportunities but also carry risks. In some countries the supporters of the old regime are no longer in a position to determine the course of events but can still impede it. In others, although they are on the defensive, they have given up on hope, and have not lost the capability, of regaining their former position. If severe symptoms of destabilization, together with economic chaos, were to persist, their opportunities would increase. They diminish if the peoples in our region, who at the moment are proving active, can carry through the crucial transformations resolutely but as calmly as possible, and above all if they can resist the temptation to try to achieve everything at once. That approach is often counterproductive.

Another danger is that of Balkanization of part of the European continent, or of the various countries, because of acute tensions between the people or states, tensions whose origins lie in the present as well as the past. If partisan or national interests were to be lost sight of, it would be a major obstacle to establishing healthy cooperation and mutual understanding in this continent of ours which is in the throes of change.

But the events in Central and Eastern Europe, although they carry risks, are first and foremost an unbelievable and historic challenge. And although obviously the challenges are mainly for us, the people of Central Europe, they are also a historic challenge and a task for the whole of Europe. The scope is vast. There is room for Western Europeans who see what we are trying to do and believe our aims. With them – with you – it will be easier to narrow the distance between us. The wall which divided free Europe from enslaved Europe is down. Now we have to fill in the gulf between poor Europe and affluent Europe. If Europe is to be a 'common home' whose door is open to all, such great disparities cannot be allowed to continue. A huge job of work awaits us all.

We now need new guidelines to guide our endeavours down a common European road, to no-one's exclusion and everyones advantage. It is not easy to chart such a course, for it takes thought and collaboration. But as, in your part of the continent, post-1992 Europe is even now taking shape, why not start thinking in terms of a Europe of the year 2000? To be realistic, what kind of Europe might that be if we unite our efforts?

It will certainly not be a European area with free movement of goods, capital and people but it might be a Europe where borders and tariffs would be much less of an obstacle, a Europe wholly open to the young. For the fate of our continent depends on what kind of young people we bring up.

It might be a Europe in which contact between creative and scientific communities, fostering permability of national cultures and thereby bringing them closer together, will be richer than it is today. It will not be a Europe with a common currency but it might be a Europe in which economies will be complementary and where differences in living standards will be smaller and international economic exchange richer. It might also be a Europe with a healthy climate, pure water and unpolluted soil, an environmentally clean Europe. But above all it will have to be a Europe which has made distinct progress towards disarmament, a Europe which will make an impact on the rest of the world as a factor for peace and international co-existence.

By applying our minds, we could find many other spheres of social life which we could arrange better in this last decade of the 20th century. We need but apply ourselves to the task.

In this continent of ours there are institutions in which a labour of this kind has long-term prospects, because it has already been going on for quite a while. One of these institutions is the Council of Europe, one of whose aims is to achieve greater unity among its members for the purpose of safeguarding and realising the ideals and principles which are their common heritage and facilitating their economic and social progress.

Now that events are speeding up in Europe, it is beginning to be possible for us – states, groups and organisations – to reflect about these matters together, and we can glimpse the possibility of and need for pan-European structures to take charge of these tasks.

I think the time has come to realise the 'common home' and the European confederation which eminent statesmen have recently proposed, it is time to establish institutions genuinely encompassing the whole of Europe.

That is why I would draw attention to the suggestion I put forward in our parliament, for a Council or European Cooperation, embracing all signatories to the Final Act of the Conference on Security and Cooperation in Europe. The council would have two functions: firstly to make preparations for summit meetings of the CSCE states and secondly to examine pan-European problems arising in between regular meetings of the CSCE states. We think this would lend needed impetus to the CSCE process and at the same time facilitate future initiatives concerning our continent and aiming to secure its unity.

Strasbourg, the capital of Europe, is a city which like our country, has often been caught up in the turmoil of history. A city which had several times changed hands and has wondered about its identity. But also a city which, though the capital of a region which has been fought over since time immemorial a place that has suffered the ravages of revolution, is now an oasis of peace and prosperity. This city is a symbol of hope for us who live in the heart of Europe, where echoes of old-age quarrels are still audible. Today the whole of Europe is faced with the historic challenge of restoring its unity. Will we be equal? That depends on us and you. Over a year ago. Pope John Paul II, addressing the Parliamentary assembly said:

> 'The member countries of your council are aware that they are not the whole of Europe: in expressing the fervent wish for intensification of cooperation, already sketched out, with other nations, particularly in Central and Eastern Europe, I feel sure I share the desire of millions of men and women who know that they are linked by a common history and who hope for a destiny of unity and solidarity on a scale of this whole continent.'

When he said this, probably no-one suspected the climate would become auspicious and that his hopes would begin to be realised.

Among Strasbourg's many symbols, on the cathedral facade, are the statues of the wise virgins. Let us be wise virgins. Let us be capable of recognising historic juncture and rising to its challenge – cautiously, boldly and clear-sightedly.

6 The North Atlantic Alliance: Yesterday, Today and Tomorrow

Field Marshal Sir Richard Vincent
GBE, KCB, DSO

YESTERDAY

The end of the Second World War, fifty years ago, left both Western European nations and their North Atlantic allies facing the challenge of economic reconstruction while at the same time viewing with concern the expansionist policies and tendencies of their wartime ally, the Soviet Union. While the Western government fulfilled their commitment to undertake the demobilization of their forces and the reduction of their defence establishments, they noted with alarm that the Soviets continued to maintain their military forces at full strength. Appeals to respect the United Nations Charter and to implement the international settlements reached at the end of the war fell on deaf ears as the Communist Soviet Government pursued its declared ideological aims. In such a situation it was not possible to guarantee the national sovereignty or independence of democratic states facing the threat of outside aggression or internal subversion. Throughout Central and Eastern Europe, as well as elsewhere in the world, the result was the repression of basic human and civil rights and freedoms, the imposition of undemocratic forms of government and the elimination of effective opposition.

The deteriorating situation was brought to a head between 1947 and 1949 in a series of dramatic events. These included: direct threats to Norway, Greece, Turkey and other Western European countries; the April 1948 blockade of Berlin which lasted for almost a year; and finally in June 1948, the coup in Czechoslovakia.

The signing of the Brussels Treaty in March 1948 by Belgium, France, Luxembourg, the Netherlands and the United Kingdom, signified the determination to resist these growing pressures by developing a common defence system and strengthening the ties between them. Negotiations with the United States and Canada then followed on the creation of a single North Atlantic Alliance based on security guarantees and mutual commitments. Denmark, Iceland, Italy, Norway and Portugal were subsequently invited to participate in this process. Finally on 4 April 1949, the North Atlantic Treaty was signed in Washington by these twelve nations. Greece and Turkey acceded to the Treaty three years later and in 1955 the Federal Republic of Germany joined the Alliance. In 1982 Spain also became a member.

Member states entered into the Treaty freely after public debate and due parliamentary process. Signature of the Treaty upholds the individual rights of nations in addition to their international obligations under the United Nations Charter. With membership comes the commitment to share risks and responsibilities along with the benefits of collective security.

The Alliance's ability to adapt flexibly to different national needs and political imperatives was aptly demonstrated when in March 1966 President de Gaulle announced France's intention to withdraw from the integrated military structure, and again in 1982 with Spain's accession to the Treaty without participation in NATO's military structure. It is of course of interest that both countries have different relationships and agreements with the military side of NATO whilst politically they are full and active members of the Alliance's political bodies. Although her forces are not part of the integrated military structure, Spain does participate with the Major NATO Commanders in order to develop her military contributions to the common defence. These unique relationships continue to evolve as the Alliance adapts to the new defence and security situation.

NATO's strategy during the Cold War era was based on deterrence and should deterrence fail, the use of collective military force to counter aggression and restore the territorial integrity of the member states. In the early years, that military force was foreseen in the form of a massive nuclear retaliation. Initially this was dependent on the strategic nuclear forces of the United States and later included theatre tactical nuclear forces.

As the situation changed, the need for a more flexible range of military responses more effectively to underpin deterrence or counter aggression was recognized and a strategy of flexible response was developed and agreed.

TODAY

The ending of the Cold War in 1990 has brought about major changes within our Alliance. Mercifully, that East-West confrontation of those earlier days came to an end without a serious international conflict – an outcome in which our Alliance clearly played a pivotal role. But in security and defence terms, these great changes now pose major challenges in redefining our defence objectives and the wider security policy to which they should respond.

Contrary to popular hopes and expectations, after the lifting of the Iron Curtain in 1990, some parts of Central and Eastern Europe – and more widely than that – have, in the absence of the rigid Cold War framework, become highly unstable and far less predictable in security and defence terms. We have not yet reached the end of all these developments, but clearly future historians will study the Cold War as a unique era. But what is not yet clear today is the sobriquet they will give to the new age that we are now entering. So there is much at stake in the new policies we are now implementing and the further changes still being considered.

ALLIANCE STRATEGIC CONCEPT

It is noteworthy that the Alliance was sufficiently forward looking to begin this process of transformation before the demise of the Soviet Union and the Warsaw Pact with the London Summit in 1990, when it formerly declared the end of the Cold War. In doing so it extended the hand of friendship to those former adversaries in Central and Eastern Europe and it directed a fundamental review of Alliance strategy in the light of the rapidly changing political and military circumstances of the time.

The Rome Summit which followed at the end of 1991 enunciated a new Alliance Strategic Concept. This new strategy redefined NATO's overall purpose and functions in the post-Cold War era in terms of the essential framework within which all other Alliance activities and development should take place. As its starting point, it reaffirmed NATO's fundamental role:

> 'To safeguard the freedom and security of all its members by political and military means, in accordance with the principles of the United Nations Charter.'

Underpinning that overall security objective, there were four key elements:

- To provide one of the indispensable foundations for a stable security environment in Europe.
- To serve as a transatlantic forum for Allied consultations on any issues that affect member nations' vital interests.
- To deter and defend against any threat of aggression against the territory of any NATO member.
- And, finally, to preserve the strategic balance within Europe.

In this process of strategic change, it was clearly recognized that the political aspects underpinning our security, including greater emphasis on arms control and other non-military measures, would become more important. But the new Strategic Concept also made it quite clear that the maintenance of an adequate military capability, both as a deterrent and, if needed, for collective defensive use, remained essential. Thus, the fundamental task of our much slimmed down forces remains today, under Article V of the Washington Treaty, to deter aggression against Alliance nations from any source, and should that fail, to restore peace and security as quickly as possible.

A NEW PEACEKEEPING ROLE

In 1992, at the Ministerial Meeting held in Oslo, a further evolution of Alliance policy was approved to allow it, on decisions to be taken unanimously in Council on a case by case basis, to support peacekeeping activities under the authority of appropriate international legal mandates. As a result, NATO forces can, if so authorized and all the nations decide, participate in international operations in response to events such as those occurring in former Yugoslavia. And today it is these two major policy formulations – namely the New Strategic Concept and the requirement to be ready, if authorized, to support peacekeeping operations – that determine the operational capabilities and organizations needed in our new emerging force structures.

COOPERATION PROGRAMME

One other significant development in NATO policy at the end of 1991 was the start of a new programme of dialogue and cooperation with the emerging democracies in Central and Eastern Europe. This initiative was launched under the auspices of the North Atlantic Cooperation Council, which was established for this purpose following the Rome Summit. And one of the most significant elements of this programme has been in the field of military cooperation.

Yet the question remained whether these limited cooperative efforts under the North Atlantic Cooperation Council were moving far and fast enough to meet the expectations and needs of our Partners to fulfil one of the key elements of our new Strategic Concept quoted earlier, namely:

> 'To provide one of the indispensable foundations for a stable security environment in Europe.'

It was this unanswered question, combined with some of the developing crises and instabilities in Central and Eastern Europe, that led to growing pressure from several countries for closer ties with NATO, including in some cases, calls for full and early membership.

BRUSSELS SUMMIT

It was against this background of continuing adaption, and increasing concern about events in the former Yugoslavia, that the last NATO Summit was held in Brussels in January 1994. This provided new leadership and direction at the highest levels on the further evolution of NATO's policies in response to these fast changing and immensely challenging international developments. The outcome of the 1994 Summit was that the Heads of State and Government made collectively the firmest recommitment to the Alliance, and gave clear direction on the new tasks and priorities needed to carry it effectively into the next century as the essential cornerstone of Euro-Atlantic Security.

At the heart of this was the strongest reaffirmation that Euro-Atlantic Security is indivisible and that the transatlantic link remains the bedrock of the Alliance; but it was also recognized that the aspirations for a greater European Security and Defence identity, following ratification of the Maastricht Treaty, would become increasingly important. In practical terms this was supported in the form of a strengthened European pillar of the Alliance through a revitalization of the Western European Union, (WEU) recently moved to Brussels, which avoided both a divergent strategic approach and unaffordable duplication and competition at a time of shrinking defence resources.

The Summit also gave clear direction on three other specific initiatives namely: Partnership for Peace; Countering Proliferation of Weapons of Mass Destruction; and the further Adjustment of Alliance Structures and Procedures.

PARTNERSHIP FOR PEACE

In considering what additional measures were needed to help project and underpin security more effectively in Central and Eastern Europe, including the Successor States of the former Soviet Union, the imaginative Partnership for Peace (PfP) initiative, agreed at the Summit, provides a means whereby partners, including OSCE members, could participate, at a pace and level of involvement which they themselves could determine, in a defined range of cooperative activities. Many of these are being offered in the military field, including joint training and exercises for peacekeeping, search and rescue and humanitarian operations, on which the wider implications will be addressed later. In addition, PfP provides the opportunity to align other aspects of defence planning and organization more closely with the Alliance, which will also help very significantly to improve our collective ability to operate together more effectively with partner nations, if authorized, in future multinational operations.

Two of the most immediate and visible signs of the changes brought about by PfP are the full time presence of representatives from PfP partner nations in the newly constructed Manfred Wörner Cooperation Wing at NATO Headquarters in Brussels, and in the Partnership Coordination Cell (PCC) at Mons. In Brussels, PfP Liaison Officers act as an important link between their nations and the Alliance, representing their nations in the various fora which have been opened to them in the Headquarters. In the PCC at Mons, the emphasis is on the practical aspects of military cooperation and covers the preparatory planning for partnership training and exercises. These are coordinated with the Major NATO Commanders who have responsibility for the detailed preparation and conduct of such military activities.

Following the 1994 Summit, three Partnership for Peace exercises were arranged, with very considerable effort. This was important politically and symbolically to give the programme early practical effect, and it reflected great credit on all concerned that so much real progress was made in all these PfP developments in that first year. Our next challenge is not just to maintain this momentum, but to expand the scope and relevance of PfP.

The opportunities made available through Partnership for Peace bring with them some very important benefits, both politically and operationally. These include a common approach to military concepts and doctrine for operations such as peacekeeping, humanitarian assistance and search and rescue; common higher training standards; increased interoperability; and greater operational effectiveness; all leading to more openness, understanding and trust at the political level, and between military forces of all ranks and levels.

This process should also secure a wider strategic objective in encouraging PfP nations to restructure their armed forces with greater transparency under democratic control and to achieve closer and more constructive practical cooperation with NATO. PfP also gives those who participate actively the important opportunity to consult formally with NATO on matters which they perceive as a direct threat to their territorial integrity, political independence, or security. This evolutionary process of contributing to a wider and more stable security architecture in Europe is now, therefore, underway through a process of relevant and political cooperation under PfP. Beyond that the purpose and modalities of the possible enlargement of NATO are now under formal internal examination. And in this regard, PfP will also represent a valuable preparatory experience for all concerned – as and when – the further extension of membership is considered under Article X of the Washington Treaty.

PROLIFERATION

It was in response to the growing concerns about the proliferation of Weapons of Mass Destruction (WMD) that the Summit in January 1994 also decided to intensify and expand NATO's political and defence effort in this area, starting with the development of an overarching policy framework which was approved by Foreign Ministers at their meeting in Istanbul the following June.

This Policy Framework recognizes that NATO has an important role to play in this field, in the realization that the increasing possibilities of trade in dual use commodities and the transfer of the related technologies, as well as the spread of expertise and knowledge of them, have made proliferation more difficult to control today than in the past.

In taking these steps better to prepare a counter to any threat posed by WMD and their delivery means, NATO will do so in a manner that supports and complements current international efforts such as the Nuclear Non-Proliferation Treaty, the Chemical Weapons Convention and the Missile Technology Control Regime.

In the development of Alliance work in this area, a balance will have to be struck between efforts made to prevent proliferation and in the complementary defence capabilities needed in case prevention fails. And, inevitably, resource constraints have to be considered here, for example, in meeting the requirements for Extended Air Defence including a potentially costly Theatre Missile Defence capability, where a NATO wide approach might offer more cost effective solutions.

ADJUSTMENT OF ALLIANCE STRUCTURES AND PROCEDURES

Following the Summit, the Alliance has also been looking again at its crisis management arrangements needed to respond more effectively to events such as those which have developed in former Yugoslavia. The growing requirement here to coordinate with the United Nations, OSCE and WEU, together with the possible need to work more closely with non-NATO nations who may participate in such multinational operations, are some of the issues which are being addressed. One of the proposals from the Summit which has the greatest potential in this area, from a military standpoint, has been the work on Combined Joint Task Forces (CJTF).

This concept involves the development of multinational, tri-service headquarters, based on deployable self-contained elements of NATO's existing integrated force structures, but adapted further where necessary to incorporate appropriate representation from Alliance nations who are not currently within the integrated force structures. CJTFs must also be capable of integrating efficiently the forces and staffs of non-NATO nations who, if authorised, could contribute with NATO to future operations.

If NATO as a whole decides that it should not or cannot act in a given situation, the CJTF must be available, on the authority of the North Atlantic Council, to provide the agreed operational support needed for WEU led initiatives. By this further adaption of Alliance forces in a manner that allows them to be separable but not separate from the existing structures, nations can avoid the duplication of very expensive command and control capabilities; and at the same time the Alliance maintains the one integrated command structure for NATO-led operations needed to ensure the continuing effectiveness of its general capability, which remains a core function under Article V of the Washington Treaty.

This need to develop a separable but not separate Combined Joint Task Force capability for NATO-led operations, as directed by the Summit, needs emphasis because there is a school of thought that peacekeeping operations are so different in character to conventional, higher intensity General Defence operations under Article V of the Treaty, that they require a fundamentally different approach in their command and force structures. While recognizing the need to adapt military capabilities to the specific needs of individual peacekeeping operations – which is, of course, precisely why the Alliance is seeking to implement the concept of CJTFs– there are two important reasons why this proposal for separate structures and procedures within NATO for peacekeeping and high intensity General Defence operations is seriously flawed:

- The first is that there are insufficient resources to create unnecessary separate structures; for today national defence budgets and the NATO common funded military budget and other programmes are shrinking, not increasing.
- But there is a second reason which is strategic in character and far more important. For to have separate operational structures for non-Article V contingency operations and General Defence (Article V operations assumes that the one will never develop into the other. If that proves to be wrong – recognizing that, historically, large conflicts have sometimes had small and unrecognized beginnings – then forces will have been committed on a basis that would be incapable of responding to such a serious escalation, forcing the introduction of fundamentally new operational structures at the very moment the crisis reaches its peak. Furthermore, the deliberate adoption of an *ad hoc* approach, outside the integrated military structure, to the command force organization for NATO led operations, leaves open the important question of who then is to be accountable for their training, readiness and ultimate operational effectiveness?

So to seek to adapt internal NATO military structures by dividing them on the basis of an artificial distinction between General Defence and Other Operations, such as Peacekeeping, would be, quite simply, strategic folly.

In the same vein, nations must beware of over optimizing their forces for lower intensity peacekeeping operations. Quite apart from the possibility of an unpredictable escalation in such conflicts, more and more nations today have been acquiring high intensity capabilities which NATO must be capable of deterring credibly, or of dealing with collectively in effective operations, should deterrence fail.

PEACEKEEPING

So much for the main initiatives which emerged in the 1994 Brussels Summit. Turning now to focus on Alliance support for United Nations operations in former Yugoslavia during the period 1992-1994. Despite the firm resolve shown by NATO, there has been continuing criticism in some quarters of the alleged lack of political will, within the Alliance collectively, to take the necessary actions to help resolve more effectively the conflict in the former Yugoslavia. This stems from a widespread ignorance about the extent of the commitment already made by NATO and a wider lack of understanding about the international strategic approach needed to deal more effectively with such difficult and complex conflicts.

The possible military responses to events in former Yugoslavia have been, of course, determined by the terms and conditions of the UN Security Council Resolutions (UNSCRs) which provide the essential legal basis on which all such operations are conducted. The fact that up until the end of 1994 there were over 60 UNSCRs related to former Yugoslavia indicates a serious lack of clarity in formulating a coherent international strategic response to this complex and tragic conflict.

To date, NATO air forces operate mainly in support of UN ground forces whose operations have been essentially of a humanitarian nature, while NATO's maritime embargo operations, mounted in conjunction with the WEU, support very effectively the enforcement of UNSCR 820 in the Adriatic. In addition to these operations, the Alliance has repeatedly stated its willingness to support the implementation of a Peace Agreement entered into freely and in good faith by the parties, under an acceptable mandate.

The reality is that NATO integrated forces currently make the largest single contribution to the international effort in former Yugoslavia. Excluding forces serving directly under UN command, there are presently over 200 aircraft, up to 20 highly capable warships and some 10 000 men and women from Alliance nations conducting maritime and air operations in support of the United Nations effort, 24 hours a day, seven days a week. And these are just the forces committed at any one time; in order to sustain them and to allow for the periodic relief of personnel and equipment, three to four times those numbers are actually required. In addition, nearly 19 000 additional personnel are contributed directly by Alliance nations to UNPROFOR operations.

Thus, out of a total of almost 49 000 personnel committed in support of UN operations associated with the former Yugoslavia at the end of 1994, about 29 000 of these – that is nearly two thirds of them – come directly or via the Alliance from NATO nations; and about 80 per cent of those are provided by European members of the Alliance.

Those who over simplistically advocate a more direct and military assertive role for the Alliance reveal their misunderstanding of what is realistically possible in such an approach and what it might achieve in terms of a long term and enduring solution to the conflict. To quote our Secretary General Willy Claes:

> '...their policy prescriptions would require a radical departure from the basic course we have been pursuing since the end of the Cold War. Instead of accepting that crises such as the Bosnian one can only be managed through a concentrated international effort, they demand that NATO act unilaterally, outside the international framework. Instead of an evolutionary process of extending security and stability to the East through a process of closer association of states to the East with Western institutions, they would have us enlarge our membership without a thought to its consequences for the wider stability in Europe'.

There is much to be learned from the incoherent international strategic response to the events in Former Yugoslavia since the crisis first developed; but this cannot be a logical reason for superficially dismissing NATO's wider purpose and utility in the post-Cold War era.

TOMORROW – FUTURE WESTERN SECURITY PROSPECTS

So a look ahead to the Future Prospects for Western Security. Put simply, is NATO now set to respond to the changing security needs of the 21st Century; or is the Alliance in danger of becoming a post-Cold War anachronism? Is NATO important any more; and if it is not, what then is to replace it?

Given the scale and pace of international developments that have unfolded since the end of the Cold War, perhaps the most remarkable thing today is that the Alliance's New Strategic Concept has withstood these testing challenges so well over these past four years. But Alliance Strategy has never stood still; nor can it today ignore the continuing international developments and aspirations that bear on its continuing relevance and evolution.

But, in this process of continuing change and adaption, there are two unique characteristics of the Alliance which should not be overlooked and which bear directly on its continuing relevance and practical effectiveness in future.

The first unique asset in NATO is its efficient multi-national military structure and, in particular, the integrated command and control capability. These are not mere military virility symbols: they provide the essential framework from which the practical force planning and, if needed, the effective mounting and conduct of really efficient multinational operations can be conducted. There are three indispensable elements which contribute to the effectiveness of the Alliance military structures.

First, the Defence Planning and Review Process is important as a means of keeping nations up to the mark in terms of their force contributions, the continuing modernisation of their forces and in ensuring the maintenance of high standards of training, interoperability and operational readiness. More widely, this key process ensures the visibility and transparency that underpins the equitable sharing of burdens and responsibilities from which the collective benefits of the Alliance ultimately derive. Adaption and streamlining of the process and organisation of NATO defence planning might be considered if that would allow it to operate more effectively, but tampering with this substance in a manner that would undermine its present rigorous application and wider value must be approached with caution.

The second important contribution that adds substance to the Alliance integrated military structures derives from the common funded programmes. These form the foundation on which effective collective military capabilities are built and they provide operational benefits that in many cases would simply not be achievable by most nations acting by themselves. A good example of this is the NATO Airborne Early Warning Force, which ensures an integrated operational capability which individually many nations could not even contemplate nationally under current circumstances for budgetary reasons. Similar considerations are bound to apply if in future it is decided, for example, to acquire a much needed improvement in airborne ground surveillance capabilities. These commonly funded programmes cost nations a very small portion of their overall defence expenditures (less than a fraction of one per cent in many cases) yet they provide immense benefits as operational force multipliers to the Alliance as a whole.

And finally, NATO standardisation programmes provide another very significant force multiplier of considerable operational value to the Alliance. It is not just the standardisation of weapons and equipment, important as that may be, which has resulted from these efforts. Perhaps even more relevant is the ability of Alliance armies, navies and air forces to work together effectively using detailed and well practised common operating procedures that have been built up painstakingly over several decades.

In a General Defence Role, under Article V of the Washington Treaty, NATO integrated forces and the benefits they derive from common funding and the overall Defence Planning Process, are irreplaceable.

Recent events in the former Yugoslavia have indicated their wider relevance and adaptability in today's less predictable security environment. Within this integrated framework, however, some aspects of the Alliance military organization can be further adapted along the lines indicated above.

Looking beyond these integrated military structures and common funded programmes, lies the second unique characteristic of the Alliance which was restated with absolute clarity at the 1991 Rome Summit, and which remains fundamental to future Western collective security interests, namely:

> 'To serve as a *transatlantic forum* on any issue that effects the vital security interests of its members.'

That is not to say that European nations should not usefully develop a stronger security and defence identity, giving it further substance. Indeed, a genuinely more effective European effort is essential if the North American Allies are to be assured that the European nations are prepared to further shoulder the burden of regional security aspirations, consistent with their wider political and economic objectives. But this European Security and Defence Identity (ESDI) needs to develop in a manner that is strategically coherent with NATO policies and capabilities, avoids wasteful overlap and duplication, and is effective at the operational level.

In this respect, practical day to day military cooperation between NATO and the WEU continues to develop satisfactorily, but the Brussels Summit directed that it be carried further, for example through the dual use of CJTFs. Beyond that, in the wider post-Maastricht approach to European defence issues, there may be a lack of realism in some quarters about what Western Europe alone can achieve in security and defence terms – though it is not popular to say so in some quarters. For it is unsound to look upon Western Europe as a geostrategic entity on its own, divorced from the North Atlantic, Canada and the US. Given the considerable uncertainties remaining in parts of Central and Eastern Europe, Western Europe on its own will not achieve an assured East-West strategic balance for the foreseeable future; nor does it possess the surveillance, intelligence gathering resources, strategic lift and power projection capabilities which NATO as a whole can achieve collectively and economically through the commitments made to it by all its members, including those from North America. Nor is it realistic to expect that these new and very costly capabilities might be developed in Western Europe at a time when, with one or two notable exceptions, most nations are still reducing their defence budgets and postponing important modernization programmes needed to keep their smaller force structures up to date.

Some would argue that the recently renamed Organization for Security and Cooperation in Europe (OSCE), which also embraces the Euro-Atlantic Security area with a much wider membership than NATO, should now take the lead responsibility for security and defence matters in this enlarged region. There is no doubt that the former CSCE has played an invaluable role in Human Rights, through the Helsinki Final Act and especially in its conventional arms control and confidence building measures achieved in the Conventional Forces in Europe Treaty and the Open Skies Agreement. And it still has important tasks ahead with regard to arms control, especially in the Balkans where no such regime currently exists; and it can, importantly, through its founding charter provide the international legal authority for others to act. But it has no forces assigned to it, nor the means of employing them effectively if they were, and with 53 member states it is proving extremely difficult, through its newly established Conflict Prevention Centre, to achieve anything like consensus to decide on action that should be taken in response to serious crises and conflicts.

No doubt there are similar movements at work on both sides of the Atlantic who believe that, with the collapse of the Warsaw Pact, the time has come to let Europe look after itself and to concentrate instead on other national interests and domestic priorities. But with longer range and more accurate and potent weapon systems; with instant media communications having an immediate effect on public and political opinion; together with our highly interactive economies and environments, the strategic reality today is that the Euro-Atlantic Security Region is even more interdependent and any moves, on either side of the North Atlantic, to develop a 'Europe only' or a 'US only' approach will, in the longer term, be fraught with strategic risks.

CONCLUSION

Regrettably, these strategic realities are not widely understood today by our publics – and even some in our governments or international institutions – which is why the North Atlantic Council recently concluded that urgent priority should be given to explaining these matters more effectively and more widely in future. In this respect, there is also a remarkable contrast in the attitude of so many nations in Central and Eastern Europe who have endured a quite different historical experience over the past 55 years, and who therefore continue to press hard for a much closer relationship with NATO – including full membership – when at the same time there is a growing complacency and superficiality in some NATO nations which questions the continuing relevance and utility of our Alliance. I have therefore welcomed the opportunity to set out how the Alliance has adapted to the new post-Cold War security environment, and how that process continues apace today. None of us working for the Alliance are complacent about the need for further change and adaption. But such important developments need to occur on the basis of a sound understanding of the strategic and operational realities to which I have referred, if we are to maintain the real effectiveness of our collective security and defence efforts in the uncertain years ahead.

7 Why We Are Here: The New NATO and Its Vision of a New Europe

General George A Joulwan

In the autumn of 1989, when the Berlin Wall came down, I was commanding the United States Army's V Corps in Germany. I remember one clear November morning particularly well. There was great uncertainty in the air. So I flew to the inter-German border to be with the troops of the famous 11th Armoured Cavalry Regiment. There, I witnessed an unforgettable sight. Lined up at each crossing site in the Corps' sector for as far as the eye could see were thousands of East German automobiles. As their occupants drove across the border into freedom, jubilant West Germans greeted them with flowers. They hugged one another and openly wept. Even the most jaded eyes shed tears of joy that day.

Two of my soldiers on patrol along the border got caught in one of the resulting traffic jams. They saw me later at an observation post near the border and excitedly told me what had happened. 'General,' one said, 'we were caught in this traffic jam with thousands of East Germans. Hundreds of them got out of their cars, hugged us, and thanked us for their freedom.' The other eighteen-year-old GI quietly observed, 'General, now we know why we are here.'

Now we know why we are here! That young soldier had discovered first-hand why millions of NATO troops had stood the long watch for four decades in a divided Europe. He had learned the true meaning of freedom and grasped the critical importance of US involvement in European affairs. He had come to see that the vast, transatlantic investment of blood and treasure had yielded the greatest dividends of all – peace, liberty and the emancipation of the human spirit.

Now, some six years later, no one doubts whether Americans and Europeans have benefited from their transatlantic ties in the North Atlantic

Treaty Organization. Some, however, are all too quick to question the continued utility of history's greatest Alliance.

After 34 years of service in America's Army and over 16 years of duty in Europe, I am convinced that NATO remains the anchor of American involvement in Europe, the linchpin of transatlantic security, and the key to the realization of a New Europe – one whole, free, peaceful and prosperous. In supporting that position, I will briefly recount the events culminating in the creation of NATO; highlight the efforts of the Alliance in the creation of a dynamic, democratic Western Europe; and examine the Alliance's role in the end of the Cold War. I will then explain why the fall of the Wall and the demise of Communism signalled not the end of history but rather the beginning of a new phase in NATO's continuing mission of collective security and defence. Finally, I will describe the new NATO and explain how its operations and initiatives contribute to the emergence of a vital New Europe. Throughout this chapter, I will argue that Americans and Europeans must perpetuate their solid transatlantic relationship and continue to pay the substantial price of peace and stability. In other words, I seek to update what that young soldier of the 11th Armoured Cavalry Regiment came to understand, 'Why we are here.'

THE TRANSATLANTIC PARTNERSHIP: THE FOUNDATION OF A NEW NATO

Three times in this century, American troops have crossed the Atlantic to play decisive roles in European crises. In 1917, we came to do battle, but withdrew immediately following the Allied victory in a war that was to end all wars. Safe once again on our distant shores, we watched in grand isolation as Europe's post-war, political structure collapsed and tyranny engulfed the continent. Only in 1941 did we return to fight and prevail. Yet, after committing the massive resources of United States and paying the price of over 863 000 casualties, America once more demobilized. By 1947, the error of our over-hasty departure became all too clear. Jolted into action by the threat of Communist domination of Europe and the imminent collapse of the Western European economy, the United States intervened for the third time. But this time there would be no pitched battles. This time the United States joined with the freedom-loving peoples of Europe to create a new institution – a new Atlantic Alliance – one that would guard the transatlantic community from totalitarianism and usher in an era of unprecedented prosperity and growth.

One man who understood the United States' crucial role in maintaining European peace was Sir Winston Churchill. In 1953, he defined the benefits of US involvement in Europe in the following terms:

'Had the United States taken, before the First World War or between the wars, the same interest and made the same exertions to preserve the peace and uphold freedom which I thank God she is doing now, there might never have been a first war and there would certainly never have been a second. With their mighty aid, I have a sure hope there will not be a third.'

The US and NATO eventually proved Churchill prescient in his 'sure hope'. In large measure, we can credit today's dramatically altered strategic landscape to men like President Harry Truman and General George C. Marshall, who believed that an isolationist United States would sow the seeds of a future European conflict. Their determination that democracy must prevail in Europe and that no power hostile to the United States should ever dominate the continent guaranteed a continued US commitment to Europe and that succeeding generations of Americans would serve a common NATO cause.

In 1947, Communist pressure on Greece and Turkey sorely tested Truman's resolve and gravely strained relations between Western powers and the Soviet Union. In response to these tensions, the President announced his famous doctrine, and aid soon began to flow to the countries threatened by the heavy boot of Soviet oppression. Simultaneously, the United States instituted the Marshall Plan to combat 'hunger, poverty, desperation and chaos' throughout Europe. But it took the February 1948 Communist coup in Czechoslovakia and the subsequent Soviet blockade of Berlin to galvanize the commitment of 12 nations who on 4 April 1949 signed the North Atlantic Treaty and gave birth to the Atlantic

Alliance. A new era in European and American cooperation dawned over the North Atlantic.

From 1949 to 1989, Western Europe enjoyed an unprecedented period of peace. During that epoch, Western Europe rebuilt its infrastructure, democratized its institutions and prospered in the marketplace. It did so under the protective umbrella of an evolving NATO.

Drawing on solid personal relationships forged during the Second World War, the Alliance's statesmen and soldiers soon created what Churchill would call an 'Allied Brotherhood' bound by common goals and values. Leaders and nations embraced the necessity of subordinating national interests to allied objectives in order to maintain a lasting peace. They realized that victory over totalitarianism lay not merely in the strength of tanks, ships and airplanes, but more importantly, in the strength of their common commitment.

They constructed a rock-solid foundation for a military-political organization rooted in the principles of openness, dialogue, and consensus. From its outset, NATO consisted of sovereign states which, after debate and deliberation, spoke with one clear, political voice. That foundation remains firm today. As US Secretary of Defense William Perry observed at the 1995 Conference on Security Policy in Munich: 'We don't agree on everything... But, when we sit down together, we hammer out our differences on security matters and forge a consensus.'

Of course, such consensus was not always easily obtained. At times, the Alliance experienced internal tension and even threats of the viability of the transatlantic link. However, with each major episode – the Suez Canal Crisis of 1956, France's withdrawal of its forces from the integrated military structure in 1967, and the serious disagreements over the introduction of Pershing II and ground-launched cruise missiles into Europe in the 1980s – the Alliance not only survived; it prevailed.

In a period spanning some 40 years, the Alliance strengthened its military force under an integrated command and control structure; trained to common standards and procedures; and learned to operate as an effective whole. It also expanded. Greece and Turkey entered the Alliance in 1952,

Germany in 1955 and Spain in 1982. Although these accessions were fraught with controversy at the time, they ultimately made the Alliance stronger. Farsighted statesmen came to a consensus that Western European security and defence demanded expansion of the Allied Brotherhood; individual states overcame their differences and once more emerged united in a common cause.

Throughout the four decades of NATO's evolution and growth, the United States provided strong leadership. At the political level, the United States stood in the vanguard as it championed the development of a more effective Alliance. On the military level – from Major NATO Commanders to the soldier on patrol – American forces served in Europe as a clear signal of the US's commitment and resolve. These servicemen and women walked their posts, did their tours of duty, and then returned home. They did so to protect American interests and to advance the common cause of peace and shared values. Alongside their allies, these American troops kept their vigil and carved out a zone of stability. They not only helped a continent flourish but also assisted in opening the Iron Curtain and burying a defunct ideology. And, remarkably, they did so without firing a shot.

THE NEW NATO: ITS CONTINUING MISSION AND OPERATIONAL ENGAGEMENTS

Almost six years have passed since the collapse of Communism and the Berlin Wall, but the dust is still settling. Europe is awash in uncertainty, instability, and change. The notions that somehow history has ended and the days of conflict and pain have been relegated to the dustbin of the past have proven tragically mistaken. What has become abundantly clear is that the climatic events of 1989-90 did not signal the end of NATO's mission. They merely marked the end of one strategic phase and the beginning of another. NATO's mission of collective security and defence continues, and it remains in the interest of the United States to support and lead a solid transatlantic Alliance.

Indeed, the United States must not succumb to the historical tendency to loosen its transatlantic bonds in the wake of another victory. As General George Marshall warned Americans shortly after the Second World War,

'We are a strong nation. But we cannot live to ourselves and remain strong.' There are many reasons why Americans cannot 'live to ourselves'. Our economic interests in Europe are enormous. Europe accounts for 31 per cent of total US exports. Fifty per cent of US direct foreign investment is in Europe. Europeans make more than 60 per cent of all direct foreign investments in America. Europe is traversed by many of the world's most vital trade routes, and the political revolutions of 1989-90 opened new markets for American goods and services in Central and Eastern Europe. Moreover, Europe is the focal point of America's political, social, and cultural heritage. There can be no doubt that a secure, stable Europe is crucial to the welfare of Americans, or that the US must continue to be a European power.

Yet equally clear is the fact that Europe remains a dangerous place. Certainly, the Alliance no longer faces a monolithic Soviet threat. Nevertheless, today's risks are still real and, indeed, even more diverse and potentially dangerous than those we faced in the past. Some 20 000 nuclear warheads, the dangerous detritus of the Cold War, are still in the former Soviet republics, where fragile, new democracies now control them. Ethnic conflict again prevails in the Balkans and has the potential to spread rapidly. The tragic events in Chechnya have created fresh concerns about the future of the Russian Federation, and the violence which racks Algeria draws our attention to the emerging risks along the North African littoral.

To protect our interests and to deal with this host of new risks, the US and NATO must act with imagination and dispatch. Our challenges in the post-Cold War world are in many ways similar to those faced by Truman and Marshall and their European counterparts in the aftermath of the Second World War. We must make good an extraordinary opportunity to follow up on democracy's victory. To use an old infantryman's term, we must consolidate on the objective. That is, we must consolidate the gains for democracy to promote stability; bring peace to troubled lands; enhance the dignity and worth of the individual; and create a climate for investment, growth, and economic prosperity for all the peoples of Europe. Simultaneously, we must grapple with the crises which inevitably plague an era of geopolitical transformation; and we must forge a new relationship of cooperation, consultation, and trust with the Russian

Federation – a still powerful country which occupies a pivotal position regarding the future of Europe. These will be difficult objectives to achieve; but history has taught us that we must exploit both national and Alliance strengths and get on with the task.

Today, NATO has vision for a New Europe; and with the help of its 16 member nations, it is getting on with its realization. The Alliance began its quest for a New Europe in 1990 with the London Declaration, a plan for internal transformation and the establishment of cooperation with the emerging democracies to the East. NATO continued its metamorphosis with the formulation of a new Strategic Concept in 1991. And, in January 1994, it launched three initiatives – Partnership for Peace, Combined Joint Task Force, and Counter-proliferation – which taken in combination with the Alliance's evolving crisis management capabilities constitute a bold, new engagement strategy tailored to achieve NATO's objectives.

In 1995, NATO stands ready to meet the challenges of the New Europe. It has a strategy, and it possesses the tools to carry out the strategy. In fact, NATO's military command structure has changed dramatically. There are now two Major NATO Commands instead of three. Allied Command Europe's Major Subordinate Commands have dropped from four to three in number. The New NATO has simplified its command structure, and developed the procedures which make it as relevant today as it was throughout its history.

NATO forces have, for example, adapted to match their missions of strategic balance, collective defence, and peace support operations. We no longer focus our attention on armoured formations forward-deployed to counter a major invasion through Central Europe. Today, the New NATO emphasizes its rapid reaction units – lighter, more mobile formations such as the ACE Rapid Reaction Corps (ARRC) and the ACE Mobile Force (Land). They testify to the birth of an agile, versatile new NATO committed to dealing with the fluid challenges of the future.

Nowhere is the utility of new NATO's military forces more apparent than in the Former Yugoslavia, where they are both out-of-area and operational for the first time. There, NATO airmen and sailors have achieved significant accomplishments in support of United Nations Security

Council resolutions. In fact, they have performed with unwavering professionalism to help create the pre-conditions for a political solution to the tragedy in the Balkans.

Under Operation DENY FLIGHT, NATO pilots have flown over 60 000 sorties to limit the scope of hostilities and to protect innocent people on the ground in Bosnia. In Operation SHARP GUARD, NATO and Western European Union ships have challenged tens of thousands of vessels, diverted nearly a thousand of them and continue to enforce the embargo in the Adriatic.

What's more, 17 000 NATO troops support the UN on the ground. These troops are not currently under NATO command but they are troops drawn from NATO member nations, trained to NATO standards, and, like the NATO airmen and sailors that are supporting them, are doing a superb job in very difficult circumstances.

Clearly, NATO has responded quickly, effectively and decisively in the Former Yugoslavia whenever the UN has requested assistance. The NAC's 1993 declaration of exclusion zones, as well as the humanitarian flights and airdrops conducted by NATO member nations, have saved thousands of lives. The March 1994 shootdown of four Serbian GALEBs by NATO aircraft provides yet another example. That action was quick, correct, and decisive. Multinational airborne controllers and fighter pilots worked flawlessly as a team. In fact, that single, five-minute engagement gave compelling testimony to the value of over 40 years of Alliance efforts at harmonizing and streamlining its procedures. NATO's subsequent airstrike on the Serb-held airfield at Udbina underscored another key point: the Alliance is committed and capable of responding robustly and appropriately to threats to UN Protection Force (UNPROFOR) troops or the safe areas in Bosnia-Herzegovina.

All told, the Alliance's efforts in the Southern Region have demonstrated that the New NATO can respond effectively to mitigate crises. NATO has the capability to operate anywhere on the conflict spectrum – from humanitarian relief, to peacekeeping operations, to protecting UNPROFOR forces, to the defence of the Alliance. Our procedures work. Our integrated command structure is sound. Given a task, we can succeed.

THE NEW NATO: REACHING OUT THE HAND OF FRIENDSHIP

As noted earlier, the Brussels Summit of January 1994 was a watershed moment for the Alliance and Europe. In their final communiqué, the heads of state of NATO's 16 nations launched three landmark programmes designed to extend the hand of partnership and cooperation to the people of 40 countries and to create the context and capabilities required to fulfill the Alliance's grand vision for a new Europe.

The Partnership for Peace initiative opened the door and invited all of Europe to join in a new, strengthened relationship with NATO. It created a mechanism by which the Alliance could build mutual trust and confidence with its former adversaries and other interested countries. Moreover, it established a means by which NATO and its partners could, over time, acquire the capability to conduct combined peace support, humanitarian aid, and search and rescue operations.

In just over a year, Partnership for Peace has gone from theory to practice. Twenty-five nations, including the Russian Federation, from all over Europe have signed the PfP Framework Document. NATO and nine partners now have agreed to Individual Partnership Programmes, and more are under negotiation. Twelve nations have liaison officers assigned to the Partnership Coordination Cell, and additional officers from other nations will arrive soon. The initial PfP exercises were quite successful. In Poland, the Netherlands and the North Sea, Alliance and partner soldiers and sailors trained side-by-side. Partners learned new military skills and saw the wisdom of adopting standard, peacekeeping doctrine. But, even more importantly, they experienced firsthand the strength of NATO's common commitment to the future. No wonder US Secretary of State Warren Christopher observed in late 1994 that 'PfP... evolved from bare idea to bold reality.'

Some commentators have said that Partnership for Peace is a halfway measure, not moving fast enough to engage new partners. Others have labelled it an enlargement programme. From the soldier's perspective, they have all missed the point. PfP is an engagement strategy in every sense of the word. Those charged with deterring conflict in today's new strategic setting and promoting stability, mutual trust and confidence in

Central and Eastern Europe, think it is right on the mark. The Partnership Coordination Cell Conference Centre at Mons, Belgium, offers an excellent symbol of the utility of the programme. Located in the old Live Oak building where, in previous years, Allied planners focused on the defence of Berlin, the Centre proudly displays 41 national flags arrayed alphabetically, from Albania to Uzbekistan. Not NATO on one side and partners on the other, but all together, alphabetically, as one. These flags arrayed in close order epitomize the new Europe and serve as a testimony to how the new NATO is helping the dream of that new Europe come true.

Many NATO nations, including the US, are also conducting significant bilateral activities to complement the Partnership for Peace programme. In the summer of 1994, US and Russian forces exercised together on Russian soil for the first time. It was a great success, not just for the training, but also for the interaction between soldiers of both countries. In December 1994, 72 mid-level officers from 14 former Warsaw Pact countries graduated from the inaugural, five-month programme at the George C. Marshall Centre in Garmisch in Germany. These officers learned about the role of the military in a democratic political system – essential knowledge if they are to contribute to a new Europe.

Another Summit initiative – the Combined Joint Task Force (CJTF) – offers still greater potential for dealing with the challenges of tomorrow. Under this concept, NATO is examining ways to adapt its command and control structures to make available a trained and ready headquarters and associated assets to handle crises situations. Such a separable, but not separate, headquarters would also be available to organizations such as the Western European Union or the UN, in those instances when NATO elects not to act.

Using a CJTF, NATO could fulfill a wide variety of missions, command both NATO and non-NATO forces and take full advantage of the Alliance's long, successful history of controlling multinational operations using its integrated military structure. What's more, with CJTF, NATO is clearly supporting the emergence of a European pillar – a European Security and Defence Identity.

But CJTF poses no threat to the viability of the transatlantic link. Regardless of the composition of the forces controlled by the CJTF or the security organization it supports, the United States would have to play a major role in any CJTF headquarters operation. Many of the combat support and combat service support assets – airlift, logistics, communications, and intelligence – can be provided only by specific NATO countries such as the United States.

As Partnership for Peace, Combined Joint Task Force Headquarters, and the new NATO's crisis management efforts go forward, we must never forget the need for continued vigilance – the accomplishment of NATO's basic missions of deterrence and collective defence. Of course, when an engagement strategy using PfP is successful, and when a CJTF, under NATO or the WEU control, deals effectively with a crisis, then, NATO will, in the truest sense, be deterring war. But there may come a day when the outstretched hand of NATO must quickly recoil into a fist to defeat an attack on a member of the Alliance. Even in the new NATO, our foundation stone remains Article V of the North Atlantic Treaty, 'an armed attack against one... shall be considered an attack against... all.'

THE NEW NATO: BALANCING MISSIONS AND RESOURCES

PfP, CJTF, operations in the Balkans, continuing Article V responsibilities all have one thing in common: they require adequately-sized, well-trained, and robustly-supported forces. If NATO is to succeed in creating the conditions necessary for the new Europe to stabilize, prosper and reinforce its democratic institutions, the necessary forces and resources must continue to flow from all NATO member nations and the transatlantic link must prevail.

Across the Alliance, there has been an understandable desire for a peace dividend after the victory over Communism; however, we may be cutting forces too quickly. In fact, it is ironic that for 40 years, NATO had a ready, robust force deployed along the German border, with little likelihood of it ever being committed; but today, when NATO is operationally committed and is increasing its missions, its force levels and readiness are declining.

This imbalance between requirements and resources has put considerable strain on many nations of the Alliance. At a great price, these countries have consistently met NATO force goals and performed yeoman's service in the cause of peace in the Former Yugoslavia and elsewhere around the world. They have paid the price because they understand that the price of complacency is even higher than the price of peace. Political and military leaders on both sides of the Atlantic must make every effort to balance missions with capabilities and match requirements with resources. It will be difficult to maintain an adequate defence in an era of austerity; but, NATO's nations must prevail.

CONCLUSION

The United States and its allies courageously stepped up to their responsibilities in the wake of the Second World War. They grasped their shared destiny and defended their common values. They sustained the Transatlantic link and, in doing so, deterred the advent of a Third World War and contained the rapacious hand of Communism. Today, some four decades later, NATO continues to promote stability and well-being in the North Atlantic area and beyond. Its mission of collective security and defence continues; and it has undertaken a bold, new engagement strategy designed to help achieve a grand geopolitical vision. Working together, the nations of the new NATO – nations from both sides of the Atlantic – are helping create a new NATO, built upon a still crucial Transatlantic link. They are writing a new historic chapter – one which promises a better tomorrow for us all. That's why we are here.

8 Thanks For The Memory

Wing Commander Andrew Brookes

PAST AS PROLOGUE

The brave new post-war world and I were both conceived around D-Day, 1944. The more important of the two took form at Dumbarton Oaks near Washington through proposals for a 'general international organization'. I was a much lesser acorn. My father, one of 3 021 000 US troops sent to north-west Europe during the Second World War,[1] lived up to the 'over paid, over-sexed and over here' maxim before devoting what energies he had left to the invasion of mainland Europe.

Yet although we were both sired from across the Atlantic, the parallels run deeper than that. My father's ancestors had settled in North Carolina long before 1944, in large part to escape from the petty, fractious squabbling that so characterized European affairs. It was once calculated that Russia had been at war in 46 of every hundred years since 901 AD,[2] and the rest of Europe seemed to fare no better on emerging from the medieval 'Dark Ages'. Throughout the 18th century the states of continental Europe were at war on average for three years in every five. Even Britain, ostensibly safeguarded by the watery Channel, found itself at war with somebody or other in Europe for 45 years of the 18th century.[3]

The French Marshal Saxe estimated in 1746 that the maximum size for a manageable army in battle was 46 000, yet 60 years later Napoleon's staff system was good enough to allow him to march 150 000 men from the English Channel to the Danube. The post-French Revolutionary release of social forces ushered in the age of total war. As he passed amongst the 62 000 dead and dying on the field of Leipzig, Metternich felt that 'the hand of God was armed'.[4] Small wonder that many fled the horrors of Europe for transatlantic pastures new, taking their aversions with them. In part this explained why, six months before the start of the US-Mexican war in 1846, the US Army had less than 7000 men under arms.[5]

As it happened, 19th century Europe after 1815 was a much more peaceful place in which to live. The Great Powers maintained an equilibrium through a combination of gentlemen's agreements and confining their squabbles to the fringes of empire. Yet this happy balancing of power was to flounder with the emergence of a united Germany that was to prove greater in its apparent designs and power than the sum of the other European nations that could be ranged against it. Once that happened, disputes over spheres of influence such as the Balkans were allowed to get out of hand. Eventually the US, as the only referee with sufficient clout, was forced to enter the ring in 1917 and 1941. In a way not foreseen by George Canning, the New World had been called into existence to redress the balance of the Old.

ALL MY YESTERDAYS

I was brought up in a different age, when flying was dangerous and sex was safe. Forget rationing and the fact that I grew up in the Lancashire coalfield when there *was* a Lancashire coalfield: despite tremors induced by the Berlin airlift and the Korean War, there was an air of certainty in an uncertain age. You can see an echo of it in *Miss Marple* episodes, with doors left unlocked and children like me free to roam where they willed. True, the crowds at the 1953 Farnborough Show look distinctly unpressed and unfashionable from 40 years on, but the air was bright with colour and optimism. Apart from the fact that *UK plc* could still boast 21 main aircraft and six aero-engine manufacturing companies, the Coronation and the conquest of Everest seemed to herald a new Elizabethan age. It was a time when a television science-fiction serial called *Quatermass*, (which, much to my chagrin, was deemed unsuitable for my tender eyes) could prophesy the return of an 80-ton British manned space rocket to earth in 20 years' time without it seeming at all unlikely.

There was no clear opening of the Cold War. The US Truman Doctrine highlighted the drift into armed camps when it declared, 'We shall not realise our objectives unless we are willing to help free people to maintain their institutions and their natural integrity against aggressive movements that seek to impose upon them totalitarian regimes'. Ernie Bevin clung to his hopes for a little longer but by the time the council of Foreign Ministers finally ceased to function at the end of 1947, even he felt compelled to exclaim after listening to Molotov's outrageous demands, 'Now 'e's gone too bloody far!'.

Yet if there was no date to rival August 1914 or September 1939, the origins of the Cold War as well as the two previous 'hot' ones lay with Germany. Inter-allied rumblings over post-war arrangements for Poland, Rumania and Bulgaria were really only manifestations of the search for a new European system to replace the one that had consistently failed to master the problem of a too-powerful German fish in a European pond. It was typical Churchillian rhetoric to declare that 'the Hun is either at your throat or at your feet', but he and his fellow leaders could not be blamed for seeking the first set of stable relationships Europe had known since 1870.

In March 1947, Britain and France signed the Dunkirk Treaty, whereby each pledged full military support to the other in the event of an attack by Germany. The following March this was extended by the Brussels Treaty to include the Benelux countries, which led in turn to the signing of the North Atlantic Treaty in Washington in April 1949. It would take another two years before the superstructure of NATO was finally erected on top, but the important fact to note is the firmness of the foundations on which NATO was built.

With hindsight, there were three reasons for this. First, the only alternative proved stillborn. Looking at the weaknesses of the League of Nations, the planners at Dumbarton Oaks intended that the UN Security Council should be empowered to deal far more robustly with breaches of the peace and acts of aggression. For example, member states would make armed forces and equipment available to the Security Council to enable it to impose its decisions when and if all else failed. In effect, the Security Council was intended to be an armed policeman of the world. Alas, fulfilment of the Dumbarton Oaks dreams fell far short of the ideal. In the absence of a world policeman, there was a need to invest NATO at least with the powers of regional special constable.

Second, although the NATO sleigh was to become firmly established on a Cold War *piste* that for many years only steepened and widened, the US remained firmly on board. In the beginning, the impetus was pure crisis response. One of my earliest memories is of the culture shock in our part of suburbia – wives in jeans, would you believe? – when the first families of Burtonwood personnel arrived in support of Strategic Air Command (SAC) B-29s on rotation to the UK. But even when the immediate Berlin and Korean crises were over, and SAC acquired bombers that could reach the USSR from the United States direct, there was no US withdrawal into isolationism. In essence, this was because goals and visions remained synchronised. Any organization which could appeal to both Democrat President Harry Truman and Republican Senate leader/former isolationist Arthur Vandenberg must have had something going for it, especially as the US had always fought shy of such 'entangling alliances' in the past. But looking back, it is interesting to note the subordination rather than the eradication of national traits. In 1949, as he sought to secure every vote he could in the ratification debate, Vandenberg told the Senate:

> 'I think a man can vote for this treaty and not vote for a nickel to implement it, because as far as I am concerned, the opening sentence of the treaty is a notification to Mr Stalin which puts him in exactly the contrary position to that which Mr Hitler was in, because Mr Hitler saw us with a Neutrality Act. Mr Stalin now sees us with a pact of cooperative action.'

This statement was illuminating on two counts. US citizens will not hand over a nickel to the federal budget for Europe or anything else without good cause, and 'personalization' of threats runs through their culture. The cohesion of NATO for 40 years was greatly helped by the fact that US public and political opinion continued to see Mr Stalin and his Soviet successors as obvious 'bad guys'.

Finally, although the division of Germany that flowed from the Berlin crisis came about through accident rather than grand design, it was not a disagreeable outcome. Given that Germany alone had been perceived to be at the core of European stability from at least 1890, neither Superpower bloc could afford to allow the absorption of all Germany into the sphere of influence of the other. Even development towards German unity in neutrality would have required more trust and credulity than was reasonable to expect. Insofar as NATO, and the Warsaw Pact that emerged in response, tended to formalize the division of Germany, there was much that appealed in the new security architecture. In essence the 'German problem' was solved by partition, and for many, be they inhabitants of Paris or Moscow, that was the *only* post-war problem that really mattered.

Consequently, the Europe into which I was born remained at peace because there was so much about its post-war security arrangements that fitted together. One could wrap it all up in fancy geopolitical paradigms but no more succinct justification for NATO has emerged to surpass that ascribed to NATO's first secretary-general, 'Pug' Ismay: 'To keep the Russians out, the Americans in, and the Germans down'. My subsequent military career was to convince me, had I been St Paul writing to the Corinthians, that the greatest of these was to keep the Americans in.

MEMORIES ARE MADE OF THIS

Looking at my log book, I see that I first went solo in one of Her Majesty's aeroplanes when the RAF had around 40 Canberra and V-Force squadrons divided between Bomber Command, Near East, Middle East and Far East Air Forces, and RAF Germany. Simultaneously, Britain could deploy 17 000 men to defend Borneo at the peak of confrontation, and in many ways it was this willingness to contribute to world security that impressed the Americans. I recall the first time I took a strategic reconnaissance Victor 2 across the Atlantic. In those days, there were two reinforcement routes to the Far East: eastabout through Turkey and Iran, which was quickest, and westabout through the US and Pacific, which took longer but was more politically reliable. On this occasion we were going westabout, and when I say 'we' that was illuminating in itself. When I joined my first five-man Victor crew as a young co-pilot, I brought the average age down to 45! The Air Electronics Officer had been one of many shot down in Fairey Battles over France in May 1940, while the captain had nightmares in Hawaii about being chased by Me 109s over the desert. It was all very surreal, as was touching down in Guam at the height of the Vietnam War. Guam boasted 'the Billy Eckstine orchestra and all the chicken you could eat for a dollar' because, every hour, on the hour, fully-laden B-52s would lumber off bound for south-east Asia. 'Being there' mattered. After I shut down at Guam, a USAF Top Sergeant came up to me and said, 'Excuse me sir, is that a Vulcan?' 'No,' I replied, 'it's a Victor,' and I went on to explain that whereas SAC had opted for the B-52 to fill its strategic needs, the British bought the Vulcan *and* the Victor. 'Gee,' he said when I finished, 'I wish we could have afforded to do that,' and he walked away mightily impressed by the RAF. Whether it was right that he should have been so impressed, given that SAC bought four times as many B-52s, was debatable, but there was no denying that the sight of V-bombers regularly hurtling skywards off bases from Goose Bay to Wake when a fully-laden B-52D used all of Guam's 13 000 ft runway to get airborne, did wonders for British prestige abroad. I learned then, and many times thereafter, particularly in relation to intelligence matters, that if you give the Americans an inch, they will give back a mile in return. But my father's people, who will not waste a nickel if they can help it, have no sympathy with any nation that expects to get anything out, whether it be military or trade protection, without putting something in. Thus it was that Washington, as it cranked up its embroilment in Vietnam, remained impressed by the fact that, as late as 1964, Britain still had more troops East of Suez than in Germany.

Not surprisingly, the British Treasury was less enamoured and saw great appeal in maximising 'bang for buck' by concentrating on the nuclear option. During the late Seventies and part of the Eighties, I was involved in the business of controlling and practising delivery of 'baskets of sunshine'. Two impressions remain vivid from that time. There was the leverage that nuclear weaponry gave where it mattered, and the hordes of people who came to admire the Vulcan wherever I displayed it, including a Soviet air attaché. Walking straight past the shiny Jaguar, Harrier and Tornado without so much as a glance, he made straight for the elderly Vulcan because, as he admitted candidly, 'that is the only one that can reach my homeland'. Power alone is one thing, but it has to be 'projected' if it is truly to impress friends and overawe potential adversaries.

It was the hydrogen bomb which inspired Churchill's famous vision of the age of mutual deterrence: 'Thus it may be that we shall, by a process of sublime irony, have reached a stage in this history where safety will be the sturdy child of terror, and survival the twin brother of annihilation.' Ironically, out of this atmosphere of Mutually Assured Destruction grew the exceptionally good relations between Soviet and US leaders that produced the INF agreement. I oversaw the 'drawdown' from 96 operational cruise missiles to none at Greenham Common, and I witnessed at first hand the growing trust between former opponents that flowed from the process. I have no doubt that there was a direct link between the successful conclusion of the INF treaty and the fall of the Berlin Wall. In effect, the pause for thought imposed by nuclear weaponry gave Europe 40 precious years to get its act together and create the framework and sense of security to solve the 'German problem' for themselves.

Tomorrow, and Tomorrow, and Tomorrow

In my lifetime the UK has moved from being able to produce three different V-bombers in response to one requirement, to a position where its major defence aerospace goal is a quarter share in the Eurofighter. Furthermore, when I learned to fly the RAF had 137 924 uniformed personnel: by the time I leave the Service, it will have reduced to just over 52 000. Yet nothing can detract from the glorious fact that for the first time in my experience, there is no longer any major threat to the collective security of Western Europe.

In essence, NATO was an alliance based on fear. It was organized, trained, equipped and justified in financial terms to counter the Warsaw Pact. NATO capability was enhanced by the enervating effect of a divided Germany: if ever there was an damning indictment of Communism, it was that it managed to make a poor country out of a nation full of Germans. Now that the fear factor has gone, and a united Germany is back on the world stage, Europe appears to be edging back towards its old ways.

Consequently, the only thing that can be said with any certainty is that the future is not what it used to be. However, my life and career to date have given me the following precepts and pointers to the way ahead.

Strategic Planning

The first requirement is for a reasoned, strategic strategy. The French have always been good at this: their long-term nuclear, military and transport goals appear to transcend party politics. The British, on the other hand, seem to stumble from short term palliative to shorter term fix under the mistaken impression that such 'pragmatism' is a badge of virtue. Yet the costs and impact of such a disjointed approach have been as considerable as they have been risible. Having forced what were 21 British aircraft manufacturing companies to combine into a single entity, Whitehall is now worried about lack of competition! If Britain alone cannot formulate effective long term strategies on issues such as aerospace, she must get it right within a European framework.

Rising costs will certainly drive nations down the cooperative road. Air power characteristics remain constant – 'stealth' is only a fancy new word for Bomber Command tactics against Hamburg at the end of July 1943. But technology does move on and space systems – for intelligence, communications and targeting – are but one essential Premier League tool that will not be fundable by any European nation alone.

Credibility

In 1864, General Ulysses S. Grant commanded five armies operating over an area half the size of Europe with a headquarters staff of 14 officers.[7] Today, five years after the ending of the Cold War, there are still NATO Central Region headquarters with staffs in excess of 3000. Refusal to face reality has led to unflattering comparisons between NATO and a bureaucracy in search of a pension.[8] Such damning impressions undermine NATO's credibility every bit as much as reverses in Bosnia.

It is said that mid-west Americans think NATO is the name of a Japanese admiral! The Alliance is of more immediate concern to Europeans, but even for them the Cold War version of NATO was all about preventing another war: they were not interested in fighting one. It is therefore counter-productive if the NATO hierarchy seeks out a nice little conflict, like actors in search of a play, if in so doing it erodes popular support for the Organization's very existence. Retention of public goodwill is crucial to military well being on either side of the Atlantic, not least because posturing on the UN Security Council can never compensate for shredding social fabric back home. There is still no glory in 'an Empire that can rule the waves but is unable to flush its sewers'.[9]

People Power

In 1964, the incoming Secretary of State for Defence, Denis Healey, found that of his concerns, 'Above all, the services were sick and tired of continual reorganization'.[10] I have rarely known any other state of affairs despite having served now in the RAF for over one-third of its existence. Service morale is not helped by those who sometimes seem to know the price of everything and the value of nothing. Soldiers, sailors and airmen do not lay their lives on the line for profit-related pay or performance indicators: they do it for the camaraderie, ethos and ideals that can never have a price put on them but which will cost a nation dear if they are too readily sacrificed for some ephemeral gain.

Yet some things will never be the same again. 60 000 British troops were lost by nightfall on the first day of the First Battle of the Somme yet the First World War still went on for two more years. Half a century later, the loss of around 56 000 personnel over a decade was sufficient to disenchant US public opinion with Vietnam. There is now a much greater unwillingness to accept loss of life in any endeavour, and as we enter an age where we can almost pick and choose our war, there is a danger that nothing will be worth dying for. My parents' generation freed Belsen and Auschwitz, but who today is willing to risk death for equally horrendous camps in Cambodia or Bosnia? All the military planning in the world will be as naught if an opponent sees it as pure bluff. How difficult will it be to initiate serious military action if, in pursuit of the cult of the individual, we reach a stage where we venerate life itself rather than the qualities and principles that make life worth living?

Realism

Recent events in Rwanda and Bosnia show that basic instincts have altered little since classical times when Thucydides wrote, 'The strong take what they will, the weak yield what they must.'[11] If only the dead have seen the end of war, then those alive must be realistic enough to build on our strengths and shore up our weaknesses.

For the foreseeable future, the Transatlantic link will remain as crucial as ever. There are three reasons for this. First, after all the euphoria on the ending of the Cold War, Mr Yeltsin now talks chillingly of a 'Cold Peace' descending on Europe.[12] Second, by their actions over recent years, European nations have shown that they alone are not yet up to the job of keeping the peace in their own backyard. Finally, Europe has no electronic command and control system, no strategic intelligence gathering capability or heavy airlift capacity to match those of the Americans. In consequence, Europe must take care not to let the US drift back from England to New England by making greater efforts both in 'burden-sharing' and by ensuring that whatever alliance the US is 'entangled' in is one that matters.

To that end, NATO's role must stay narrowly focused and clearly defined. In essence, NATO achieved its greatest success as the overarching nuclear umbrella for the region and that is how it should stay. The umbrella will become useless if too many holes are torn in it over unrelated matters such as out-of-area peacemaking. These issues should be left to separate organizations such as the UN or OSCE.

Having ensured that NATO remains the bedrock of European security, the *status quo* cannot be maintained in its entirety. Despite common culture, economic and political heritage, the US and Europe have drifted apart on issues such as Bosnia. Having reached the age of the Coalition of the Willing, talk of Combined Joint Task Forces to allow small groups of European NATO countries to work together in military operations in which the US does not wish to take part are timely.

But Europe does need to get away from the impression that its counsels are both uncertain and incoherent. Europe must build on the US-given breathing space conferred since 1949 to really put its house in order. This means enhancing another 'entangling alliance' in the shape of an expanded and strengthened European Union (EU), a single market more populous than America's and more valuable than China's. On all counts, the EU has plenty of 'value-added' and that is the way to go.

CONCLUSION

It was the Transatlantic alliance which made me and sustained me. I am eternally grateful for the fact that I have never known anything but peace, whereas my mother had endured two world wars before she was much over thirty. That said, I am also a committed European who would have no difficulty serving in a European Air Force. NATO has thrived for 40 years on the basis that 16 nations will come to each other's assistance in time of need – if we cannot build on nations' individual strengths to develop a European defence architecture that we can all rely upon in time of need, we may as well give up.

There are some who begrudge the fact that Britain's net contribution to the EU budget had risen to just over £2bn by 1992.[13] But this is far more than the admission fee for a seat at the top table. It is impossible to set a figure on the full financial costs to Britain of the Second World War: suffice to say that just one element – the amount Britain owed the US for mutual aid – came to around $21bn at 1946 prices.[14] But for someone like me, whose father never came back from the invasion of Europe, the costs run deeper than that. I also knew only one maternal uncle because all his brothers had died serving with a West Yorkshire Pals battalion in the First World War. I well remember that gaunt, cadaverous man who never seemed to know how to smile and whose cold, grey eyes had seen Passchendaele, mustard gas, a POW camp and heaven knew what other hells. If past enemies such as Germany and Britain put into the EU communal budget far more than they get out, it is a small price to pay for ensuring that Europe has a future to enjoy rather than the dismal prospect of a re-run of the past.

NOTES

1. Ellis, J., *The World War 2 Database*, p. 229.
2. Pitirim Sorokin, quoted in Blainey G, *Causes of War*, p. 1.

3. Cole D.H., & Priestley E.C., *An Outline of British Military History, 1660-1936*.
4. *Memoires, III*, p. 311.
5. Casdorph, Paul D., *Lee and Jackson*, p. 53.
6. Vickers Valiant as well as the Avro Vulcan and Handley Page Victor.
7. Montgomery of Alamein, *A History of Warfare*, p. 438.
8. Alan Clark, quoted in *The Sunday Times*, 11 December 1994, section 3, p. 4.
9. St John Broderick on 2 October 1900, quoted in Gilbert M., *Winston S Churchill*, vol 1, companion vol 2, p. 1204.
10. Healey, D., *The Time of My Life*, p. 261.
11. *History of the Peloponnesian War*, Book 5, 89.
12. Organisation for Security and Cooperation in Europe (OSCE) Meeting, Budapest, 5 December 1994.
13. *Whitaker's Almanack*, Edition 127 1995, p. 757.
14. Hancock W.K., & Gowing M.M., *British War Economy*, p. 547.

9 European Security

Major Nicaise

Nietzsche observed that Europe would only come together at the graveside. Since his time, two fratricidal conflicts within less than a quarter century have been necessary for Europeans to become aware of the need to pool their strengths to build the continent. More recently, the idea of European security has been given new urgency by the geostrategic upheavals and the proliferation of new and diffuse dangers.

This European security must be supported by an organization strong enough to be credible, yet sufficiently flexible to preserve the freedom of action of each individual state. It should not be dependent on *ad hoc* coalitions, neither should it be shackled by a structure of federal type. But the effectiveness of the European alliance depends on the Common Foreign and Security Policy defined in the Maastricht Treaty being given concrete form.

A brief overview outlining a Europe of variable geometries will present the need for a strong alliance, which embodies the European identity yet respects national independence. It will then be possible to develop the European defence 'machinery' to be placed at the service of this common security policy.

EVOLVING EUROPEAN STRUCTURES

Before elaborating a concept of European security, it is appropriate to define the Europe in question. Is it the Europe of the 15 or a widened WEU, or does it include eastern Europe or even Turkey or certain states of the Maghreb? In the face of the diversity of opinions, probably nobody can state how Europe will look in 2010 or 2020. It is therefore appropriate to retain the idea of a Europe of 'variable geometry', capable of expanding in the years to come. In view of its present character, it must be concluded that Europe will not acquire a federal structure within the next 25 years.

On the other hand, it could come together *en bloc* in areas of common concern; in particular in order to confront threats affecting the European Union as a whole.

Following the geostrategic upheavals of 1989, all observers agree that we have passed from a world without risks but with a clearly-defined threat to a world of risks without any specific threat. The dangers we face are now highly varied and diffuse, but real nonetheless. They arise out of the proliferation of nuclear or chemical weapons, the growth of international gangsterism, with its links to narcotics and its encroachment on certain national economies. In a more complex Europe, whose face changes with each vote, security can no longer be conceived around one single organization, created in other circumstances to confront a single specific threat scenario.

SECURITY STRUCTURES FOR A EUROPE OF 'VARIABLE GEOMETRY'

First of all, it should be stated that Europe cannot depend for its security on the United Nations alone, even if filled out by alliances of circumstance. Europe has already suffered the consequences of the weaknesses inherent in an organization like the League of Nations. But neither is Europe ready to take on a federal organization, owing to the continuing strength of national loyalties. It is not enough to say (as President Mitterrand did in January 1995) that 'nationalism is war' for nationalist ideas to be eradicated. Recent referenda are enough to show, if proof be needed, that the idea of a federal Europe can still inspire a certain fear. An alliance which is non-federal is thus needed at European level to guarantee security. Can this be provided by NATO, WEU or OSCE?

The recent geostrategic transformation has called into question NATO's very existence, by removing the menace which gave this integrated military organization its foundation. There are those who are consequently tempted to reduce its role without putting in place another instrument reliable enough to guarantee Europe's security. Others take the opposite line, seeking a new legitimacy for NATO by means of enlarging its responsibilities. An objective comparison forces one to the conclusion that Europe has the choice today between NATO on the one hand, a proven and efficient alliance, but one suffering a legitimacy crisis and essentially unsuitable for the new challenges, and on the other a renascent WEU, more flexible, but immature, inexperienced and deprived of means. It would therefore be unreasonable to make an exclusive choice in favour of one of these organizations over the other. Today, these two bodies actually have complementary roles. NATO is indeed alone in its ability to assure the continent's security against a major threat. At the same time, WEU appears better suited to intervene in a purely European framework against threats of lesser magnitude.

As for the OSCE, without wishing to overlook its function as a consultative forum, it cannot aspire to resolve Europe's security problems on its own within the foreseeable future.

WEU must thus be progressively developed in such a way that its complementary *vis á vis* other organizations, notably NATO, is maintained. At the same time, the development of the only purely European security organization, is required by the establishment of the Common Foreign and Security Policy as set out in the Maastricht treaty. This means that WEU is to grow into the military arm of the European Union. At this point it will also need to be able to draw on the appropriate military capabilities to allow it to act autonomously, more specifically to manage crises in situations when the Alliance is unwilling or unable to act as a whole. The successive creations of Eurocorps, Euroforce, Euromarforce and the Franco-British Euro Air Group all amount to concrete steps in this direction.

A DEFENCE INSTRUMENT OF FOUR PILLARS

Having defined an institutional framework for European Security in relation to the Common Foreign and Security Policy, it is possible to add more detail to the instrument at its disposal. This should consist of four pillars:

- nuclear and conventional forces, and a doctrine suitable to meet all threats;
- a sustained effort in all spending pertaining to European Security;
- a defence industry to guarantee Europe's independence in military equipment; and,
- finally, a 'European' culture of defence and security.

A means of defending the European heartland against all threats

Within any time parameters in question, it is impossible to conceive of Europe's defence not including a nuclear deterrent. Western Europe is today protected by the US nuclear umbrella, with only France and the United Kingdom holding deterrent forces of their own. The result, as President Mitterrand has indicated, is that 'the conception of a nuclear doctrine for Europe will fast become one of the major questions concerning a common European defence'. Indeed, all European countries aspire to some form of nuclear protection. It is therefore necessary to adopt some concept of expanded deterrence so that each European state should benefit automatically from this protection in the event of aggression. The British and French nuclear forces could be placed at the service of European deterrence. This would leave the secondary – but complex – question of final decision-making. Should this be some collegiate system of multiple keys, or left in the hands of a single authority?

But Europe's defence depends equally on a significant quantity of conventional military force. Taking into account the force reductions which have affected all Europe's member states, it is vital that it become possible to pool these forces at very short notice. This implies a high degree of interoperability, which can only be attained by uniformity of operating procedures, intensive common training, identical logistics – which in turn demands commonality of equipment – and the means to project significant force within Europe and beyond, wherever major European interests are at stake. Nevertheless, the accent on interoperability should not lead to an exaggerated degree of multinational integration. The experience of the Franco-German Brigade shows that brigade or divisional level represents a practical limit. European forces should thus be composed of national formations of up to brigade or divisional level, with only headquarters, certain support units and specific forces being made multinational.

In parallel, there are two areas requiring development as a matter of priority: the use of space and anti-missile defence. Since the Gulf War, everyone has been persuaded of the importance of space for intelligence acquisition and for communications links, but this is also true for verifying treaty compliance. The same cannot be said of anti-missile defence, which is a subject that still encounters much opposition. And yet Europe does not simply have to contend with an unidirectional threat, as was demonstrated in 1986 by the Libyan missile launched against Italy. Nuclear deterrence is unable to meet all the threats that might be posed. Europe's populations will not tolerate being left without protection at the same time as theatre anti-missile systems are being developed to shield military forces. Following the example of Israel's population, they will only be inclined to support governments if they are guaranteed the greatest possible chances of survival. It is therefore desirable to create a 'bubble' of anti-missile protection covering Europe, at an estimated cost of some FFr200bn or the equivalent of between two and four per cent of Europe's annual equipment budget.

These two sectors of space and anti-missile defence, both of which remain beyond the reach of any single European state, require a cooperative approach on both financial and technological grounds. As a result, they could serve a catalyst function for European defence by forging solid links between European countries under a common shield without this entailing reliance on an external power. This, however, should not be deemed to rule out cooperation with Europe's major allies.

The structure should be flexible enough to allow each State continued freedom of action. The resulting organization and its force structures must be simultaneously coherent enough to meet a serious threat to the European heartland while remaining sufficiently flexible to leave each state a certain autonomy to manage its own more distant interests. France, for example, is still linked by accords and treaties to a number of African countries. It must be able to intervene without necessarily involving Europe. The principal of subsidiarity applied to the Maastricht Treaty must also be applied to European security and its means for crisis management. It is therefore important that 'reservoirs' of forces and alliances be kept available to address conflicts which do not strike at the heart of Europe's vital interests.

The budgetary effort must be evenly sustained throughout the European level; it would not be acceptable that the financial burden for Europe's defence be unevenly distributed among the member states. Naturally, the economic crisis and the geostrategic transformation have driven countries to look for a peace dividend. But there exists an irreducible threshold if this defence is to hold credibility.

Defence organized at a European level should certainly allow substantial economies to be made, by virtue of a better distribution of the costs, a degree of force specialization and, above all, standardization of equipment. Thus Ballistic Missile Submarine (Nuclear Power) patrols could be closely coordinated between British and French boats with the aim of reducing the overall number. Amphibious operations could be made the responsibility of a certain group of European countries and airmobile operations of another. Finally, equipment standardization would be a beneficial consequence of the creation of a unified European defence industry.

It is therefore vital to create a European defence industry so as to guarantee Europe's military independence, above all in such sensitive areas as nuclear or missile technology, space or anti-missile defence. The absence or loss of know-how in these spheres would mean surrendering Europe's autonomy to manage its own security. Considering the bitter competition at global level affecting the defence industries, and the fall in equipment investment, these industries are condemned to regroup and specialise or else to disappear. The next combat aircraft, like the next tank, will be either European or American (or Asian). Regrouping in a single European industrial base will admittedly entail painful sacrifices for everyone, but there will also be ample rewards in the form of major savings.

Finally, European security can only come about by the development of the requisite common culture of European defence. Bismarck said that the whole of the Balkans was not worth the bones of a single Pomeranian grenadier. History has shown us the penalties of such reasoning and this is a lesson on which Europeans must reflect in the light of today's new Balkan crises. In other words they must accept that they belong to a single unity in which individual and common interests are interlinked. The inculcation of a European defence culture first requires a solid acquaintance with the characteristics of each nation. For the military, exchanges of officers should be further encouraged between staffs and training colleges as deepening an understanding of the various national psychologies. In this respect France's high-level College Interarmées de Défense, some 40 per cent of whose students are foreign officers, constitutes a viable forum for exchanging ideas; this is an example which should be developed further in universities and schools.

If so much as one of these pillars were to prove faulty, the stability of the whole security organization would be greatly jeopardised. The importance of this mission is such that it should mobilise all Europe's energies, particularly those of its diplomats and military.

CONCLUSION

As Napoleon remarked, nations, like individuals, gain enlightenment only as a result of direct experience, and more often as a result of misfortune. It is to be hoped that Europe can draw on the lessons of history so as to overcome its nationalisms, local differences and economic rivalries so as to construct a solid European security. This should rest on a Common Foreign and Security Policy and a robust, non-federal organization which leaves states with the autonomy to manage crises of a secondary nature which do not threaten the European heartland. Pending the WEU's growth to maturity, NATO and WEU should fulfil this role in a mutually complementary manner.

A recast 'machinery', founded on the four pillars of conventional and nuclear weapons, defence effort, armaments industry and a supporting European culture, would therefore be an effective instrument in the service of a Common Foreign and Security Policy. A first step in this direction will be the publication of the forthcoming European White Paper.

10 Out of the Past Grows the Future

Major Ralf Jung

My task is to look back on events of the recent past from a personal viewpoint and to hazard a guess as to the near future. I would like to sketch in the post-Second World War policies of the three most important West European countries (Great Britain, France and Germany), around which Western Europe has revolved since and show that these policies continue to have repercussions, even after the revolutionary developments of 1989. First of all, however, I should like to recall some of the past events, whose fifty year anniversaries were commemorated in 1995.

In January, we were reminded of the Red Army's liberation fifty years ago of the remaining survivors of the most notorious extermination camp at Auschwitz.

Fifty years ago on 4-11 February, the Yalta Conference also took place. This resulted not only in the entry of the Soviet Union into the war against Japan but also meant the lifting of the border demarcation of the Russo-Japanese war of 1904. It is idle to speculate on whether or not Yalta's demand for unconditional German surrender prolonged the war in Europe. It was justified in order not to repeat the mistakes of 1918. The territorial transfers imposed upon Germany, however, led to the flight and expulsion of thousands of Germans. What today is described by the euphemism 'ethnic cleansing', was at the time gruesome reality.

The 13 and 14 February was another commemorative date in 1995. On that night fifty years ago the old German city of Dresden was destroyed by a massive bombing raid. Even in Great Britain today, there are different appraisals as to the necessity of this raid. Remembrance of this terrible event has become part of German-British relations. This was made clear by the participation of both the Duke of Kent and the German President at remembrance ceremonies this year.

On 15 April 1945, British soldiers liberated the notorious concentration camp of Bergen-Belsen and war correspondent Richard Dimbleby brought home the horror at what they found through his famous radio broadcasts. It became clear that the massive extermination of human beings in German concentration camps was no mere invention of British war propaganda but corresponded to an almost incredible reality.

The ceremonies which took place on 6-8 May marked, of course, fifty years since the end of the insane war in Europe which had been forced on the world by the National Socialist 'Third Reich'.

On 26 June fifty years ago, the Charter of the United Nations was signed in San Francisco. Through the Charter, the assembled nations sought to remove war from the powers of states. The purpose of the United Nations was declared to be to 'secure world peace and international security'. (That we haven't lived up to this agreement is shown not only in the history of the last fifty years, but also in the seeming helplessness with which we confront contemporary crises and conflicts.)

The war in the Pacific, instigated by the expansionist nationalists of the Japanese Empire, ended in their defeat fifty years ago on 15 August 1945. Among those commemorated on this anniversary were the nearly 100 000 British soldiers and civilians who perished in Japanese prison camps (a third of those interned). 14 November also marks the half century which has passed since the start of the Nuremberg Trials.

Looking back, it may be that the most far reaching action was the decision at Yalta to partition Germany and its capital into zones of occupation. The foundation stone for the later partitioning of Europe between East and West was laid at this time, a partition which found its symbolic expression in divided Berlin.

In a recent essay, Sir Michael Howard described the development of relations between the three great West European powers by saying that 'French, British and German national self-consciousness has been largely determined, indeed, by conflict and contrast with one another.' Mutual opposition on the part of Britain and Germany to France in particular, characterised the early history of this relationship. In the face of British opposition, however, Germany then strove for world power status towards the end of the nineteenth century. This led eventually to the First World War and brought about a realignment of allegiances between the three countries. After 1918, French attempts to keep defeated Germany as weak as possible for the foreseeable future ran contrary to the British policy of appeasement. The result of the run-down in British armed forces throughout the 1930s was that Britain was unable to prevent the traumatic experience of French military defeat in 1940. The collapse of France left Great Britain to shoulder alone for a while the main burden of the developing war.

Even after the defeat of Germany and the destruction of the Third Reich in 1945, the Alliance of Dunkirk in 1947 and the signing of the Treaty of Brussels in the following year gave expression to the lingering fear of Germany regaining strength.

Fear of Germany lessened, however, as the old powers were helplessly confronted by Soviet expansion. European politics was fundamentally altered with the British initiative to bind the United States to Europe through the North Atlantic Treaty Organization. Washington DC became the 'Capital of the West'.

The price for this was high, however, and meant the re-arming of Germany just five years after the War's end as well as Germany's integration into the Atlantic Alliance, something which the French objected to enormously. A plan to tie German armed forces to a European defence community, promoted primarily by the French government, failed due to lack of support in the French parliament. The Alliance was saved by British readiness to permanently station substantial armed forces on the Continent. The state of affairs finally arrived at was summed up by the famous epigram which described the purpose of the North Atlantic Alliance as being 'to keep the Russians out, the Americans in, and the Germans down'. The integration of Germany into the European Community, which developed political characteristics beyond its original role as a method of economic cooperation, has contributed decisively to the reduction of tensions within Europe.

The historical achievement of Adenauer and de Gaulle was to have taken the post-Second World War path of reconciliation between France and Germany. The German-French treaty of 1963 symbolised the end of centuries-old hostility. This treaty created a close relationship between both countries that has been watched closely, with occasionally justifiable concern, by Great Britain and the United States. The 'Europeanization' of European defence, an end towards which both France and Germany have become engaged for different reasons, was inevitable. The form that this should take, however, has not yet been decided.

If the United States should withdraw from Europe, then one can only hope as Sir Michael Howard has that the three major European powers 'will have settled into a relationship that will represent something more than an uneasy equilibrium'.

I began my national service in 1978 as a young conscript in a *Panzerartillerie* battalion and was stationed at a small barracks located approximately 30km east of Celle in Lower Saxony, near what was at that time the inner-German border but which is today in the middle of Germany. During my tour of duty as platoon commander in an armoured reconnaissance battalion, we had among our normal duties the reconnaissance of positions along the inner-German border in accordance with NATO's General Defence Plan. It was with mixed emotions that we reported on positions over which we would have to go into battle for and which, in so doing, might have transformed our country into a decisive battlefield for conventional and, presumably also, nuclear weapons.

As I excitedly and joyously watched the fall of the Berlin Wall and the unbelievable speed with which this lead to German unification, I never dreamt that in a short while I would be among the first *Bundeswehr* soldiers sent to the new Federal States to dissolve the National People's Army (NVA) and to integrate into the *Bundeswehr* part of its personnel and wide range of equipment.

I took up my duties with the Reconnaissance Battalion 1 of the now defunct (NVA) in Beelitz, a small town near Potsdam. This battalion bore, in typical communist fashion, the 'honourary' name of Dr. Richard Sorge.

On the day that I arrived, I was greeted by officers still wearing the uniform of the old NVA. At midnight they changed into new uniforms. Changing their preconceptions and convictions was, however, to take somewhat longer.

The experiences of the following six months were unforgettable, in particular the way in which we in the *Bundeswehr* won the trust of soldiers faced with the problems brought about through the NVA's dissolution. I watched, for example, a former NVA battalion commander entrain his last T-54 himself as no driver could be found and pondered his fate as he left army life for the uncertainties of a civilian future. I shall not forget driving past rows of Russian soldiers loitering in front of the Red Army's hospital near Beelitz and wondering in which of the anonymous hospital rooms behind them sheltered Eric Honecker, the leader of East Germany and builder of the Berlin Wall. A similarly unforgettable moment occurred when a Russian colonel approached me with an invitation to a Soviet Army Day celebration. We spoke no common language and, wanting to engage him in conversation, I sought an East German interpreter. This proved to be very difficult as there suddenly seemed to be no East Germans willing to speak Russian anymore.

Although many problems remain unsolved, the *Bundeswehr* can well claim to have shouldered the burden of unity in an exemplary way and the description of the *Bundeswehr* as the 'Army of Unity' is fully justified. Based on this achievement, the *Bundeswehr* will be able to tackle issues relating to structural adaptation as well as orienting itself towards 'new tasks'. *Bundeswehr* soldiers' self-image and the current debate on the role that they should play in international politics has been affected by the post-Second World War years. The demilitarization of Germany decided at Yalta continues to influence this debate and the often entrenched positions on this issue within German society can be traced back to this decision.

Germany finds itself in a new and difficult position following the withdrawal of Allied troops from Berlin, the withdrawal of Russian troops from the new federal states and the end of the temporal limitations of the 2+4 Treaty. It has once again slipped back into the middle of the continent. Old fears, even those of our allies and friends have not completely disappeared. The effort of Germany to lose its front-line status in Europe and the desire by the emerging democratic states of Eastern and Central Europe for quick integration into the European Union and into NATO is neither without problems, nor accepted by all of the present member states. The demise of East-West, bi-polar confrontation has pulled the West's attention away from its exclusive focus on Eastern Europe. France and its neighbours, for example, are expressing increasing concern over developments in the North African states and the Mediterranean region in general. Two further examples are the NATO partner states of Greece and Turkey. They continue to confront each other with suspicion and take different views of the bloody conflict in former Yugoslavia. Turkey faces, in addition, important internal difficulties which have prevented it from assuming a more prominent role in the Middle East.

The Alliance must address these questions even if it is difficult to arrive at a consensus among the divergent interest groups within NATO. The already considerable pressure from the states of Central and Eastern Europe to join NATO is being further strengthened by the unpredictable behaviour of Russia. As a result, the question of NATO's relationship with Russia becomes a decisive one. Furthermore, since Finland's accession, the European Union now has a direct land border with Russia. Whether the present security organizations can rise to the challenges presented by the collapse of the Yalta settlement in Europe appears doubtful. This is so not only because of developments in former Yugoslavia. It must not be forgotten, when faced with the apparent helplessness of these organizations, that they are only reflecting the consensus of interests within their constituent member states. National interest determines the handling of the situation. While this might be regrettable, it remains the only starting point if more is to be achieved. One thing which must not be undone, however, is the transatlantic connection. There can be no credible European defence capability without American back-up.

The special relationship that exists between the major West European nations, and between them and the US, is indispensable for a stable and secure order in Europe. Whether military integration can and should play the role of forerunner to a still weak political integration is, with justification, debatable. Military integration once entered into, however, is difficult to reverse and at least forces a permanent improvement in political understanding.

The path taken by Germany towards integration of its land forces into multi-national or bi-national corps is, with military hindsight, not without criticism. It is, however, a way to break down existing, and in my opinion, unjustified fears regarding increasing German military power. The German-Dutch Corp, whose official language interestingly is English, can be viewed in this light. It is also appropriate that the German-Dutch Corp was founded this year, fifty-five years after the *Wehrmacht* marched into the Netherlands and fifty years after the Netherlands was liberated by allied soldiers.

11 Repression to Rejuvenation: Eastern Europe in a New Continent

His Majesty King Michael of Romania

On the 23 August 1944, I took upon myself the fateful decision to remove Romania from its enforced alliance with the Axis power, and join the nations fighting for Europe's freedom. Much literature and many falsifications have been written about this act ever since, but, in reaching my conclusion in that hot August, I was driven by two fundamental considerations: that Romania's place should always be on the side of those promoting democracy and that Hitler's war was not our own. The act was supported by the entire nation, including the leaders of all the political parties, and all the armed forces. We fought heroically: we ousted the Nazis, and went all the way to Czechoslovakia. Yet, no sooner had the war ended, than Romania's huge contribution to the Allied victory cause counted for nothing. As the man responsible for my country's destiny, I had no means of knowing that, by 1945, the map of the continent had already been drawn. The Second World War began, ostensibly, over the independence of Poland. For the next four decades and more, however, Poland languished under a Soviet-imposed dictatorship. It was the same for my country, and for all our neighbours. I will never forget the sacrifice of our soldiers, the faces of our men and women who fought heroically and died, persuaded that they did this for a good cause. And I shall always remember the haunting picture of my country, devastated by war, only to be pillaged by the advancing Red Army. The anniversary of the end of the war brings back bittersweet memories for all East Europeans: it was a time of a triumph against Hitler, but it was also the time when another dictatorship began in earnest. The problem for Europe today is not to relive history but, rather, to draw the appropriate lessons for the future. And, although the dangers today are very different from those in 1945, the difficult task of recreating a continent whole and free remains as elusive a goal as ever.

In the minds of many, Eastern Europe is yesterday's story. The countries of that region held their first post-communist elections and their leaders are getting on with the ordinary tasks of any politician: handling the economy, mediating between competing interest groups and, of course, confronting each other. The Western media now concentrates on issues that appear to be much more crucial: the spread of weapons of mass destruction and the prospects for an economic recovery. I have, however, one fear: that between the genuine but temporary difficulties which the West is currently experiencing and the challenges still to be faced elsewhere in the world, Eastern Europe could, yet again, be forgotten.

We have many reasons for satisfaction. Only five years ago, we were debating not the future of democracy in the Eastern half of Europe but, rather, the more modest task of persuading the then ruling communist parties to share power with an emerging popular opposition. We may be horrified today at the prospect of war in other parts of the world and, indeed, at the carnage in Yugoslavia. But we must also remember that, due to the people of Eastern Europe and the policies of all of NATO, the spectre of an all-out European war now seems remote. It is now fashionable in the West to assume that all our institutions, from the European Union right through to NATO, have been discredited; they were supposedly built for yesterday's world which no longer exists, and they have all failed to predict or prevent the disintegration in Yugoslavia. My experience of Eastern Europe remains, however, very different: the people of the region, far from dismissing Western cooperation structures, are pushing even harder to join. And, far from being the prisoners of their own history, the people of Eastern Europe have drawn the correct lessons from their past experience: only by being closely bound to the West, only by becoming full members of both NATO and the European Union, can they avoid isolation and disaster. The task of reconstructing the continent belongs to all of us, both East and West. And it cannot be postponed any longer.

I am aware, however, that sentiment alone cannot govern the conduct of foreign policy. And I think that I am realistic enough to understand that the West's long term interests require us to concentrate, if only for the moment, on other parts of the world, particularly the situation in Russia, which is growing increasingly complicated. But I would like to point out that the problems of Eastern Europe have not disappeared and are unlikely to do so even if they no longer command so much attention in the press. These problems are neither intractable, nor unmanageable. They require application, a good knowledge of the aspirations and fears of the people concerned and much perseverance. And they need to be solved not out of any altruistic motive, but simply because Eastern Europe's problems are also your own.

One of the greatest pitfalls in handling future relations with Eastern Europe is that of generalisation and stereotyping, usually based on insufficient knowledge of the region. It is true that all East European countries are relatively small and poor. And, yes, all of them have to travel the long and arduous route to real democracy, a navigation in uncharted waters with no rules and plenty of potential storms. For decades, these countries were not the West's problem. The West may have decried the violations of human rights and expressed the hope that, one day, Eastern Europe would be free. Nevertheless, Western governments (and often Western nations as well) basically considered the prospect of liberation to be remote. The West relied on a strong NATO, based on genuine consent and mutual security interests and developed – albeit after some reservations – close economic relations and free trade areas. The West grew richer as the East became poorer but, since war was unthinkable, that was the way things were going to stay.

The revolutions in the East surprised us all. The courage of the people of Eastern Europe, their determination to be free, were a source of inspiration for an entire continent. Yet, as the walls came down, some appeared only too ready to resurrect them under different guises. How many were prepared to believe that German unification would come about less than a year after the collapse of the Berlin Wall? And how many would have expected to refer to the *'former'* Soviet Union so quickly? But, as the pace of events gathered speed, the ranks of the self-doubters in the West grew. No, we were told, the problems of Eastern Europe cannot deflect our own national agendas. And no, we cannot do much for them, since their national reconstruction will take decades.

The old European continent was torn by warfare many times. The graves of your brave soldiers dot cemeteries throughout the world, as a silent tribute to the Western democracies' determination to defeat dictatorships originating in Europe. Europe and the United States collaborated in that war, and in the Helsinki process, that conference which led, after many tribulations in the 1970s, to the creation of a more durable security in Europe. From the Atlantic to the Urals, Europe is now officially free of communism, free of weapons aimed across borders. Yet the continent is not united in any sense. One half – especially the 15 members of the European Union – are rich, while the other half – ruled by communist dictatorships imposed on them from the East – still suffer in poverty. I have no doubt that an equalisation of wealth between East and West, desirable though it may be, is not feasible any time soon; it is pointless to provide mere slogans, for the reality goes much deeper.

When I frequently point out to people that Europe does not end at the Alps, I usually get the reply that it is difficult to define the borders of the continent. Indeed, as a result of the Soviet empire's disintegration, the Organization for Security and Cooperation in Europe (OSCE), that institution sponsored also by the West in order to create stability, now includes countries stretching as far as the borders with China. Most probably a new definition of Europe's frontiers will ultimately emerge. And I suspect that this new Europe will not include all the countries currently represented in the OSCE. My greatest fear is that when this happens, some nations in the continent's eastern half will be left out. A new policy of differentiation is emerging. The countries of the so-called Central Europe, Poland, the Czech and Slovak republics and Hungary, are deemed more able to join the European Union and NATO, while other states – such as my own – are relegated to the bottom of the pile. While fully aware that Romania's progress has not been as fast as that of other former communist states, I wish to reiterate my conviction that the continent should not be divided into first and second-tier countries. Such a policy of differentiation, even if applied just in practice rather than in strictly legal terms, would remove any incentive for reform and perpetuate instability. What hope do I have to explain to my people, the Romanians, that they must suffer more on the path of economic and political regeneration if the ultimate result will still be relegation to a turbulent and increasingly ignored corner of the Balkans?

I am sure that many will agree with these sentiments, at least in principle. But they will point out that the problem is not the principle. Rather, it is the mechanism by which a democracy can be consolidated and a market economy created. And – they will suggest – until these two preconditions are fulfilled, any talk of integration either into Europe or into the world market economy will remain purely academic. Besides, they will point out, Eastern Europe has some specific problems which it needs to iron out first. Territorial demands, ethnic problems and decaying social structures are usually at the top of this particular list. I am also told that some countries are simply not made for democracy, as though a system of government is somehow inherited in one's genes.

Throughout the last 47 years spent in forced exile, I have learnt to endure calumny, humiliation and threats to the life of my family. I have been accused by communists of collaboration with the Fascists, and by relics of right-wing dictatorships of collaboration with the communists. Yet nothing has pained me more than hearing the idea – to which many in the West still subscribe – according to which Romanians are different from other Europeans. Supposedly, they do not know what democracy means; apparently, they would be content with any system of government, as long as it provided basic food and heating. I need not remind you that very similar thoughts went through the minds of Europeans when analysing Asian and African countries. There, as well, democracy was viewed as a peculiar luxury, something which may arrive at a later stage, but something which is not particularly necessary as long as a state had a supposedly low level of education and economic development. Africa ended up with neither democracy nor economic development; parts of Asia are experiencing a higher level of economic development, and they will not be able to ignore claims for political freedom for much longer.

I have never accepted the notion that some people are not predisposed to democracy, partly because I never thought that a person must be particularly well educated or economically advanced in order to desire freedom, and expect to be treated with respect. The distinction between so-called economic rights such as work and a decent standard of living – and human rights – such as the right to free speech and assembly – was always a false one. Eastern Europe is the best example of one simple fact: without democracy, there is no long-lasting economic development and without a decent standard of living, democracy remains fragile. The two concepts are inter-related and, indeed, inseparable. My countrymen are neither backward, nor naturally inclined towards dictatorship. Their present economic predicament may be unique on the European continent, but that is hardly their personal fault.

They were ruled by a regime which used terror more extensively than anywhere else in Eastern Europe and underwent a period of enforced industrialisation of a kind hardly experienced elsewhere. The aim was to transform Romania, to fit existing realities into the utopias concocted by Marx in London, perfected by Lenin in Zurich and applied by Stalin in Moscow. The Romanian communist party never experienced even the brief period of liberalisation which followed the death of Stalin in other East European states. It never considered relaxing its political control, because it never had any instrument or idea how to engage in a serious dialogue with its people. I would not like to suggest that Eastern Europe's other dictators were better, because I do not believe that dictatorships deserve to be distinguished in these subjective terms. However, I would like to point out that, while the dictators of Hungary, Poland, Czechoslovakia and East Germany at least attempted to appease their people by providing them with some consumer goods, the Romanian dictators did not consider this necessary. Instead of a dialogue, they sponsored rabid nationalism and racial hatred; instead of food, they provided the Romanians with defaced flags and a forged history.

The system perfected was a bizarre mixture of nationalism, Marxism and pure Byzantine-style nepotism. It was a rule which completely destroyed not only cultural life, but penetrated and manipulated all social structures. The system relied on compromising people not merely by forcing them to participate in a gigantic cult of personality, but simply by forcing an entire nation to witness this process of national degradation. Yet communism failed to isolate my country from the mainstream of Europe. Those who poured into the streets in December 1989 sought not merely to overthrow a hated dictatorship; they also assimilated the aspirations of their fellow Europeans. Ceausescu liked to wave the national flag at every opportunity, but the crowds which rose against the regime waved the very same flag back at him.

Both before and after the miraculous year of revolutions, I have often heard that some East Europeans are morally and socially 'sick' and that they will need a long period of convalescence. I do not agree with this analysis for two reasons. First, if they need a lengthy period of convalescence, I fear what will happen during this period. Secondly, to suggest that a society is just sick is hardly illuminating, for it tells us little either about the disease or the possible cure.

In reality, democracy is more than a system of government; it is a way of life. It is a mechanism of self-denial, an agreement between those governing and those governed about rights and obligations. This agreement is neither open-ended nor indefinite, and its application depends on a whole host of other mechanisms, all of which place checks and balances on the government of the day. To be sure, this includes an independent judiciary, a free press, impartial armed forces and a great deal of toleration throughout. But it also includes an economy which can meet the growing needs of people and a vision of a better future. These ingredients are inseparable, as I am sure all East Europeans understand very well. They are now engaged in nothing less than a new process of national self-definition, a rebuilding of state structures. I think that the West must be patient; it must understand that this process can be set back temporarily but that, given the right encouragement, it can also advance fairly quickly. You should not be afraid of the problems ahead, partly because they are unavoidable, and partly because they are also open to solutions.

I will not deny that the problem of nationalism and ethnic conflicts occupies us all at the moment. For many in the West, the rekindling of such issues is regarded as a backward step, a return to problems supposedly solved in Western Europe decades ago. I hardly need to remind Europeans, however, that this is a mistake, at least for two reasons. First, because many other nations are still seeking solutions to ethnic difficulties and secondly, because any direct comparison between the recent historical experience in East and West is misplaced. Because it had been free since 1945, Western Europe could start solving its difficulties because it was free since 1945, while in the East, similar problems were allowed to fester under the guise of 'workers solidarity'. Furthermore, many Western countries have enjoyed a long independent existence, while the East Europeans' states are relatively young and naturally sensitive about their frontiers and internal cohesion. Ultimately, prosperity allowed Western Europe to smooth over many of these difficulties, while in the East, economic decay exacerbated ethnic conflicts.

It is clear that what the West fears most is the spectre of ethnic tension spilling over into violence, rather than the mere existence of these tensions. Yet the danger of violence can and must be prevented with the help of two essential steps: first, the elaboration of a security framework which encompasses all East Europeans and, second, the engagement of the newly freed states in a vast programme of economic reconstruction which harnesses their energies to more profitable ends. We must not repeat the mistake of ignoring ethnic and territorial differences. On the contrary! These should be discussed openly and frequently. Our main yardstick should be the prevention of the use of force, and the creation of a mechanism by which such differences are constantly debated, if not ultimately solved. We cannot expect a quick solution to problems steeped in history, nor should we be so daunted as to abandon them to fortune, for luck has not usually smiled upon the East Europeans.

I think that I hardly need to convince anyone that the creation of a new security system is imperative. A variety of arrangements is currently being debated, all intended to answer various security interests. Let me tell you some of the East European worries, for they are simple. For decades, they belonged to the Warsaw Pact, an alliance which did not answer their security needs. This alliance has now evaporated, but the void created will have to be filled. The East European states need a security structure which on the one hand accommodates their independent existence and, on the other, prevents any one larger power from re-establishing a hegemony over their region. I am aware of the fact that this very simple set of desiderata presents the West with immense difficulties. Everyone, and particularly politicians in North America, are now openly wondering if they still need to contribute to Europe's security as actively as before. The decision must be theirs, but I am convinced that we need to look at the problem in its entirety. Security is indivisible and in an age of modern missiles, it is bound to affect someone living in Paris as much as someone living in the Balkans. Everyone assumed that the war in Yugoslavia, as tragic as it may have been, would not affect Western European security. Three years after Yugoslavia erupted, Western soldiers were in the Balkans in their thousands, seeking to keep a peace that did not exist, hoping to achieve a peace which continues to be elusive.

The second potential danger is to offer the East Europeans various stages of association in existing institutions. The concept has some attraction: after all, it preserves existing Western security structures which have worked well. Yet, before deciding on the potential treaties of association that the West may offer Eastern Europe, it should consider carefully what they may actually entail, and make sure that the East Europeans understand Western intentions correctly. As a young man in Bucharest in 1939, I remember vividly certain guarantees offered to my country at the time. If new guarantees or treaties are envisaged, we must remember that no security is worse than an imaginary one. The East European states must not become the playground for wider games played either on the West or Eastern extremities of our continent. Any other approach could spell disaster for us all.

The difficulties of helping the transformation of East European economies also loom large. Again, the initial mood of euphoria has been transformed into deep gloom. Economic experts forecast millions of unemployed in Eastern Europe, tens of thousands of bankrupt factories – in short, an industrial desert. Suddenly, the pennies are counted at home. A relatively prolonged economic recession and the delay in reaping the 'peace dividend' from disarmament all seem more important. To those in North America who are about to embark on seeking re-election, I can only say that I understand their predicament and sentiments. However, I would also like to remind them of what is at stake in the long run.

The newly elected leaders of Eastern Europe also had to face re-election. More importantly, they had to show that democracy meant not only better newspapers and noisier parliamentary sessions, but also at least the promise of a better life. Nobody expected the West to bankroll Eastern Europe. Indeed, I believe that the debate on economic assistance has concentrated too often on charity. The sight of children dying of AIDS in infested Romanian hospitals was, indeed, heart-rending, and I cannot find enough words to express my admiration to those who helped. Yet in the long run, such dreadful sights can only be eliminated through the integration of the East Europeans into the world economy, and through the establishment of a myriad of contacts between businessmen.

Western governments have been right all along to insist that economic contacts should only take place once a framework of a market economy is apparent. This is so not only because a market economy is best at identifying opportunities and allocating resources, but also because the system is essential in order to break down the concentration of political power at the centre and safeguard democracy. I also see nothing wrong in the fact that Western governments should ultimately continue to condition the granting of aid on progress towards democracy and a market economy. But the other side of the same coin must surely be that progress is an evolutionary concept, and it must be helped along by positive involvement.

In the second round of elections, East Europeans overwhelmingly voted for the return of their former communist leaders. With the exception of the Czech republics, former senior communist members are now back in power in every other East European state; indeed, in my country Romania, they have never left power even for a brief interlude. But this development, as galling as it may be for those who believed in a swift transformation, is neither sinister, nor irredeemable. The reality is that nobody believes in communism; few people ever did. The problem is not one of ideology but, rather, of democratic expectations: the people of Eastern Europe have had all the pain associated with economic reform, with fewer of its benefits. And even more tragic is the situation in some countries such as mine, where the pain of reform has been sustained without much of the proper reform either. Faced with such difficulties, people tend to cling to the known past, to the people who suggest that it is possible to have both economic prosperity and the fairly painless certainty of the past. I am not particularly concerned about the return of former communist officials, partly because I suspect that this will be a passing phenomenon, and partly because the governments of the region are discovering that they do not have as many alternatives as they originally pretended.

Eastern Europe is currently divided into two main blocks: those who have started on the road of economic reform and are already reaping the first tangible benefits, and those who have not, but will be forced into doing so soon. Eastern European leaders, including the former communists who still rule in my country, have already discovered that they cannot reinvent the wheel: the third way between market reform and a command economy leads to the Third World. Romania, for instance, has both a high rate of inflation and a large unemployment problem despite persistent efforts to avoid economic reform. The retention of some conditions on the supply of aid and credits is necessary in order to shorten this period of political learning, and it is also crucial in order to ensure that no reversal to authoritarian practices takes place. Eastern Europe is in a curious half-way position: the old dictatorships cannot return, but democratic practices remain fragile. It is in everyone's interest, therefore, to tilt the balance towards democracy, and to do so quickly.

Very often, this will entail carrots, as well as sticks, offers of cooperation, as well as limits to what may be tolerated. It is in this context that I welcome the European Union's recent decision to accelerate the process of integrating the countries of the East, including my own. Granting or denial of economic aid and trade concessions are never separated from political aims, but we must always remember that they are most effective when they serve as an encouragement, rather than merely as punishment. I also readily agree that the budgets of Western countries are limited and coming under increasing strains. Clearly, what is required is the creation of a framework which will encourage private businesses to trade with Eastern Europe on mutually advantageous grounds.

I have set out many imperatives and it is natural for Western Europeans to ask if the effort is really worthwhile. After all, the West's current problems are now very different, ranging from difficulties over trade with Asia and North America, and a variety of deeper social problems which confront us all. My answer to this is an emphatic 'yes'. During the Great Recession of the 1930s, Eastern Europe was forgotten. A few years later we were surprised at the number of dictatorships which confronted us on the continent. I am sure that we can learn from that lesson and avoid similar pitfalls.

Romania was not as lucky as its neighbours. When communism fell in December 1989, it did not have a writer-turned-politician, or a trade unionist with years of experience in opposing dictatorship. No doubt, some of the mistakes which took place since then were unavoidable. Yet I continue to blame those who assumed control over Romania's government in December 1989 for one cardinal crime: the fact that they sought to continue as before, and showed little interest in instituting real democracy. Instead of confronting the thorny problem of personal responsibility for former crimes, they executed Nicolae Ceausescu and his wife in a sham trial and sought to avoid any discussion of their own communist past. And, instead of encouraging the creation of opposition parties, they terrorised and intimidated those who sought to compete with them in politics. The same techniques were applied to my person as well. The authorities claimed that I represent a past which will never return. Yet at no point did they dare ask the people whether they wanted a return to the monarchy, as it existed throughout their history, or whether they preferred the republic imposed by the communist regime. Instead, they resorted to traditional subterfuge. First, they appointed a temporary head of state. Then they proceeded with the election of a president before a constitution existed. Only then did they impose a constitution voted upon by barely half of the population and supposedly decreeing that the republic will continue for ever. A sham election, a sham democracy and a sham constitution rushed through parliament and voted upon by only barely half of the electorate. I hardly need to repeat the story of what followed thereafter. Romania's new leaders quickly discovered that no foreign aid was forthcoming and, while they could use miners in order to disperse demonstrators, they could not offer Romanians food and work. The government disintegrated and former collaborators are now accusing each other – ironically – of communism.

It hardly needs emphasising that such techniques will not produce the stability which Romania needs. After two refusals, I returned to my country and was greeted by hundreds of thousands of well-wishers, ordinary Romanians who were not put off either by communist propaganda or present intimidation. Startled by this unforeseen welcome, the government has persistently refused to allow my return, precisely because it knows that the institution of the constitutional monarchy is growing in popularity.

Yet the past is not my main concern. Our country will hold parliamentary elections next year and, hopefully, embark on a new start. What Romanians need most is reassurance and hope. Reassurance that they could be ruled by a head of state who is truly impartial, and a government which is truly responsible to parliament. And hope that, if they manage to achieve this feat, the world will extend them a helping hand. After Poland, Romania remains the biggest East European state, a country with vast economic potential and plenty of natural resources, a state which remains solid in an area now beset with turmoil. If a new government is elected in a genuinely democratic way, it should be welcomed as Europe's equal partner. I, for one, will continue to abide by the oath given to my people back in the torment of the Second World War: to defend their interests and protect them, impartially and at all times. Nothing will prevent me from fulfilling this oath and every effort should be made by Europe to welcome Romania and all other East European countries into the family of the world's democracies. Fifty years after the end of the War, this is the best tribute that we can offer to those who died for our freedom.

12 Brute Force and Genius: The View From The Soviet Union

Dr Christopher Bellamy

By May 1945 the armies of the Soviet Union, numbering more than 11 million in total, had reached the river Elbe. In four years of ferocious fighting, during which their efforts had never faltered, they had grappled with 65 to 70 per cent of the total strength of *Wehrmacht*, and defeated it, though at appalling cost. For 1418 days, since 22 June 1941, those armies had fought with an incongruous mixture of bone-headed determination and cunning; of the most basic logistics and some very slick and ingenious technology; of futuristic tanks and horsed cavalry; of sullen resignation and fanatical determination; of tactical clumsiness and brilliant generalship – in short, of brute force and genius. The Berlin operation from 16 April to 18 May 1945 was almost the last of 160 distinct offensive operations – Prague and Manchuria followed. In its final, furious dash for Berlin alone the Red Army had lost 78 290 dead and more than 274 000 wounded.[1] Averell Harriman, the US emissary to both Churchill and Stalin, congratulated the 65-year old Soviet dictator on the capture of the Third Reich's capital, Berlin, which now lay in ruins. 'Alexander I got to Paris', replied Stalin.

It was a characteristic and telling allusion. The parallels between the Great Patriotic War of 1941-45 and the Patriotic War of 1812, which also impelled Russia westwards as a key player in an international alliance against a dictator, were many and obvious enough.

Soviet preparations for the total war had begun in 1925. The blueprint for the conduct of the Great Patriotic war was published in 1926 and 1927, in *Strategy*, by Aleksandr Svechin (1878-1938), a former Tsarist Major-General, who later disappeared, like so many, in Stalin's purges. But *Strategy* remained the only book allowed to bear that title until 1962, when it was supplanted by *Military Strategy* by Marshal Vasiliy Sokolovskiy (1897-1968), the result of a ten year study of nuclear war.[2]

Svechin understood that in modern war a knock-out blow was unlikely, certainly in a war involving the Soviet Union, and that victory would only come after a series of hammer-blows, like those which rained on Germany from the east. War was not 'a medicine for a state's internal illness', wrote Svechin, 'but a serious examination of the health of its internal politics'.[3] War would permeate the entire state. Not only would armies have been immobilised for the front, but the police and the Interior Ministry would need to adopt draconian measures in the rear. It was a grim, Orwellian picture, which accurately predicted the war the Soviet Union raged. Svechin was attacked and imprisoned at the behest of the flamboyant and cruel Marshal Mikhail Tukhachevskiy (1893-1937), but Tukhachevskiy stole most of the ideas and used them in his own seven volume study *Future War*, and *New Questions of War* – studies of protracted war.[4]

Well before the war was over, Western observers noted with a mixture of admiration and alarm how the Soviet Union was throwing everything into the conflict, with no pity on its people and no conservation of resources for the future. They never fully understood what Pasternak called Russia's 'infinite capacity for suffering'. Lieutenant General Sir Giffard Martel, who led the British military mission to the Soviet Union in 1943, wrote secretly:

> 'You will remember that the Bolsheviks were really frightened lest the US and ourselves would not continue lease-lend to them after the war. Without this their standard of living will remain at the present pitifully low level and the Bolshevik government may easily be kicked out...Russia expected lease-lend for three years after the war to raise their standard of living. Here is a weapon which we could surely use to make them behave with a little decency'.[5]

The British Foreign Office, assessing the likely direction of Soviet policy after the war, in April 1944, had not entirely agreed with Martel:

> 'The USSR will have made immense sacrifices for victory in men and material. The wastage will have been enormous. None the less, the USSR will emerge from the war (i) as the strongest land power in the world and one of the strongest air powers; (ii) as the very successful exponent of a new economic and social system and a new type of

multi-national State; (iii) as the great Slav power (as in the past) and the heir to much besides from the heritage of the old Russia. She will have great prestige and very great pride in herself. All the indications are that the regime will be strengthened by the war; it will be well adapted to deal with the problems resulting from the dislocation caused by war; it seems most unlikely that it will be faced with any serious internal dissension.'[6]

The dislocation was more serious than predicted – equivalent to a medium-sized nuclear war. Since the late 1980s, Russian and Western historians have begun to lift the veil on the true losses, and they were even more staggering than Khrushchev's often quoted '20 million dead' – military and civilian. The 'global loss' – including indirect losses through hunger, disease and the low birth-rate during the war years – is agreed to have been around 48 million – 23 per cent of the population. Battlefield dead accounted for 8.5 million, to which 18 million wounded, shell-shocked and frost bitten must be added. Millions of civilians had died – nearly a million in the siege of Leningrad alone. Five million prisoners of war fell into Axis hands: only two million came back – most to fall into another category of casualties: the victim of internal repression, Stalin's own war against his people, which resumed in earnest after victory over Germany, although it had continued throughout.[7] And these figures do not include the invisible legacy of wars, a legacy we are only now coming to recognize: psychological casualties, nervous diseases and 'post traumatic stress disorder'.

In the Russian Republic (RSFSR) alone, 1.8 million civilian inhabitants were wiped out and 2.4 million taken for forced labour in Germany.[8] In the unconquered part of the country, the war economy took everything. And the cost of industrial migration – uprooting whole factories and relocating them in the east, and of an estimated 15 million evacuees fleeing eastward from the German advance, has never been calculated.[9] When victory dawned in 1945, gangs of orphans roamed the countryside and there was a cruel imbalance between the numbers of women and men, which had its own impact on the population.

The most productive part of the country had been occupied by the Germans and laid to waste. In occupied areas of the Soviet Union the invaders destroyed 1710 towns, 70 000 villages, 32 000 industrial plants and 65 000 kilometres of railway.[10] In the Russian Republic alone 23 000 schools had been razed. Damage to basic industry was particularly heavy, with between one-half and two-thirds of the total capacity of the Soviet Union being put out of commission. Mines with an annual output of over 100 million tons of coal and 20 million tons of iron ore were wrecked and factories producing 19 million tons of steel were completely or partially destroyed – as much as total Soviet production at the end of 1945.[11]

But there was no rest. Reconstruction would prove as demanding as war. But the Soviet Union had to do more than rebuild. It had to capitalise on its new international position – a position in which it could hardly have expected to find itself four years before. It could not just stop, but had to keep going. And, shortly after the end of the war in Europe, it had to contend with the appearance of the atomic bomb, as it has already begun to contend with the ballistic missile.

A 'vigorous Government drive for sustained and even higher output' began immediately after the surrender of Germany and the subsequent announcement of the new five year plan. Some of the Soviet soldiers and civilians who had come into contact with foreign ideas and higher standards of living – particularly in Germany – wondered why the Soviet system had not been able to produce the same material benefits as the capitalist world. Holidays were again permitted and an eight hour day reintroduced, but real holidays were impossible because of the dislocation of the transport system and, with higher output targets, the eight-hour day simply meant cramming more effort into less time.[12]

Stalin's May Day order of 1945 called on the Soviet people to 'heal wounds of war quickly' and to 'increase the power of the Soviet state'. Newspapers repeatedly stressed the enormity of the task ahead. Immediately after the end of the war in Europe, there was no relaxation of efforts and peace did not bring any tangible advantages, but people remained confident in their leaders and in the future.[13] On 23 June the Supreme Soviet passed a law demobilizing the thirteen oldest groups on active service (men between 40 and 52(!)) stipulating that they should receive work within one month, at least as good as before enlistment, and specifying gratuities to be paid, food rations, coupons for meals and loans for house-building. When a member of the British embassy staff asked a Soviet journalist 'How things were going' he replied with a wry smile: 'Peace has come but it has not yet turned into something tangible'. Citizens would 'have to wait some years before they can enjoy the fruits of their labours and their Government's long term planning', wrote the *Chargé d'Affaires*. 'But they are buoyed up by pride in their recent victory, by confidence in the wisdom of their leaders, by the conviction that one day things will be better, if not for them, at least for their children'.[14]

It did not last long. But what ordinary people thought did not matter, anyway.

In July 1945 the Soviet Union had a regular Army of 11 365 000. Demobilizing and re-absorbing several million returning soldiers – seven to eight million by March 1946 – proceeded less smoothly than expected. Some of the soldiers were dissatisfied with the jobs provided for them, others found they were not treated with the respect which they felt they had earned. As Sir Archibald Clark Err, the British Ambassador, noted on 4 December, 'Moscow is now experiencing a real wave of hooliganism'. The more unruly elements among the demobilized soldiers were partly to blame but in the wake of amnesties for prisoners declared after the war, it was likely that 'habitual criminals and recently amnestied jailbirds are taking advantage of the situation to operate even more actively than usual'.[15]

A few days later he wrote this dissatisfaction:

> '...is, however by no means new in the Soviet Union, because, for various reasons, the country has been living under a scarcity economy for the greater part of the past twenty-eight years. But people seemed to have hoped that in some mysterious way the war would lead to an immediate and great improvement in the standard of living. Now that they realise that this improvement will inevitably be much slower than they had imagined, and that the main emphasis in the new five years' plan is to be a reconstruction, capital goods industries and the development of railways, their spirits have sunk, and at the moment there is certainly a mood of depression and at times even protest.'[16]

However, such discontent was assessed – correctly – as unlikely to deflect the Soviet leadership from the path they considered necessary. 'They know they have Slav passivity, victory in war, the efficiency of the NKVD (the Interior Ministry) and other important factors on their side'.[17]

On 26 May 1945 the State Defence Committee ordered the gradual conversion of military to civilian production, but this process of conversion proved difficult. Defence output fell 68 per cent in the last quarter of 1945 while civilian output only rose by 21 per cent. Furthermore, output measured in terms of quantity does not give a full picture. As the British Embassy reported in March 1946:

> 'It is probable, in view of the re-equipment of the armed forces, the slowness of reconversion of war factories and new preparations for the production of the atomic bomb, that armaments account for a higher proportion of total production now than in 1940'.[18]

Western intelligence, prone as ever to over-insure, believed the Soviet Union would avoid a major war until 1950 – the end of the five-year plan. Stalin said he would avoid one until 1960. In his February 1946 speech he said it would take at least three five-year plans to prepare for 'all contingencies'. He clearly believed that it would take the world a similar period to recover from the Second World War as it had recovered from the First. And at this stage he saw a great war originating in the rivalry between imperialist powers again. He did not foresee the dominant position the US was to acquire in the capitalist world, and, even, the full effect of its massive lead in the nuclear weapons field.[19]

THE COLD WAR

By 1944 it was clear that 'the war has given the Soviet Union the opportunity of transforming themselves from a revolutionary Power, to a great extent isolated from and suspected by the other great powers – something of a pariah – into one of the four leaders of the world'.[20] Co-operation with the other three – the US, Britain and France – would give the Soviet Union a better assurance than any other method of freedom from external pressures while it was carrying out its own industrial and social development. There were signs that such a policy had some attraction for the Soviet Leaders.

Immediately after the end of the war, Western Governments were inclined to appear firm but friendly to the Soviet Union, so as not to alienate it. War was unlikely as long as the US and UK remained sufficiently strong to discourage any adventures and provided the internal situation did not deteriorate to the point of persuading the Soviet Government that if it did not act 'now' it might later have to defend itself against a stronger and aggressive coalition.

However, the Soviet regime was recognised as 'dynamic', and the Soviet Union as still expanding though, admittedly, not yet beyond areas where Russia had interests before the Revolution. Nevertheless, it seemed obvious that Soviet and Western interests would collide. Britain and Russia had a long history of hostility and suspicion. There was no such tradition between the Soviet Union and the United States, and a good deal of admiration (as there still is) for American industrial and technological prowess. But the ruling Soviet elite feared American economic expansionism, hated American business and high finance and distrusted the international role the US might wish to play after the war.[21] Except in the extremely unlikely event of Germany or some other power again becoming a deadly menace, there was no longer much likelihood of British and Russian interests being automatically drawn together as they were in 1812, 1914 and 1941. The Soviet Union's attitude to the UN would depend on how far it advanced Soviet interests. They regarded the core of the UN as three-power cooperation between themselves, Britain and the US. Finally, the Soviet Union would become a threat to Western colonial interests, in the longer term. It was predicted that the Soviet Union would be strong enough to launch a war for the liberation of colonial peoples after three five-year plans, by 1960, when the colonial powers' own troubles might lead them to launch a war against the Soviet Union. At the beginning of March 1946, when the growing movement towards Indian independence was in the news, many Soviet people wrote to the Kremlin offering their services as volunteers for the 'forthcoming war for the liberation of India'.[22]

The Soviet Policy was described as 'like eating an artichoke', picking the leaves off one by one. But they do not want war and will proceed step by step, preparing the political ground in advance (like Jenghiz Khan did)...'[23]

By 5 March 1946, when Churchill made his famous 'Iron Curtain' speech at Westminster College, Fulton, Missouri, the hopes of a changed Soviet attitude to the West and friendly cooperation had evaporated. By that time, the shape of the Cold War was clearly defined.

> 'It is not a matter any longer whether divisions stationed here can cover such and such territory; it is a matter whether we can afford to allow a power with such ambitions and such lack of scruple to control such colossal manpower and industrial potential. Mr Roberts [the British Chargé d'Affaires in Moscow] thinks that the Russian ambition is to control the whole of Germany looking east and under Soviet influence. I believe that would be an almost irresistible menace.'[24]

A year after the end of the European war, the world picture being given to the Soviet public had clearly changed considerably from that portrayed in 1945 or even before Churchill's Fulton speech. It was still defensive. Soviet commentators considered they had achieved three out of four main war aims: the enslaved peoples of Europe must be liberated; liberating peoples must be given the chance of building a new democratic society (in fact, measures to model the Government of East European states on the Soviet had been pursued with the utmost energy); and war crimes must be punished. The fourth – that there must be no rebirth of aggression in Germany – had been held up by 'reactionary influences' in Britain and the United States.[25]

By the end of May, the Soviet Government had clearly come out against friendly cooperation with Europe and America. Livinov told the US Ambassador that in his view 'the best we could hope for was an armed truce'.[26] It lasted forty years.

THE BOMB

In his book *Stalin and The Bomb*, David Holloway has drawn a striking parallel between the beginning and the end of the Great Patriotic war. In

1941, Stalin received good intelligence about the imminent, cataclysmic German invasion, but ignored it. In 1945 he had also received good intelligence about the Manhattan project, and although Soviet scientists were working on a bomb, Stalin largely ignored that intelligence too.

The successful detonation of the *Gadget* – the first atomic bomb – in New Mexico on 16 July 1945, coincided with the Allied summit at Potsdam. On 24 July President Truman told Stalin 'that we had a new weapon of unusual destructive force'. Accounts of Stalin's reaction vary. He undoubtedly knew what Truman was talking about, but he probably did not make the connection between a new weapon of war – with greatly increased firepower – and the diplomatic and political revolution it would unleash. Only when the Americans dropped one on Hiroshima on 6 August did it become obvious, in Alexander Werth's words, that it was a 'New Fact in the world's power politics'.[27]

Pravda and *Izvestiya* carried a brief Tass report that an atomic bomb with more destructive power than 20 000 tons of TNT had been dropped on Hiroshima (in fact, the yield was about 13 kilotons). The cost and difficulty of building the bomb and the need to use atomic energy to safeguard world peace were cited. It was immediately apparent to Stalin that the Soviet Union had to have a bomb too, and on 20 August the State Defence Committee decreed that a Special Commission be set up to direct all work on nuclear energy. It was to be chaired by Lavrentiy Beria (1899-1953), the head of the NKVD, who had been responsible for the deaths of millions in the purges. He would report to Stalin once a week on the progress of the project.[28]

With hindsight it is difficult to appreciate that neither Western observers nor the Russians were convinced of the overwhelming decisiveness of nuclear weapons at the time. The Japanese had exaggerated the effect of the bomb to excuse their surrender: the Americans to overawe the Russians. One remarkably consistent view, expressed by Field Marshal Sir Alan Brooke and by the Russians as well, was that because of their construction Japanese cities were far more susceptible to the hot wind from a nuclear explosion than cities with brick and concrete structures would be. Many of the Japanese casualties could have been saved with prompt medical attention, and many were due to secondary effects on the population which was quite unprepared for a surprise attack by a single, high-altitude aircraft – houses collapsed with gas stoves still burning.[29] One of the two Soviet scientists in the Special Commission, Peter Kapitsa (1894-1984), wrote to Molotov in December 1945:

> 'The effectiveness of atomic energy against military targets, as used in Japan in the form of bombs, has not yet been proved. This is not only because its production is not proportionate to the cost, as technology will evidently soon overcome this problem, but mainly because, as calculations and experiments show, in a nuclear 'burst', thanks to its small mass, only a part of its energy goes into the shock wave, which therefore does not have the expected destructive power. A great part of energy is lost as radiation [sic. – surely heat and radiation], which incinerated so many people and houses. One may safely say that if the Japanese had not lived in 'paper houses' and had they not been taken by surprise, the casualties would have been considerably smaller, because one can protect oneself against the radiation [and heat, presumably] of an atomic blast.
>
> It is also interesting to note that in the atomic bomb in its present form the most precious elements, which are necessary for the production of atomic energy, are barbarously and irretrievably wasted.'[30]

Kapitsa's comments were loaded: he argued that atomic energy had to be used for peaceful purposes, not least because its military use was inefficient. He requested permission to publish an article on the matter: he was told to 'wait a while'. It was never published, and his letter remained a secret until 1990.[31]

At least the atomic bomb fitted into the strategic bombing which the Western Allies had been pressing. As the revision of the British report of 30 January 1946 noted, 'the most obvious result is that the bombing of towns and industry now give a far greater return for war effort expended and may therefore become the most profitable type of war'.[32] By contrast, the effects of Hiroshima or Nagasaki type bomb on army targets appeared to offer little return on the investment. Dispersed and well-dug in fighting troops might be disabled out to 1200 yards: columns of vehicles on roads might be destroyed over a length of four miles – 120 vehicles, if they were 50 metres apart. Atomic bombs, it must be remembered, were very rare: by June 1946 the US had nine, a year later, 13.[33]

The Russians, who had used air power overwhelmingly in support of ground troops, had no tradition of strategic bombing to destroy the enemy's war making capacity. Nor did they have an intercontinental bomber force capable of delivering bombs to the United States. Like Britain and the US, however, they recognized the value of its potential as a political and diplomatic weapon. A Soviet Air Force officer, Major-General E Tatarchenko, linked the emerging paradigm change with an earlier one, and the first recognizable nuclear arms negotiations:

> 'The Second World War was the first mechanized war or war of engines. But the Second World War was, along with that, a war, in which the widespread use of atomic energy *(vnutroatomnaya enegiya)* did not occur. However, two atomic bombs...on Hiroshima and Nagasaki and also the experimental atomic bomb detonated in New Mexico...were harbingers of new methods of waging war.
>
> Almost simultaneously with the birth of the atomic bomb appeared a new term – 'atomic policies'. The problem of utilising atomic energy is discussed in the Security Council of the United Nations Organization.... In their presentations eminent American scientists have quite rightly spoken of the very risky attempt to monopolise work in the area of atomic energy.... In one of their speeches the American scientists say, correctly:
>
> 'We cannot pretend to a prolonged monopoly in relation to the atomic bomb. Other scientists can use the basic principles and, maybe, even more successfully, than we have.... The unique bit, which remains secret – this is the technical processes of factories and equipment.'[34]

Two other reports received by the Soviet government in 1946 also played down the effects of nuclear weapons. One covered the US tests at Bikini Atoll in July 1946, at which M G Meshcheriakov and Anatoliy Aleksandrov, both physicists, were present as Soviet observers. They wrote of 'general disappointment' with the results of the explosion, when a plutonium bomb was detonated over a group of warships. In August, the Allied Control Commission for Japan visited Hiroshima and Nagasaki. A Soviet intelligence officer attributed many of the casualties to surprise and the lack of precautions.[35] But in the longer term the existence of the bomb was to profoundly influence the development of the Soviet Union's Armed Forces.

AIR POWER AND BALLISTIC MISSILES

At the end of the Second World War, the United States and Britain had long-range bomber fleets and carrier-borne aircraft which would attack the Soviet Union. The Soviet Union had no means of attacking them directly but had vast land forces which could possibly overrun Europe before nuclear attacks on its war-making potential were effective. During the latter part of the war, Stalin had shown a keen interest in the British and American strategic bombing campaign and at the end of July 1944 an American B-29 Superfortress – the most advanced long-range bomber in the world – was forced to land near Valdivostok, while in November two more crash landed in Siberia after their crews had bailed out. Early in 1945 – before Hiroshima – Stalin ordered the development of a four engined bomber with a range of 3000 kilometres, but in 1946 he changed his mind and ordered his designers to copy the B-29.

Foreign ideas undoubtedly had some influence immediately after the war. In mid-1946 Major General Tatarchenko cited an article in the British Journal *Army Quarterly*, which had suggested that the nuclear weapon had sounded the death knell for battleships, aircraft carriers and possibly heavy cruisers, but would lead to an abundance of 'flying fortresses' (in fact, aircraft akin to the B-29 Superfortress which the Russians were busy copying to make the Tu-4) and maybe even larger aircraft.[36]

Tatarchenko noted the potential of jet engines for operating at 'super-height' and 'super-speed', leading to 'super-long-range flight'. In order to enable future aircraft to fly at very slow speeds as well as supersonic, he believed that aircraft would have both jet and non-jet engines, something which has not materialized.

Developments in the US were noted, which by 1946 included machines automatically controlled from the ground, that is, robot aircraft and guided missiles, the modern term *upravlyayemy raket* already being in use. He mentioned the possibility of missiles like the German V-2 in future homing in on light, heat or metal, foreseeing infra-red and laser guidance. Television guidance for bombs was also mentioned. The atomic bomb, jet propulsion, radar and radio were identified as the four elements with greatest potential at this stage.[37]

In 1944, even before the German V-2 ballistic missile offensive against Britain began in September, the extremely talented Major-General G Pokrovskiy published a remarkable article on 'The Use of Long Range Rockets' in a young people's magazine. Long range rockets firing beyond visual range were relatively inaccurate at that time and Pokrovskiy believed they would be unsuitable for use against moving targets. But they could devastate comparatively larger areas as weapons 'of mass destruction', the term now used for nuclear, biological, chemical and some incendiary weapons.[38] By implication, they would be used, like the V-2's and as proposed for the earlier nuclear missiles, against 'soft' civilian and industrial targets. Pokrovskiy portrayed a barrage of several such rockets, to compensate for inaccuracy. The individual missiles were each mounted on some kind of vehicle, launched at an angle of about 30 degrees, and not vertically. US intelligence reports of 1948 indicate that the Soviet General Staff continued to believe that, given the technology of the V-2 type rockets with which they were experimenting, this would be their *modus operandi* in a future war.[39] In October 1944 and March 1945 the journal *Air Force Technology* published details of the jet powered, unmanned V-1.[40]

By 1946, even an airman had to ask whether long range bombers would be completely replaced by missiles. Guided surface-to-air missiles and high speed jet fighters would probably stop the 'giant bomber' from being a cost-effective means of attacking distant targets. Missiles would probably be cheaper, and the Russians noted that from 1944 London and southeast England had been attacked with rockets only. The Germans had also planned to attack New York and other conurbations on the eastern coast of the United States with missiles.

To the Russians, behind the British and Americans not only in the technology of building long-range bombers but of navigating and controlling them, missiles were a very attractive alternative. The strength and prestige of their artillery arm also had influence on the emphasis on the missile development:

> 'Undervaluing this new powerful means of waging war would be a fatal mistake. It should be clear to every moderately well-informed person that this weapon appeared in 1944-45 in its most primitive, initial form. One can scarcely doubt that in future it will receive significantly greater development.'[41]

However, missiles would not totally replace bombers. 'Of course not!' As with navies, the appearance of a new system did not mean that others would disappear. There would be several types of giant aircraft: bombers, troop-carrying and cargo-carrying.[42]

The plan for rocket development, concentrating mainly on the development of long-range missiles, was drawn up at the end of 1946, concentrated at Scientific Research institute (NII)-88. It was here that most of the captured German rocket scientists who had worked on the V-2 project were brought. The Soviet army had captured an entire German rocket factory in Thuringia at the beginning of 1945, and brought 200 scientists back to the Soviet Union.

Although the Soviet Union had advanced work in the field of rocketry to build on, the Germans had produced a working ballistic missile in large numbers and that offered a faster route to an operational missile. Western intelligence noted there was 'little or no return to the research and study of fundamentals but instead the Soviets seem to be engaged in a vigorous programme of getting missiles to the hardware (test vehicle) stage with a minimum of research, the trial and error character of such a development programme might result in considerably greater performance in shorter time than the Soviets might be able to develop by a return to research in fundamentals.'[43] The main problem was developing a missile with the required range: the V-2, with a range of 200 miles, had been able to hit London from the Netherlands, but was useless to the Soviet Union except as a tactical weapon. In March 1947 the chief designer, Sergei Korolev, who had narrowly escaped death in the purges, proposed to solve the problem by separating the war head from the missile after the boost phase, so that the body of the missile did not have to be made robust enough to withstand re-entry. But they also investigated possibilities for improving the range of V-2 type rockets by using different propellants. A liquid oxygen-anhydrous hydrazine combination in the V-2 might give a 70 per cent increase in range and nitric acid-anhydrous hydrazine combination 45 per cent.[44] Intercontinental ranges were only attained with multi-stage rockets. The first large post-war Soviet rocket, the R-1, appeared in October 1947, looking exactly like the V-2 on which it was based. However, Korolev's team was also working on the R-2, a significant advance on the R-1, with double the range – 600 kilometres. The first flight tests took place in 1949 and it entered service with the Soviet Army in 1951.

These early missiles were not equipped with nuclear warheads but in late 1947 or early 1948 Stalin convened a meeting with three senior Marshals of Artillery, Sergei Kovalev and Igor Kurchatov (1903-1960), a physicist on the Soviet nuclear programme. This suggests that they were discussing putting nuclear warheads on missiles, and in 1948 there were a number of tests to see if cosmic rays would set off nuclear warheads at high altitudes.[45]

CONVENTIONAL FORCES

For the moment, however, Soviet planning concentrated on conventional forces. There is little evidence that the Soviet Union's leadership really feared an attack from the West, or that it planned to push on into western Europe. Its plans centred on consolidating control of territory newly acquired – including the Baltic States and 'western Ukraine' (formerly Poland), where the Soviet Government faced active guerrilla opposition, though that was the job for the Interior Ministry, not the Armed Forces. At the end of 1946 and the beginning of 1947, the Soviet General Staff presented the Supreme Military Soviet with a 'Plan for the Active Defence of Soviet Territory'. The overall strategic plan coincided with the Top Secret plan for the Group of Soviet Occupation Forces in Germany signed by Marshal Sokolovskiy dated 5 November 1946, which was published under the policy of '*glasnost*' in 1989.[46] The overall plan demanded the Armed Forces 'repel aggression and guarantee the integrity of the frontiers established by international agreement after the Second World War; be ready to repel enemy air attack including the possible use of nuclear weapons; the Navy will be prepared to repel possible aggression from the sea and support land forces, acting in coastal regions.'[47] The forces were divided into three groups: the 'repulsion Army' *(armiya otpora)*, including forces in fortified regions; the reserve of the Supreme High Command; and second line forces and new formations to replace combat losses. Soviet forces in the occupied zone of Germany numbered 17 divisions in four armies, which were concentrated between 50 and 150 kilometres back from the border with western Allies' occupation zones. Third Shock Army and Eighth Guards Army were forward, First and Second Guards Mechanized Armies further East. The published orders do not give final objectives, but list the positions of the main enemy concentrations while the maps do not show operations beyond the Inner German border.[48]

Even at the end of the 1940s, neither the Soviet Union nor the United States believed that a nuclear attack on the Soviet Union would win a war. The first US plan, dated 4 September 1945, envisaged 20 nuclear targets in the USSR and the Soviet occupied territory. In 1949, the 'Dropshot' plan for war with the Soviet Union was formulated, envisaging an attack with some 300 atomic bombs. But in 1951, a Soviet Colonel, P. Fedorov, argued that the damage inflicted by the Allied air offensive against Germany was assessed at equivalent to 330 atomic bombs: that was more bombs than the United States possessed – and more than the Soviet Union thought they possessed. And that had not defeated Germany. In the first four months of war in 1941 the Germans had captured or killed millions of Soviet soldiers and seized 60 per cent of coal, iron and steel production facilities – far more damage than an atomic air offensive at *that time* would inflict on the Soviet Union. The Soviet Union had survived and fought back, to win. The vision of a future war in 1950 looked very like the Second World War: an initial Soviet success, overrunning much of mainland western Europe, followed by a build-up of British-American strength in the United Kingdom, under cover of superior air, sea and, now, nuclear bomb power.

Soviet Military Doctrine concentrated overwhelmingly on conventional war. The 500 divisions the Red Army had fielded at the end of the war were reduced to 175, but they were much strengthened and went over completely to motor transport – the Red Army, like Wehrmacht, had relied heavily on horses during the Second World War. By 1953, any mechanized corps had the same mobility as a World War II Tank Army – the elite armoured spearheads in the Soviet operations.[49]

The 1948 Field Service Regulations, worked out at a conference in autumn 1947, made no mention of atomic weapons, although senior officers studied nuclear weapons effects and defence against them. An important meeting in April 1947 dealt exclusively with reforms to conventional forces, and stressed the importance of economic factors in waging protracted war.[50] It was in 1949-50 that Stalin took the important decisions to increase Soviet forces in Germany, build up the armies of the Soviet Union's new satellite states in Eastern Europe and expand the Navy. The creation of NATO in April 1949 added to East-West tension and formally committed the US to the defence of western Europe. That in turn stimulated Soviet naval expansion to cut the transatlantic lines of communication that would guarantee US support for Europe.

But Stalin and his advisers still thought in terms of a conventional war, with some nuclear attacks on the Soviet Union. In order to minimise the effects of atomic bomb attacks, an enormous effort went into the development of air defences. The first jet fighters were tested in April 1946 and the first high altitude jet fighter, the Mig-15, in December 1947. In February to March 1947 a meeting of senior air defence officers was convened to discuss the defence of the country against strategic attack. In April 1947 it was decided that the fighter planes would remain under PVO command, but would be subordinated to the Air Force for training and maintenance: in July 1948 all strategic air defences, both fighter planes and artillery, were placed under the command of a separate service, equivalent to the Army, Navy and Air Force, a measure of the importance defence against atomic attack had acquired. Early warning radars and anti-aircraft artillery also received high priority, but the sheer size of the country made it difficult to deploy a radar screen.

It was not until 1951 that the Soviet Army held its first exercise to investigate the effect of nuclear weapons on combat in the field, the only one before Stalin's death in 1953. Another was held in the Carpathians in 1954, in which both sides attacked the other's lines of communications, and the umpires declared that the war had ground to a halt. Nuclear weapons, it appeared, had not yet made war unthinkable, but with the total chaos nuclear strikes would cause they had made it impossible to fight.[51]

On Stalin's death on 5 March 1953, Georgiy Malenkov (1902-88) assumed the mantle of command. In December 1952 the US had detonated its first thermonuclear device – a thousand times more powerful than the bomb dropped on Hiroshima. On 12 August 1953 the first Soviet hydrogen bomb was detonated. It was probable that the vastly increased power of thermonuclear weapons changed Soviet views. Malenkov himself seems to have changed his view and after he was deposed in February 1955 the way was clear for a radical revision of Soviet attitudes. Nuclear weapons were now cardinal to the possible conduct of future war. But they were so terrible they really did make it unthinkable as a rational tool of policy.

THE WIDER WORLD

The expansion of the Soviet navy was the one Soviet post-war innovation that the British Foreign Office failed to predict in 1944. They believed that increased economic collaboration between the Soviet Union and other countries would 'make her interested in expanding her mercantile marine and in security of access to open seas during the period of relief and reconstruction'. Therefore, however, 'it is possible that the importance of maritime communications may diminish, as Soviet economic internal development progresses.'[52] The rapid expansion of the Soviet merchant fleet in the post war period continued until the break-up of the Union in 1991.

However, Stalin used Red Navy Day on 23 July 1945 to issue an order which indicated he was interested in expanding the Soviet Navy. During the 1930s the Soviet Union embarked on what was meant to be expansion of its fleet. On 15 January 1938 Molotov told the Supreme Soviets that, 'The mighty Soviet State ought to have a sea-going and ocean-going Navy commensurate with its interests and worthy of its great cause'.[53] These plans, which involved the construction of two 59 000 ton battleships and two battle cruisers, were cut short by German invasion in 1941. In July 1945 the British Embassy reported:

> '...the Soviet Government's growing interest in naval bases and strategic waterways such as Königsberg, Kirkenes, Bear Island, Bornholm, the Bosphorus and Dardanelles and Port Arthur, in the disposition of the Italian and German fleets, and in the construction of new ports and the repair of old ones...can almost certainly be taken as a sign of their determination to develop the policy of building an ocean-going fleet worthy of their interests and power.'[54]

The embassy staff had 'little doubt that the Soviet Union will now make great efforts to increase her naval strength.' The Soviet Union would certainly wish to profit from the German defeat and to become the dominant naval power in the Baltic, thus realising the aims of Peter the Great. This would certainly be coupled with a close interest in Denmark and in freedom of passage through the Baltic into the North Sea. The Soviet Union would equally wish to reassert its naval superiority in the Black Sea and to secure freedom of egress into the Mediterranean through the Dardanelles. The war had shown the importance of Murmansk and Archangel as the emergency life-line for the Soviet Union very clearly, and it would certainly try to ensure liberty of action for its fleet in northern waters and might want bases in Bear Island and northern Norway. It was 'too early yet to say' what the Soviet intentions in the Far East were but the interest the Soviet Union had already shown there in the future of Port Arthur and Korea suggested a 'definite intention to increase Soviet naval strength in the Pacific.' However, for some years to come the Soviet Union would be fully occupied restoring its naval position in the Baltic and Black Sea where, it was also thought, the majority of the merchant fleet would be concentrated.[55]

At this stage the expansion of the Soviet Navy was a distant prospect, and based on the idea of a Navy as a status symbol combined with a pragmatic desire to exploit the unexpected gains from the world war. Later, the need to defend against foreign attacks launched from across the oceans or from aircraft carriers provided a more urgent incentive to develop a Navy which could go out and meet the threat. After the US naval blockade of Cuba in 1962, the need for a navy as a means of projecting power – a view closer to that prevailing in 1945-46, reasserted itself.

The need to push any potential threat away also meant that the Soviet leadership wanted to build up a defensive belt of subservient, or at any rate friendly, states. Western intelligence assessed that:

> '...such an aim implies a gradual but continual broadening of the belt. For instance, when domination of Turkey and Persia has been achieved, she [the Soviet Union] will probably seek a measure of domination in Syria and Iraq. It is therefore thought that it would be wrong to assume that the belt will include only those countries contiguous to her boundaries'.[56]

The Soviet Union was expected to take much more of an interest in the Middle East, and did so after the war. The war had shown how dependent the Soviet Union was on the oil resources of the Caucasus, and any British or American activity in the area was likely to provoke suspicion. But by 1944 the oil resources of Iraq and the Persian Gulf were forecast to become the centre of world oil production. The Soviet Union, like the United States, wanted to conserve its own oil resources, for strategic reasons. Post-war industrial development and a raised standard of living – including more cars and trucks – were expected to increase its requirements substantially, which, it was assumed, would lead to a conflict of interests in the Middle East as the Soviet Union, Britain and the US converged on the oil resources of the area.[57]

In spite of the flood of volunteers for the anticipated 'war of liberation' in India, the Soviet government had discarded the 'world revolution' propaganda it had tried to spread in the Second World War and was cooperating with the British Government to some extent. As plans for Indian independence and division developed, the Soviet Union was expected to oppose the creation of a strong Muslim Pakistan because of the repercussions this might have in central Asia. At the time, it caused no serious problems, but the concerns about 'Islamic fundamentalism' hinted at then surfaced prominently in the 1980s.[58]

The Soviet Union's position as a Pacific power was understood and accepted by Britain and the US. The British proposed a conciliatory approach. The Soviet Union's direct interests lay in North Manchuria, Korea, Sakhalin and the Kuriles and the Western powers took an 'understanding attitude' there so that the Soviet Union would not 'make trouble for us in the southerly regions where our own interests lie'. Any attempt to oppose Russian security interests in the North Pacific might be met with Russian interference in Japan, so it was not a good idea to try.[59]

The likeliest post-war area of conflict in the Far East was between Russia and China, but in August 1945 Stalin concluded a treaty with Nationalist China and in 1949, after Mao's victory in the long Chinese Civil War, concluded a new one with the Communists, which set the scene for the Korean war. It was not until the mid-1950s that the two Communist giants began to fall out.

It is unlikely that there was any hard-and-fast world view that Stalin and his small ruling cliqué felt obliged to follow. Stalin believed that the post-war period would resemble the inter-war period, leading perhaps to another conflict in 15 or 20 years. He certainly did not foresee the bi-polar world which would evolve, and which has now disintegrated.

THE LEGACY OF WAR

In 1944 Churchill, who was no Russophile, told the British Parliament that the 'guts of the German army had been largely torn out by Russian valour and generalship' – a recognition of the colossal Russian capacity for suffering and, in one word – 'generalship' – their mastery of the conduct of large-scale war.

At the time of its victory in 1945, the Red Army looked like the force that, more than any of its Allies, had broken the Third Reich on land. In photographs and film you see men who look as if they know what they are doing. Marshals, like Zhukov and Rokossovski, in high-collared uniforms that convey authority in a way the ungainly British battle-dress never could, with the gold shoulder boards reintroduced in 1943, cloaks worn with a certain swagger, every infantryman, just about, carrying an automatic weapon, and tanks like the JS-3 that look modern, even now. And large numbers of women, more than in any other Army and Air Force, as military police, political officers, snipers, even night bomber pilots – the 'Night Witches'. Fifty years on, you see no women soldiers anywhere near a Russian operation.

It was their finest hour – the Soviet Union's gargantuan effort in the Great Patriotic War followed by their frantic effort, brutality, purges and collectivisation of the inter-war years. But there was no break, no rest. The years that followed were as hard, and many of those who had fought their way to victory were promptly arrested. The Soviet Union finished the war as one of the four 'great powers'. Within a few years, thanks to nuclear weapons, it was one of the two Superpowers. But it was always part illusion. Germany, with 100 million fewer people, had very nearly defeated the Soviet Union in 1941-42, and had in a very short time overrun an area larger than that conquered by Alexander the Great. Without the British and Americans diverting the German war effort in 1942-43, the Soviet Union would have lost, and although the Soviet Union could, in time, probably have won the land war on its own from 1944, the British and American air offensive was vital to divert the German war effort which would otherwise all have turned east.

Fifty years and two generations later, Russia is reaping the consequences of going that extra mile – a mile too far. In the race to rebuild and develop the economy and technology, an environmental catastrophe as bad as that inflicted by the Germans has taken place. People now want what people expected in 1945. Comfort, consumer goods, security, leisure. But they also want the respect that goes with being a great power. Russia has the potential to be the richest nation on earth. The expectations of 1945 were disappointing, so were those of 1991. With hard work, massive foreign investment – of a kind the Soviet Union was counting on in 1945 – and a massive effort to clean up, those expectations might one day be fulfilled – maybe in another couple of generations. But, like the victors of 1945, those responsible may not get much thanks. They never do. As Aleksandr Solzhenitsyn, an artillery forward observation officer, in war, recalled:

> 'While we had been ploughing through the mud out there on the bridgeheads, while we had been cowering in shell holes and pushing periscopes above the bushes, back home a new generation had grown up and gotten moving. But hadn't it started moving in *another* direction? In a direction we wouldn't have been able and wouldn't have dared move in?...
>
> Our generation would return – having turned in its weapons, jingling its heroes' medals, proudly telling its combat stories. And our younger brothers would only look at us contemptuously: oh, you stupid dolts!'[60]

On the road into Grozny, in Chechnya, near Russia's southern border, heading from the west, there is a war memorial. Down the road, the Russian Army and Interior Ministry were engaged in another 'internal' operation. *1941-1945. Nikto ne zabyt. Nichto ne zabyto* – 'No-one is forgotten. Nothing is forgotten', proclaimed the war memorial. Sadly, it has been unable to keep its promise.

NOTES

1. John Erickson and David Dilks, ed., *Barbarossa: The Axis and the Allies,* (Edinburgh University Press, Edinburgh, 1994), pp. 265, 266.
2. Aleksandr Svechin, *Strategiya*, (2nd ed., Voyenny Vestnik Press, Moscow, 1927). Preface to the first edition was written in 1925; A Ageyev *'Voyenny teoretik i voyenny istorik AA Svechin'* ('Military Historian and Theoretician A A Svechin'), *Voyenno-Istoricheskiy Zhurnal (Military-Historical Journal- VIZh),* 8/1978, pp. 126-28, use until 1960s, p.127; Marshal of the Soviet Union V D Sokolovskiy, *Voyennaya Strategiya* (Voyenizdat, Moscow, 1962, 1963, 1968); E L Raymond, *Soviet Preparations for Total War 1925-1951* (ph.D, University of Michigan, 1952).
3. *Strategiya,* 2nd ed., p. 38.
4. See in particular the graphic passage in *Strategiya,* pp 46-47. Tukhachevskiy *Budushchaya voyna* (Upravleniye shtaba RKKA,

Moscow, 1928) (7 Vols) and *Novye voprosy voyny* (New Questions of War) (unpublished, 1931-32), are both available from East View Publications, Minneapolis, E00100 and B 001203, respectively. See also extracts of the later published in VIZh 2/1962, pp 62-77; Col R A Savushkin *'Zarozhdeniye i razvitiye sovetskoy voyennoy doktriny'* ('The Birth and Development of Soviet Military Doctrine'), *VIZh* 2/1988, pp. 19-26, on *Budushchaya voyna* cited Central Military Historical Archive (TsGASA) F 33988, p. 2, p.682.

5. Memorandum from the British Mission in Moscow to Lt Gen Sir H Ismay, War Office, 21 January 1944, papers of Lt Gen Sir Giffard Martel in the Imperial War Museum *GQM* 4/4. Martel made the same point many different times, for example, in his book *The Russian Outlook*, (Michael Joseph, London, 1947).

6. *Probable Post-War Tendencies in Soviet Foreign Policy as Affecting British Interests*, Foreign Office, April 29 1944, N 1008/183/38, in FO 371/43335.

7. Erickson and Dilks, *Barbarossa*, pp. 256-74.

8. *Ibid.*, p. 273.

9. M A Garelov, *'Otkuda ugroza'* ('Whence the Threat?', *Voyenno-istoricheskiy zhurnal (Military Historical Journal – VIZh)*, 2/1989, pp. 16-31, these figures p.16.

10. FO 371/43335 *Some Probable Post-War Tendencies*... p.3.

11. FO 371/47925, Roberts to Bevin, 21 September 1945, printed 29 November 1945.

12. FO 371/47925, Sir A Clark Kerr to Bevin, N 17305/627/38, 9 December 1945, printed December 20 1945, p.1.

13. FO 371/47924 Roberts to Bevin N 10185/627/38 printed 11 August 1945.

14. *Ibid.*, pp. 1, 2, 5.

15. FO 371/47925, Despatch of 4 December 1945. July 1945 Strength: Garelov *'Otkuda ugroza'* p. 17. Seven to eight million demobilised FO 371/56831 N 3799/605/938 dated 24 March 1946.

16. FO 371/47925 Clark Kerr to Bevin, N 17305/627/38, printed 9 December 1945, p. 1.

17. *Ibid.*, p. 2.

18. David Holloway, *Stalin and the Bomb*, (Yale University Press, New Haven and London, 1994), p. 367; FO 371/56831, from Frank Roberts in Moscow No. 1090, 21 March 1946 commenting on Joint Intelligence

Committee (JIC) paper.
19. Holloway, p. 151.
20. FO 371/56831 No 1090 of 21 March 1946.
21. *Ibid*; FO 371/43335 of 29 April 1944 pp. 7-8.
22. FO 371/56830, Roberts to Warner 2 March 1946.
23. FO 371/56831, R.M.A. Hankey covering minute on Roberts from Moscow of 20 March 1946.
24. *Ibid.*, 25 March 1946.
25. FO 371/56833, report of lecture by the well known commentator Yermashev 7 June 1946.
26. *Ibid.*, Roberts to Warner, (5 June 1946 on conversation between US Ambassador and Litvinov 'about a week ago').
27. FO 371/43335 of 29 April 1944 pp. 5-6.19. Holloway, pp. 116-17, 127, 129, citing Alexander Werth, *Russia at War 1941-1945*, (Pan, London, 1964), p. 925.
28. *Ibid.*, pp. 134-35.
29. *Ibid.*, p. 227.
30. 'An Absurd Situation', *Vestnik: Soviet Magazine for Politics, Science and Culture*, June 1990, pp. 58-64. This includes a facsimile of Kapitsa's 18 December 1945 letter to Molotov, held in the Soviet foreign Policy Archives, ref. 13134/19. XII-45g., with Molotov's notes in green pencil.
31. *Ibid.*, p. 64, transcript of telephone conversation between Podtserob, Molotov's aide, and Kapitsa, 25 December 1945.
32. PRO Defe II 1252, *Examination of the Possible Development of Weapons and Methods of War*, TWC(46)3 (Revise), 30 January 1946, Part II 'Effects on Warfare', p. 8.
33. *Ibid.*, Part 1, 'Matters of Fact Relating to atomic energy, section B(e) 'Effect on Army Targets'; Holloway, p. 228.
34. Maj. Gen. of Aviation E Tatarchenko, *'Nekotorye problemy razvitii vozdushnoy moshchi'* ('Certain questions of the Development of Air Power'), *Vestnik Vozdushnogo flota (Air Force Herald)*, 5-6, 1946, pp. 60-63, this p. 61.
35. Holloway pp. 226-27.
36. Tatarchenko, p. 61.
37. *Ibid.*, p.62.
38. Major General of Technical Services G Pokrovskiy, *'Primeneniye dal'noboynykh raket'* ("The Use of Long-Range Rockets (Missiles)'), *Tekhnika molodezhi (Youth Technology)*, April 1944, pp. 7-8.

39. *HQ USAF Air Intelligence Reports* in possession of Air Historical Branch Ministry of Defence, 100-13/9-100 dated 4 August 1948 (15 June report), p.12.

40. *'Detail konstruktsi inemetskogo samoleta-snaryada V-1'* ('Details of Construction of the German 'aircraft-shell' V-1'), *Tekhnika vozdushnogo flota (Air Force Technology)* 1/1945, p.8. For description of the V-1, *TVF* 10/1944.

41. Tatarchenko, *'Nekotorye problemy...'* p. 63.

42. *Ibid.*

43. *HQ USAF Air Intelligence Reports* 100-13/9-100 4 August 1948, p. 10.

44. *Ibid.*, 13/10-100 dated 15 November 1948 (15 September report), 13/11-100 dated 9 February 1949 (15 December 1948 report).

45. Holloway, pp. 246-49.

46. Garelov, *'Otkuda ugroza'*, pp. 24, 26-31 (full GSFG plan).

47. *Ibid.*, p. 24.

48. *Ibid.*, and map inside front cover.

49. Holloway, pp. 231-32; Maj-Gen A Kho'kov, *'Istoricheskiy opyt v razvitii voyennoy nauki'* ('Historical experience in the Development of Military Science'), *Voyennaya Mysl' (Military Thought)* 6/1990, pp. 28-36, developments in 'The first post-war period', p. 31.

50. Army General M A Gareyev, *'O voyennoy nauke i voyennom iskusstve'* ('On Military Science and Military Art'), *Voyenno-istoricheski zhurnal* (Military-Historical Journal – VIZh), 5/1993, pp. 2-8.

51. Garelov, p. 17; Holloway, pp. 237-42; Ferdinand Otto Miksche, *Atomic Weapons and Armies* (Faber, London, 1955), pp. 17-18.

52. FO 371/43335, 29 April 1944 p. 4.

53. FO 371/47924, Roberts to Eden 25 July 1945, printed 7 August, N 9839/627/38.

54. *Ibid.*, p. 2.

55. *Ibid.*, p. 3-3.

56. FO 371/56831, for the Joint Intelligence Committee from Director of Intelligence 23 March 1946.

57. FO 371/43335, 29 April 1955, pp. 11-12.

58. *Ibid.*, pp. 12-13.

59. *Ibid.*, p. 13; Holloway, pp. 274-76.

60. Aleksandr Solzhenitsyn, *The Gulag Archipelago, 1918-1956*, (trans. Thomas P Whitney, Collins/Fontana, London 1974), Part II, p. 615.

13 Resistance and the Re-emergence of German Democracy

Manfred Rommel

Nowadays, the vast majority of Germans, aware that the crimes committed under Hitler would have continued in the case of a German victory, understand that it was better for Germany to have lost the war than to have won it. The situation was different after the First World War, when Germany had just become a republic and a democracy. From the very beginning, the young German democracy had to face terrible political and economic challenges. The democratic politicians were falsely blamed for Germany's misery and they had to fight extremists on both sides. On the right wing, there was a strong political movement that aimed at re-establishing monarchy or a government that functioned like a military headquarters. On the left wing, there was Lenin's and Stalin's communism as practised in the Soviet Union. In the eyes of many Christians, the Soviet Union was the empire of evil and the enemy of God. A revolution in Germany after Lenin's manner, by the way, would not have been a source of happiness to mankind either. Many convinced democrats dreamt of a better democracy than the one which existed in reality. There was also a tendency to leave the most unpopular decisions to rival parties. The military defeat of 1918 was not widely accepted. The Treaty of Versailles, in particular its provisions for immense German war reparations, was considered an attempt to pauperise and humiliate Germany forever. There was the belief that the army had not been defeated, but stabbed in the back by traitors.

The *Weimar* Constitution endowed the Republic's President with more powers than the head of government, the Chancellor. The President could dissolve the parliament and he had the power to enact provisional legislation in order to preserve public order. The more pressure the foes of democracy on both ends of the political spectrum were able to exert on the democratic parties, Social Democrats, Catholics, and Liberals, the greater the rift grew between them on fundamental issues of the economy, social welfare and defence. The more frequently crucial decisions failed to find a majority in parliament, the more the public's view was confirmed that parliament was a failure and that the fate of the nation rested upon the office of the President.

The last government to have a parliamentary majority collapsed in March 1930. All further governments existed at the sufferance of the President. The first President of the *Weimar* Republic, the Social Democrat Friedrich Ebert, was a man of high morals and democratic commitment. After his death in 1925, he was succeeded by Field Marshal von Hindenburg, a symbol of past military glory. Nearly eighty when he first assumed the presidency, Hindenburg collected around him advisors, some of whom were General Staff officers, aiming at a new non-parliamentary government. This took place against a background of growing public opinion in favour of a strong leader to save Germany. The gate was being unlocked for the 'saviour' Adolf Hitler.

After the First World War, the German army was reduced to a hundred thousand soldiers in accordance with the Versailles Treaty. In addition to the official army, some more or less private military units, called Freikorps, were in existence. They fought communists in the Baltic states and marched against communists in the Ruhr area, in Saxony and in Bavaria. In March 1920, Freikorps members attempted a *coup d'état* against the democratic government in Berlin, but failed. Some political parties also developed armed detachments of their own. The stormtroopers commanded by Hitler and the militant units of the communists were a permanent threat to the Republic's stability and security. The official German army, the 'Hundred Thousand Man Army', was designed as a non-political army. Professional soldiers were excluded from elections and, as they were used to safeguard domestic public order, were not permitted to be members of any political party. The virtues taught in all armies, including the German army at the time, of loyalty, obedience, discipline, courage and reliability are all good virtues so long as they are focused on the defence of democratic institutions. It is fundamentally different, however, when dictatorship takes the place of democracy, as happened in 1933. After 1933 it would have been better if the army had been less loyal, less obedient and less disciplined. Hitler promoted the secondary virtue of loyalty as a primary one. He caused primary virtues, such as respect for human dignity and worth, to disappear.

The so-called 'Enabling Act' in March 1933, which changed the *Weimar* constitution, was passed by a two thirds majority in parliament, against the votes of the Social Democrats. The Act, in effect, transferred legislative power to Hitler's government. Many pieces of draft legislation which hadn't a chance of parliamentary approval, were now simply signed by Hitler. In only a few weeks, radio, newspapers, films and the theatre, all of which had been a source of criticism under democracy, and even under the German Empire, had become tools of government propaganda and brain-washing. No more bad news, only good news. It is shameful to admit it, but a wave of optimism began to spread throughout Germany as more people married, more children were born, jobs were created and the economy seemed to flourish. The German public was not aware that Hitler's economic policy was bound to end in disaster as it was based on government orders, especially for rearmament, and financed by printing money. Step by step the organization of society intensified enormously. Men and women, workers, managers, lawyers, students, children, all were organised into paramilitary units. On Saturdays and Sundays there was trumpeting, piping and drum beating in the streets by marching units and their bands. Soldiers' songs, that had previously been sentimental, became 'optimistic' and aggressive. Works of art displaying a critical attitude towards war disappeared, to be replaced by products praising heroism.

Buried under propaganda was the fact that, from the beginning of the Third Reich, Jewish citizens were discriminated against, mistreated, expropriated, insulted and killed. Political opponents of the regime and dissenting artists and journalists were forced to emigrate or disappeared into hastily erected concentration camps. At first the churches tolerated Hitler. Many Christians were happy that the threat of communism had disappeared from Germany and that Christian values seemed to have been saved. Many Protestants were particularly impressed by Hitler, who had declared himself a Christian believer. Many of these, however, woke up once Hitler tried to incorporate Protestantism into Nazism. There was more scepticism among German Catholics, but in July 1933 a concordant was brought about between the Hitler government and the Holy See in Rome.

After Hindenburg's death in 1934, Hitler merged the offices of Presidency and Chancellery. The majority of army officers watched Hitler's stormtroopers with concern and irritation. They felt relief when Hitler ordered the killing of the 'Brownshirts' most important leaders in 1934, thereby reducing their influence considerably. The army did not foresee that a new danger was to come in the form of the 'Schutzstaffel', or 'SS'. Hitler's most important ally was success. Unemployment disappeared almost completely, war reparations ceased to be paid – Hitler could profit from what his democratic predecessors had achieved. The German fear of falling victim to the superior arms of neighbouring states disappeared as German rearmament was no longer limited by restrictions. The dream of uniting Austria with Germany became true. Even the risky occupation of Czechoslovakia ended without war. Increasingly Germans saw in Hitler a miracle worker.

The history of the German resistance began in 1933. During the early years, communists, in particular, organized a highly efficient underground resistance, although its structure was constantly battered by the police. Thousands of opponents risked and sacrificed their lives by distributing leaflets and pamphlets against Hitler and by organizing secret groups. Many conservatives as well were aware, or in the course of time became aware, that Hitler's intentions were inhuman and illegal and that his ultimate aim was war. In November 1939, Georg Elser, a man with no links to any resistance group, thought that he could save the world from war by assassinating Hitler. The bomb that Elser detonated in the *Bürgerbräukeller*, a Munich beer hall, succeeded in killing several of Hitler's companions, but the dictator escaped unharmed.

The German resistance had little chance of success. Hitler's system of government, including his secret police, was a triumph of organization. Its increasing efficiency severely handicapped the ability of dissenters to organize and communicate with one another. A veil of propaganda was spread over reality. News about concealed facts was difficult to obtain and dangerous to repeat. In Berlin and other large cities, as well as at universities, the chances of organizing conspiratorial groups were better, but still not easy. This situation worsened with the onset of the Second World War.

Dependence on official propaganda grew considerably in war time. Those listening to foreign broadcasts were liable to severe punishment, particularly if they were caught disseminating what they had heard. Hitler's government found this necessary in order to protect German morale from being undermined by hostile influences. Any German voicing criticisms against the government was equally liable to severe punishment. There was a strong feeling of solidarity among the majority of Germans at the start of the war. Added to this was national pride felt in the victories achieved during the first two years, especially the victory in France of 1940. As the Second World War ran its course, many Germans began a long intellectual and emotional path which led them away from thinking that Germany should and would win to thinking that it might be better if a Germany under Hitler, in fact, lost. Among the German anti-Hitler resistance were many men and women who had travelled along this path.

The attack by Germany and its allies against the Soviet Union in June 1941, brought about a fundamental change. From the very beginning, the Russian campaign was a struggle for existence as both sides fought with cruelty and toughness. German propaganda described the attack on the Soviet Union as a crusade against evil, of the morally superior against wickedness and of civilization against barbarism. Soviet atrocities were detailed and widely reported by the German media. Throughout history the crimes of 'crusaders' have often been worse than the crimes crusaded against. This describes the German campaign in Russia when one takes into account the activities of special SS units in exterminating Jews, Russians and Poles. Of course these atrocities on the German side went unreported in Germany. As it is not possible to kill millions of people in total secrecy, news of these crimes leaked out and spread terror and disbelief in Germany. People who heard of such things were well advised to keep it to themselves if they valued their lives. Many men and women who had heard of or seen such things, however, joined the resistance movement to Hitler. This was the case with a group of army officers in Berlin, among them Count von Stauffenberg, and also for a group of students at the University of Munich, led by Hans and Sophie Scholl. The resistance group founded by Hans and Sophie Scholl, 'The White Rose', sought with meagre means to reveal the crimes of Nazism with leaflets and pamphlets. Theirs was a blind revolt of moral indignation against the immorality of their times. Hans and Sophie Scholl were arrested and executed in 1943.

The majority of Germans, however, felt that Hitler had 'burnt their bridges' behind them and that nothing save final victory would save them from total devastation in the event of a German defeat. This was certainly the case after the war in the Soviet Union turned against Germany and the Red Army began advancing westwards. German soldiers, in particular those fighting on the Russian Front, felt this way. Hitler's overthrow held less appeal for those fighting in Russia than those fighting in France. Furthermore, there was hope that peace might still be something which could be negotiated if Germany's armed forces remained strong (not that Hitler ever considered a negotiated peace). The hope grew in resistance circles that the Allies might offer a reasonable peace if Hitler could be eliminated and a more acceptable government placed in power. Representatives of the Western Allies contacted by German resistance members in 1944, however, gave little hope that anything short of unconditional surrender would be offered to Germany, even in the event of a successful plot against Hitler.

As early as 1938, facing a threat of war over Czechoslovakia, a plan to remove Hitler had been worked out by Generals Beck and Halder. The plan was not executed because Hitler came to an arrangement with the British and French governments, averting immediate hostilities. It remains unknown whether this plan could have worked and whether German troops would have allowed the generals to lead them against Hitler. Certainly, once fighting began it was hopeless to try and order them to march against Hitler's government. Loyalty and obedience had been preached so relentlessly that my father, for one, believed it impossible for generals to turn the army against the leadership in Berlin. He thought it only possible to surrender troops in a situation of military disaster.

The German military was an imperfect tool of revolution for another reason. Although the army enjoyed a certain degree of autonomy with respect to the Nazi government, during the war there was no professional soldier as supreme commander. Hitler had appointed himself as supreme commander of the armed forces in 1938 and supreme commander of the army in 1941. He was a master of 'divide and rule'. Very rarely, if at all, did the top military commanders in the field have an opportunity to meet each other and exchange views. Some of them also disliked each other and there was rivalry between them. The idea of the German *Wehrmacht* being capable of defining something such as a political '*volonte generale*' was not realistic.

Under the suspicious eyes of dictatorship, it was not possible to organize the German resistance in a highly structured way. Nevertheless, a remarkable degree of structure was achieved under the circumstances and links were made between organizations which, otherwise, operated on their own. One of the spiritual leaders of the resistance was Carl Goerdeler, the conservative and Protestant Christian mayor of Leipzig. Both Carl and his brother, Fritz, were eventually executed for their part in the 20th of July Plot. In 1933 Goerdeler was highly esteemed in Germany and would have been welcomed by Hitler as a supporter. Goerdeler, however, had rejected any co-operation with National Socialism from the beginning and recognized that Hitler's intention was to destroy the Christian religion and the ethical foundation of German civilization. He further saw that Hitler was aiming at war and that his ultimate goal was an empire of oppression and inhumanity. With great courage Goerdeler talked to many people about his fears and hopes. In the 1930s he wrote letters and memoranda to American and British politicians, in which he warned of the bellicose intentions of Hitler. Goerdeler viewed with dismay the confusion among Germans. In 1937 he wrote that, even among the most fervent Nazis, no one really knew the true meaning of National Socialism. For Goerdeler it was essential that Germany return to a constitutional state and to the rule of law. Goerdeler pointed out that every legitimate government was based on the ethics of God, as documented in the Bible. He spoke with generals about their responsibility and he attempted to unite the various groups comprising the German resistance by encouraging co-operation and a common vision of what could and should come after Hitler. Goerdeler was a great man and it borders on the miraculous that his numerous activities in the resistance were not discovered by Hitler's police until 1944.

The group of army officers hostile to Hitler, which from 1938 onwards centred around former army chief of staff, General Beck, was most important. Included among them were officers from army headquarters and from officers of various military agencies in Berlin, such as the headquarters of the Reserve Army and the Army General Office, responsible for supplies and army administration. Linked to these resisters were civilian groups representing nearly all of the opposition circles whether conservative, liberal, socialist or religious. In clandestine meetings they discussed ways of getting rid of Hitler and his government and what should follow. They produced drafts for a new constitution and a general vision of the future that might be acceptable to their differing political views. They also drew up lists of names of who they thought should constitute a replacement government to Hitler's. They were also in touch with individuals from neutral states and even from the United States and Great Britain. Their moral disgust at Hitler's crimes, of which they were well placed in Berlin to be aware of, was their main motivation for conspiring.

The crucial question was how to end Hitler's government. There were three possibilities. First, Hitler could give up hope and resign. Second, the German Army could surrender in France after D-Day. Third, Hitler could be killed. Increasingly the Berlin conspirators became convinced that any plot would have to be based on a successful attempt at assassination. The confusion arising from Hitler's death would increase the chances of success of a rather complicated strategy.

The plotters decided to use for their own ends an official plan already in existence to have the Reserve Army suppress any public disorder that might arise. The official plan had the code name 'Valkyrie'. The intention was for the conspirators to order troops at their command to attack the government under the mistaken impression that they were defending it. This might have worked in the confused atmosphere arising from a successful assassination attempt, but as Hitler wasn't killed by Count von Stauffenberg's bomb, the conspirators' plan failed. The guards' battalion in Berlin turned against them. The military commander in Paris, General von Stulpnagel, had ordered members of the Gestapo arrested once he learnt that Stauffenberg's bomb had gone off. Realising that Hitler still lived, he attempted suicide, failed, was arrested and executed. Prior to 20 July 1944, Count von Stauffenberg had planned two earlier attempts to kill Hitler, on 11 July 1944 in Berchtesgaden and on 15 July 1944 in Rastenburg, both of which had to be cancelled. He was, in my view, the most important personality in the German resistance. Officers of the Berlin group had long plotted the assassination of Hitler, but it was Stauffenberg who brought the plotting into the realm of active reality. That his third, and this time executed, attempt at assassination failed, was a tragedy for the thousands who had participated in or supported the German resistance movement and a tragedy for the millions of soldiers and civilians who were to die in the months to come before the war finally ended.

A short remark about my father. On 20 July 1944 my father was out of action and in a military hospital; he had been severely wounded in a British fighter attack near Livarot on 17 July. Two days earlier, on 15 July, he had produced a message to the COC West, Field Marshal Von Kluge and to Hitler, which he ended with the demand that the consequences be drawn from the German defeat in the West. Since late 1943, my father had several contacts with opposition circles. When he came home after his release from hospital on 14 August 1944, he was still badly handicapped. The Gestapo was observing our house day and night. Talking to us, my father expressed the opinion that continued fighting in the West was a disaster for Europe and Germany. He said that he had been against killing Hitler because to do so ran the risk of making him a martyr and then a dead Hitler might be more dangerous than a living one. He said that his intention had been to surrender in the West and let the Allied troops advance as far as possible into Central and Eastern Europe. He thought that such a plan was feasible after the Allied breakthrough which was certain to come and which did come at St. Lo. I think that he told us only what he felt was good for us to know. On 14 October 1944, two generals came to see my father and informed him that there was sufficient evidence that he was implicated in the conspiracy. Due to his war record, however, Hitler was giving him the choice of taking poison, in which case the usual measures against his family and his staff would not be taken. My father accepted the poison and was dead half an hour later.

There is no other period in human history in which more wrong events were produced and more wrong arguments uttered than during the time of Hitler and his Third Reich. It pulled many millions of people into the abyss of disaster because it was almost perfect in suppressing criticism.

Had the Germans, particularly the German media, the freedom to express their true opinions in 1943 or 1944, Hitler's dark government would have come to an end. Carl Goerdeler was correct when he wrote in 1943, 'If the truth could be spoken, this entire nightmare would be over'. As it was, the German resistance movement was not successful and this remains a tragedy. What should also remain though are some lessons. In my opinion the most important lesson is that democracy, uncomfortable though it may be at times for the governing class, should never be corrupted and abandoned. Today, technological advances applied to communication and social organization allow modern dictators to exercise enormous power. Under these conditions, the ability of people to liberate themselves becomes nearly impossible in the short term and, taking a longer view, is possible only once the dictatorship begins to lose confidence. Those who despise dictatorship must do what they can to stabilize existing democratic systems and not be tempted to escape from reality into an imaginary paradise, which, however carefully it might be designed, is always a fool's paradise.

After the Second World War, the victorious nations, the United States, Great Britain and France, gave the Germans freedom and helped the re-establishment of democracy in Germany. I will never forget this noble action. It allowed me the privilege of living as a good democrat, in a time very different from the past. This is something that our fathers in Germany did not even dare to hope in July 1944.

14 France in the Aftermath of War

France in 1945

PIERRE MIQUEL

On 9 May 1945, France was present at the signing ceremony in Berlin. Her territory had not been uniformly liberated the previous summer; the battle continued to rage throughout the winter to the north of Strasbourg and in the Colmar salient. The 'Atlantic pockets' on the west coast held out until the very final moment. It was now the task of de Gaulle's provisional government to place a country ravaged by four years of war and suffering back on its feet.

The ports and communications links lay in ruins, and reconstruction demanded industrial means which had yet to be restored. A loan of two billion dollars in gold was immediately arranged from the United States thanks to the efforts of Jean Monnet. A re-equipment and modernization plan was drawn up to return French levels of production to those of 1929. De Gaulle's ordinances of 1945 made it possible to nationalize the key energy sectors of coal, gas and lighting. Air transport was also brought under the state control, through Air France, as was the SNCF rail network. So too were the systems of credit; the four largest deposit banks and the insurance companies were also nationalized. The private status of the Banque de France was also ended on 2 December 1945, and the National Credit Council became responsible for overseeing investment and protecting the currency. Only certain deposit banks and merchant banks, such as Rothchild's, Paribas and the Banque d'Indochine escaped nationalization.

The manufacturing industries also now came under state authority; Renault motors, for example, and Gnome-Rhone engines. Responsibility for working conditions and social matters was given to industrial committees

---

The RUSI expresses its gratitude to Armées d'aujourd'hui magazine and its editor-in-chief, Cdr Philippe Weber, for permission to reproduce these articles, which first appeared in the April 1995 edition of the magazine.

set up during the year. These committees, dominated by the trade unions (the Communist-led Confederation Generale du Travail was then five-and-a-half million strong), were evidence of a new France, partly collectivised and characterised by state socialism and the social advances according to the norms of north-west Europe and Labour-governed Great Britain. Churchill, after all, had just been displaced, whilst negotiating at Potsdam, by the new Attlee administration. The wind at that time was blowing to the left.

A STRICT PURIFICATION

The Communists, strengthened by their very many sacrifices in the Resistance, constituted the most organized political force in the country. With the Francs-Tireurs Partisans and the 'Patriotic Militias', they had presided in numerous regions over rapid dispensations of justice in advance of official investigations. The latter were severe but occasionally slow, and allowed the bigger fish to escape (such as Vichy Police chief René Bousquet, who succeeded in delaying his trial), while instead striking assorted small-fry 'collaborators', not always by design. The real cleansing was yet to come. The trial and execution of Vichy's erstwhile head of government, Pierre Laval, the clemency shown to Pétain and the arrest of some 30 000 people gave this operation a precipitate character which has necessarily been questioned. Deportees returning from the camps were surprised to learn that some of those responsible for their misery had escaped justice and fled abroad. Meanwhile, the summary executions in the countryside gave the impression of expedient justice, politically-driven, or of scores being settled.

As well as being accused of hatching plans to place themselves by such means at the core of the administrative system and of the police and the army, the Communists had at their disposal the collaborationist newspapers that had been seized. They now edited a large number of publications, particularly those for youth and female readers. In the provinces they possessed daily papers with patriotic titles like *La Marseillaise* and *Le Patriote*. *L'Humanité* at that time had a readership of 456 000. The party could also count on able members or sympathisers in the state radio, which had been nationalized in 1945. In October 1944 de Gaulle had secured the dissolution of the Patriotic Militias, but authorized the return to France of Communist leader Maurice Thorez, who had been condemned for slipping away to the USSR in 1939.

FRANCE SPLIT IN THREE

The Communists believed themselves capable, with socialist support, of reconstituting the Popular Front of 1936 and of more besides, since the right had been largely compromised by collaboration and barely still existed. Radicals, men such as Daladier and Herriot, were held responsible for the defeat of 1940. The council elections of April saw the new Christian Democrats of the People's Republican Movement (MRP) unite the anti-Marxist vote on the promise of organizing an opposition to the dominance of the left. This tendency was to be confirmed at the parliamentary elections in October: the MRP had as many deputies (some 150) as the Communists in the constituent assembly. The Socialists had 142. France was split three ways.

Did de Gaulle desire this return to the system of parties? In a long letter to the Socialist leader Leon Blum, he had accepted their legitimacy. But he wished for a constitution with an effective executive to allow the country to be governed, and a restrained legislature. The Communists, on the other hand, hoped for a parliamentary regime with a government rigorously subordinated to a unicameral majority. The new constituent assembly had unanimously elected de Gaulle to the presidency of the provisional government. Alongside his own followers Jacques Soustelle and André Malraux, he had been forced to include Communist ministers, among them Thorez. Which of them would give the new Republic its constitution, de Gaulle or Thorez?

In the end, it was to be neither of them. The Communist plan was rejected, as indeed was that of de Gaulle. The Fourth Republic would adopt a mixed regime. The President of the Republic would not be directly elected, neither would there be a single omnipotent assembly, but instead a bicameral parliamentary system, allowing the Senate to survive as the Council of the Republic. The country would vote for a constitutional model cooked up by Georges Bidault and the MRP. In the short term, the French people proved content with this, pleased to be given back the right to vote which Vichy had taken away from them. Indeed, they had been unable to do so since 1936. But were the deputies, many of them veterans of de Gaulle's wartime consultative assembly in Algiers – genuine ex-Resistants like Bidault, Vincent Auriol, and René Pleven – aware that, in opting for tripartism, they were heading for a split with de Gaulle? He had re-established democracy. He had no intention of being the powerless President of a weak Republic; one already subject to the system of parties and their exclusive influence, and to a sort of dilution of responsibilities. He doubted that such a system could rebuild France's power and allow the country to assert itself abroad. In January 1946 he left power, declaring: 'My mission is over. The exclusive party system has returned. I reject it.'

Thus drew to a close the first phase of the restoration of the republic, by a damning departure. The man referred to in the antechambers of the Fourth Republic as the 'hermit of Colombey' would wait twelve years for power to fall back into his hands, to rebuild the state and to give back France her greatness.

****

France and Germany Reconciled
JEAN GUITTON

In my early years, before 1914, my grandparents used to tell me of the war of 1870. In my childish dreams, I would see the Uhlans ride into our sleeping cities. The map of France that hung in my classroom was in a state of mourning, and the purple that covered Alsace and Lorraine was to remind us that these provinces had been torn from us by defeat of arms and that we should have to fight to take them back.

All that has changed. We are no longer warriors drawn up against one another. In Europe we have become brothers. Brothers that are required to overcome enmity, to become reconciled.

When the Germans invaded, I was serving as an officer in Clermont-Ferrand, in the very heart of France. Seeing them arrive in the town – I was filled with terrified anguish.

This France, a nation so ancient, so noble and so sure of herself; the eldest daughter of the Church; France, protected by her frontiers for so many centuries, which had beaten the most powerful army in Europe in the previous war of 1914-18; France which had suffered the parades of Cossacks or Prussians in Paris only at rare intervals; this same France which had signed the peace in 1918 in the belief of abolishing war once and for all by her victory... now saw herself at a stroke and without warning humiliated, led astray, struck down by a German corporal. In her open cities and her deserted countryside, my country appeared dead.

And yet I felt within me a ray of light, a timid love like a germ that drew me towards Germany. This love for Germany was hidden deep down in my heart, as indeed it must have lain hidden deep in the heart of France.

I was a professor of philosophy. Each year I was required to comment before the students at the Sorbonne on the Discourse on Method, the most famous text of the *philosophie française*. Descartes records:

> 'I was then in Germany; it was at the time of the wars which have not yet ended in that country. The beginning of winter caused me to halt in a place where, finding no conversation to entertain me and being untroubled by passions of any sort, I stayed constantly in a manner of stove (i.e. a most well-heated room).'

When they wish to go to the very limit of their intelligence, each of our two nations has need of the other so as to become fully itself. It is a paradox, this attraction of the genius of Germany for the culture of France and that of the genius of France for the culture of Germany.

And I believe that the secret of this double attraction is defined by the following thought:

> 'It is towards one's brother that one needs to show generosity. This brother may be an intimate enemy. But in what is best in this brother, he reveals to us the best in ourselves since he is the half that has been torn away.'

****

The Construction of Europe 1945-1950
ELISABETH DU RÉAU

In his book *Unite or Die*, published in 1929, Gaston Riou made the case for a union of the states of Europe as a pressing necessity. If Europe proved unable to bring down economic barriers and if nationalism rose up again to create walls among states or hostile blocs, the European continent, already confronted once with extinction, would sooner or later be condemned to irreversible decline. Foreign Minister Aristide Briand proposed at the League of Nations in 1929 that 'a sort of federal link' be created between the states of Europe, but his project was never to see the light of day. Ten years later Europe went to war, a total war of global dimensions, from which it was to emerge bled white, still more butchered and weakened than after the first conflict. In the 'Year Zero' of 1945, it could fairly be asked whether Europe indeed still had a destiny.

The Europe that emerged between 1945 and 1948 was a new space, remodelled and fractured. Those who had hoped for a just and lasting peace saw their hopes collapse during 1947. On the 5 March 1946, in front of an American university audience at Fulton, Churchill gave a speech whose analyses were still a premonition at that time:

> 'A shadow has fallen upon the scenes so lately lighted by the Allied victory. Nobody knows what Soviet Russia and its Communist international organisation intends to do in the immediate future...From Stettin in the Baltic to Trieste in the Adriatic, an iron curtain has descended across the Continent.'

From the hopes at the liberation to the early moves of the Cold War, initial expectations were modified.

In July 1944, some weeks after the allied victory in Normandy, representatives of resistance and anti-Nazi movements in Czechoslovakia, Denmark, France, Germany, Italy, the Netherlands, Norway, Poland and Yugoslavia drew up a common declaration in favour of federal union, stating that:

> 'Only a federal union can safeguard the democratic institutions in such a way as to prevent countries which have not grown to democratic maturity from endangering the general order.'

Indeed the two years between the end of the War and the final break between the two blocs were to be marked by major changes in Europe's political, economic and diplomatic landscape.

It has become recognised that the Yalta conference of February 1945 was not a some kind of global carve-up agreed between the giants of the US and USSR, and assented to by the United Kingdom. But if it is right to denounce the myth of Yalta, it must also be remembered that in the immediate aftermath of this agreement, the Soviet Union intervened in Romania to install a government in which Communists were given the key posts. The British and Americans, joint members of the control commission with the Soviets, offered no overt criticism of this violation of the Declaration on Liberated Europe.

THE BIRTH OF THE FIRST EUROPEAN MOVEMENTS

Between winter 1945 and autumn 1947 the balance of forces in eastern Europe shifted steadily in favour of the Soviet Union, which progressively extended economic and military control by means of unequal bilateral treaties with its 'partners' – 'people's democracies' which were by now scarcely independent any longer.

At the time of the birth of the first European movements, such as the European Federalists' Union (November 1946), New International Teams (March 1947), and the Movement for a United Europe (May 1947), the early accent was on building a Europe within its full geographical dimensions. The links forged between western European democrats and representatives of exiled governments which had fled Nazi oppression explained why there were those who refused a purely 'Western' approach. For this reason Britain's Labour party and certain French Socialists were reluctant to take initiatives which could force a break with Moscow. Within the Socialist Movement for a United States of Europe, led by André Philip, European doctrine was based on Socialist values and envisaged building a united Europe by a planning structure for core industries and investment.

In June 1947 President Vincent Auriol and Premier Paul Ramadier, while attracted by the American offer of the Marshall Plan, were anxious to avoid rupture with Moscow and agreed to an invitation to the Soviet leadership to visit Paris. On 11 June, Auriol declared that 'an over-restrictive definition of Europe is dangerous'. However, the Soviet delegation that came to Paris rejected the Marshall Plan at the beginning of July 1947. Diplomat Hervé Alphand recorded in his Journal:

> 4 July 1947. Seeing Molotov coming down the steps of the Quai d'Orsay, I told myself that we were entering a new era; one which might continue for a long time and even take a course dangerous for peace. Against our wishes, the character of our links with the East would be modified by economic necessities.

By September 1947, the break appeared complete. The sixteen states of Western Europe accept the Marshall Plan, and in eastern Europe the Soviet Union created the Cominform. Europe had split in two for more than the next forty years.

CREATION OF THE OEEC

The greatest consequence of the entry into the Cold War was the strengthening of the Euro-Atlantic axis. It was in the economic field that American aid was first sought from spring 1947 onwards. With the agreement of President Truman, anxious to stem the expansion of Communism into Europe, US Secretary of State General George Marshall proposed a European Recovery Programme, to apply to all European states, in his Harvard speech of 5 June 1947. The condition set by the US was that a conference be convened and a permanent structure for European cooperation be put in place. This was the origin of the Paris Conference, which brought together sixteen west European states during the summer of 1947 following the Soviet refusal; for their part, the states of eastern Europe wishing to participate were obliged to decline the invitation.

In April 1948, the Organization for European Economic Cooperation (OEEC) was formed, with 16 countries and a seat in Paris, to permit the Marshall Plan to distribute more than $12 billion over four years. The institution was a European one, an intergovernmental body with a ministerial committee and a secretariat. In 1960 it would be enlarged to include non-European members, thereby becoming the Organization for Economic Cooperation and Development or OECD.

Cooperation was also pursued in the military field, and the policy of the Western Allies evolved rapidly between 1946 and 1948. Until the beginning of 1947, the hazy threat was seen as a resurgence of German militarism; thus the Treaty of Dunkirk, signed between Britain and France on 4 March 1948, designated a German adversary. One year later, the view had shifted and the danger was being judged to emanate from the Soviet Union.

The Brussels Treaty, concluded on 17 March 1948 between the Benelux states, France and the United Kingdom, was a defensive treaty of alliance which foresaw mutual assistance by member states in the event of aggression. In the Treaty's preamble, the five signatories committed themselves to defend the democratic principles, civic and individual liberties and the respect of the law that constituted their common heritage. They endowed themselves with permanent institutions, forming the Western Union, with headquarters in London. From summer 1948, the crisis triggered by the Berlin blockade caused the Union's Consultative Council to consider establishing a permanent military staff at Fontainebleau.

A UNITED STATES OF EUROPE

But the aggravated split between East and West and the rise of the Soviet Union, which became a nuclear power in 1949, caused the members of the Western Union to turn towards the United States. Early negotiations began in autumn 1948, leading to the creation on 4 April 1949 of the Atlantic Alliance between ten countries of western Europe, and the United States and Canada. One year later the organization was strengthened to become the North Atlantic Treaty Organization.

Both the European institutions created in 1948, the OEEC and the Western Union, foresaw cooperation between the member states in an intergovernmental framework. But among the advocates of the idea of a

European Union, some movements and individuals were arguing in favour of a different, federal model of European union. The formula of a 'United States of Europe', used by Victor Hugo in 1849, had resurfaced during the inter-War period and was re-launched by Winston Churchill at the University of Zurich in September 1946. The aim of the federalists was to see a single European government established over time, and they were prepared to see the sovereignty of states curtailed in the interest of the central institution. Taking their inspiration from the system in the United States of America, they envisaged certain responsibilities being passed up to federal authority; but on the means of achieving this, they remained divided. The 'maximalists' hoped to see a European constituent assembly convened; others instead favoured the conclusion of a federal pact between national governments.

In December 1947, the International Committee for the Coordination of Movements for European Unity decided to call a major congress for the following spring with the aim of promoting dialogue between the different currents of support for a European Union. The Congress of The Hague, which met from 7-10 May 1948, was a private initiative of the highest importance. It unfolded in the presence of some one thousand people, eight hundred of them delegates of various movements. The political resolution finally adopted by the Congress was a compromise between the cooperationist thesis and that of the outright federalists. The creation of a Council of Europe was proposed, to consist of an intergovernmental council and an assembly.

How the national governments of western Europe would react was another question. The French government was enthusiastic; Georges Bidault, now Foreign Minister, suggested on 19 July to the Western Union that a Council of Europe be created to allow 'the peoples of Europe' to come together and to give expression to public opinion by means of a European assembly. Little progress was made between Summer and Autumn 1948 owing to British opposition to such an assembly, but negotiations were finally concluded at the end of the following spring. On 5 May 1949, the Council of Europe was set up by the Treaty of London. This intergovernmental body was to comprise of a Committee of Ministers and a consultative assembly with limited powers. The ten signatories (the five partners of the Brussels Treaty, Ireland, Italy and the three Nordic countries of

Denmark, Norway and Sweden) proposed the creation of a closer union between members states 'so as to safeguard and create the ideals and principles that are their common heritage'. They committed themselves to work to further human rights; shortly thereafter, in 1950, this was to lead to the establishment of the European Convention on Human Rights and the Court of the same name.

WIDENING EUROPE

At the Assembly's first session in Strasbourg, the federalists expressed their disappointment that their vision had not been triumphant, but they still judged that the Council could function as a useful theoretical laboratory, a tribune from which to exchange European ideas. At the session's opening, Bidault had listed the countries that made up the assembly; as early as August 1949 he was already outlining a future Europe expanded to the full dimensions of the continent and anticipating, in the very near future, the entry of a Germany which had returned to the ways of democracy.

On 9 May 1950 Bidault's successor, Robert Schuman, surprised a press conference at the Quai d'Orsay by announcing a major Franco-German initiative with the words:

> 'Europe will be made neither at a single stroke, nor by building an all-encompassing structure; it will come about by concrete achievements that create a genuine solidarity. Bringing together the nations of Europe first requires the elimination of the centuries-long opposition between France and Germany. The measures undertaken must first and foremost affect France and Germany.'

The Foreign Minister went on to expand on his thinking and proposed a plan, the basis of the establishment of the European Coal and Steel Community among the new Federal Republic of Germany, the Benelux states, France and Italy. Five years after the signing of the armistice in Berlin, Schuman was setting the seal on the reconciliation between France and Germany to permit the creation of the founding Community of the six. Hailing this noble initiative in *Le Monde*, Maurice Duverger rightly noted that 'Europe is leaving behind the dreams, the storm clouds and the speeches and is taking shape in a concrete project'. The treaty establishing the European Coal and Steel Community was signed in Paris on 18 April 1951, a decisive date in the history of the European construction. At the heart of Europe a magnetic pole had come into being. As events continue to show, it remains to this day the 'hard core' of the European Union.

15 Sweden's Neutrality – A Debatable Balancing Act

Lars Hjörne

I was only ten years old when Adolf Hitler ordered his war machine to attack Poland, but I remember all too well the upheaval which followed the outbreak of war. Above all, I remember the blackout, the food rationing, the air raid alarms when German war planes violated Swedish air space, the sound of guns from the convoys being attacked at sea outside my home city, Gothenburg, the arrival of ships under safe conduct with supplies – and the suitcase packed in case I had to be evacuated in a hurry.

The privations of the Swedes were, of course, minor compared to the sufferings of people in the countries at war or under German occupation. At the same time, the uncertainty about Hitler's intentions for our country was for years a heavy psychological burden for the government and people.

Including Sweden, 20 European nations declared their neutrality at the outbreak of war, but only six escaped being dragged in. Apart from Sweden, these were Switzerland, Eire, Spain, Portugal and Turkey. This last country was a borderline case since Turkey declared war on Germany in February 1945, when the outcome was no longer in doubt. The difference between Sweden and other small neutrals lay not so much in what they wanted, as in their position outside an area which a big power had marked out as a sphere of defence or economic interest.

Reactions to the official policy of neutrality differed in various parts of Sweden. In Stockholm, for instance, the government had greater support than in Gothenburg. The reason was the traditional economic and cultural ties with Britain across the North Sea. In the past centuries many Scots had settled in the city and on the West coast, and brought with them new skills and profitable trade.

In Gothenburg people are proud that their city is sometimes called 'Little London'. They grin with pleasure when people on the East coast say that Gothenburgers reach for their umbrellas whenever possible that it may rain in London. During the war they were certainly not neutral at heart: their sympathies lay with Western Allies.

The Germans were well aware of the British influence in Gothenburg. In a report to his Stockholm legation – duly noted by the Swedish security service – their Consul General complained that the people of Gothenburg were all too deaf to the preachings from Berlin because of their traditional ties westwards.

I grew up with *The Manchester Guardian* and *The London Illustrated News*, which were always on the library table in our home which was part of the editorial building of the daily *Göteborgs-Posten* (*Gothenburg Post*) in central Gothenburg. My father, Harry Hjörne, chief editor and majority owner of the paper, was born in Waukengan, Illinois, in the United States, the son of Swedish emigrants. Thanks to a scholarship, he spent some time in England in the 1920s as a young journalist and gained contacts in the Liberal party. He also closely followed an election. Such was his interest – and his memory – that he recalled practically every parliamentary constituency in the post-war general election in 1945. From those early days he retained a deep admiration for the British and especially the British parliamentary system. He had no time for Hitlerism or its policy of violence.

Most people regarded him as an out and out civilian. None the less, he applied to join at once when the Swedish Home Guard was formed in 1940. On his application form he even offered to defray the cost of his own rifle! To his surprise, he was asked to take command of the North Gothenburg district, where the majority of recruits were workers from the shipyards. At about the same time, my mother Anna was given charge of the attached women's organization, and my brother Bengt served as a dispatch-rider. To my great disappointment, I was too young to take part.

Against all my expectations, my father turned his troops of 800 men into an effective partisan force, and he was immensely proud when his unit won the first countrywide Home Guard competition. The enthusiasm with which the creation of the Home Guard was greeted took the government by surprise. Estimates of the number of recruits had been about 40 000. The number turned out to be well over 100 000, so it was clear that people wanted to defend themselves and their country. The volunteers were, of course, additional to the regular defence forces and the many tens of thousands called up for military service during the war.

Despite my youth I was very conscious of the tension and the anxiety in the country during the early war years. Our exposed position became abundantly and painfully clear after the German attack on Norway and Denmark on 9 April 1940. Many people thought it was Sweden's turn next.

The country was badly prepared for an attack because its defences had been run down in the thirties. The fortifications of the sea approaches to Gothenburg were not even manned on 9 April! A resourceful chief of police ordered cars on to the runways of the airport so as to prevent the landing of German military planes – just in case.

The situation was grave enough without the government making it even more tense. Yet immediately after the outbreak of war it was decided to take emergency powers. On the strength of that, a new security service was created. This meant that citizens were subjected to a supervision which they had never had before. Telephone tapping and censorship of letters and telegrams were met with daily.

At the same time, the authorities began to subject the press to supervision. In a speech the prime minister, Per Albin Hansson, underlined that the government would not tolerate statements which might shake foreign confidence in Sweden's neutrality. This was an open warning to writer and journalists to stop criticising the Nazi regime – something that Berlin regarded as a departure from neutrality.

Sweden was – and possibly still is – the only country in Europe to have press freedom enshrined in its constitution. Now people found this tampered with by the enforcement of a doubtful interpretation of one single paragraph. As a result printed material could be confiscated, frequently without legal redress.

As early as the autumn of 1939, the first seizures of book and newspapers took place. Twelve papers were confiscated after publishing 'improper criticism' of the Berlin regime.

Germany also attempted to rein in Swedish opinion by diplomatic complaints, usually containing disguised threats. In one month alone, September 1940, the German minister, Prinz von Wied, handed fourteen notes to the Swedish foreign minister Christian Günther. Practically all were complaints about the attitude of the Swedish press. The German line was that the authorities themselves were responsible for what was written in the country's newspapers. The official attitude conveyed from Berlin was that neutrality of the press should be an integral part of 'total neutrality'.

The German propaganda minister, Joseph Goebbels, further developed this theme with barely disguised threats in a speech in Berlin in February 1940. He castigated as totally unreasonable the idea that neutral governments should permit criticism of a German at war. He also underlined that it was against the concept of neutrality to differentiate between opinion in a country and the attitude of its government. His words were dutifully reported in the German press and made a strong impression in Sweden. They contributed to a decision, taken in fear, by the Swedish parliament to adopt a censorship law and to add further restrictions to the law of press freedom.

Without a doubt, the government felt itself under strong pressure, and there was continuous and grave concern in official circles. The Swedish legation in Berlin added to these feelings by sending a stream of alarmist reports. A typical example was a dispatch from the then envoy to the foreign office in Stockholm on 7 April 1940:

> 'I must emphasize most urgently the warnings in my recent private letter. I caution specially against provocative statements or anti-German expressions in the newspapers or on the radio. This is a situation of the utmost danger for Sweden's existence.'

A spokesperson for the German Foreign Office contributed to the feeling of impending menace by openly declaring: 'There must be a change in the attitude of the Swedish press. Otherwise there is danger ahead.' At one stage the Swedish foreign minister threatened to resign if certain newspapers did not modify their harsh criticism of Germany.

As a consequence of the seriousness with which the German threats were regarded, the stopping of papers and magazines was largely directed against those which were openly critical of the Nazi regime and its brutalities. They constituted 79 per cent of total seizures. A balance of sorts was created by also including some local National Socialist papers and pamphlets.

As Sweden was thought to be under threat of imminent attack by Germany, the government felt it had no other choice. Derogation from the press freedom law and the use of confiscation method were considered justified, as long as Germany was victorious and able to carry out its threats.

The control of the Swedish press was exercised by a state directorate of information. It issued in total 150 'directives' to the press to keep silent about events for which the Germans did not want publicity. Defiant papers ran the risk of total suspension. The following is a short summary of the directorate's activities:

- In 1939: 12 newspapers confiscated, of which two were freed after court appeal.
- In 1940: 25 confiscations, nine papers freed. The British *Nyheter från Storbritannien* (*News from Great Britain*) was confiscated on 27 May 1940 because of an article and pictures from bombed Norwegian villages under the headline 'German Cultural Monuments in Norway'.
- In 1941: 81 papers confiscated, of which five were freed.
- In 1942: A climax was reached with 139 confiscations. In March alone, 38 papers were stopped because of articles about German cruelties against Norwegian patriots in Norway.
- In 1943: 29 confiscations.

During a meeting off the record at the Swedish Foreign Office, my father asked the foreign minister how credible were the reports of German torture. The reluctant answer was that far worse things had happened than had been reported in the papers which had been confiscated. Among the victims in Norway was a great friend of our family, the author Erna Holmboe Bang. She survived, but carried for the rest of her life the marks of injuries inflicted on her by the Germans.

The Swedish press was forced to keep silent about such atrocities because of the German threats. It took the turn of the war, and the beginning of German losses in 1942, to reduce the number of confiscations. Soon they ceased altogether. From early 1943, the new German minister in Stockholm, Dr. Hans Thomsen, was less inclined than his predecessor to attempt to rein in Swedish papers by means of diplomatic protests.

Remarkably enough, relations between government and press were fairly smooth. Editors of the major papers were frequently called to the Foreign Office in Stockholm to be informed confidentially of the situation and the government's relations with Berlin and other capitals. This show of openness resulted in a general acceptance – with some notable exceptions – by the papers of the government's balancing act, even when it was felt to be dubious. By and large, the Swedish press had to accept the necessity of restraint.

My father's paper, *Göteborgs-Posten*, belonged to the category prepared to show understanding of the official attitude, even when this was repugnant. Although he felt he had to support the policy of appeasement, it had no effect on his personal sympathies. Democracy and the parliamentary system were still ideals he held sacred. Earlier he had taken part in the battle against the fascist Lappo-movement in Finland. Earlier still he had demonstrated his intense dislike of Mussolini and Italian fascism. After Hitler had gained power in Germany, he stood up against the system and its attempts to suborn authors and artists, and to drive dissenters into exile.

In Finland he was detained several times by the Finnish political police, when taking part in meetings with the 'Peace-opposition' movement round the country. While Finland was allied to Germany during part of the war, the authorities wanted to clamp down on such efforts.

My father strongly disapproved of the concessions made by Sweden while Germany was at its strongest. At the same time he felt that the critical situation required him to publicly show support for the government and official policy. This pragmatic stance was shared by most responsible journalists, whatever their opinion in private.

For him it was very important to follow the situation in Denmark and Norway during the years of German occupation. Unusually for the time, he employed a Danish journalist, Knud Rye, and a Norwegian, Sigmund Stafne. Their sole job was to keep tabs on news and events in their countries and to report on them in his newspaper. Stafne was often invited to our home. Once when he did not turn up at short notice, I asked why. It was in December, and the answer was surprising. He was busy 'picking blueberries' – which I quickly understood to mean that he had gone over the border in secret to contact the Norwegian resistance. The Norwegian border is less than 200 miles distance from Gothenburg and has thinly-populated forest areas, where it was possible to avoid German guards.

Another memory I have is the flood of propaganda sent from Germany to Sweden, which one could not escape seeing. It was yet another crude attempt to influence Swedish opinion. Its flagship was the periodical *Signal*, controlled by the German war machine, and mainly filled with semi-official front reports and photographs. At its most expansive, *Signal* had a print run of two and a half million copies, translated into 20 languages including Swedish. As the propaganda message was undisguised, the important Swedish dailies soon refused to give it advertising space. *Göteborgs-Posten*'s refusal took place in the autumn of 1941 – at the time a provocative stand.

The Germans regarded Sweden as an important propaganda target. The direct sale of German newspapers was not very successful, but some Swedish language periodicals fared better, notably a German weekly review and a publication called *Tyska Röster* (German Voices). The radio station at Königsberg also sent out daily news bulletins and propaganda in Swedish. A great number of books and glossies were also produced, lauding the German Wehrmacht as 'invincible'. It was considered important to try and make Swedes believe that a German victory was inevitable.

The somewhat more modest British reply was the Swedish language paper *Nyheter från Storbritannien*. It was circulated widely and became popular, as it was free from direct propaganda. An air-mail edition of *The Times* was sent over and became required reading among as many as could get hold of it. There were also a number of booklets on the British war effort, while an important source of British news and opinion was the daily bulletin in Swedish from the BBC in London. A great number of listeners also tuned in to the BBC's programmes in English.

After the battle of El Alamein we began to get more British publications, this time on Allied successions and German defeats. At long last the Germans came off second best in the propaganda war. But German pressure was still there. It was only when the tide of war had visibly turned, and the Germans were in retreat, that Sweden could draw breath. The government had succeeded in keeping the country out of the war, even if only just, and with the Swedish banner somewhat soiled.

Many of the concessions made to the Germans early in the war were abhorred and made people despair of the government. The most flagrant case took place in 1941, when permission was given for the transit on Swedish railways of a German fighting division from Norway to Finland, which took place after the German attack on the Soviet Union.

Another clear departure from Sweden's neutrality was to permit the transportation of German soldiers on leave to and from Norway. They were supposedly unarmed, and equal numbers were required to travel in either direction, so as not to add to the occupying forces. There were many clenched fists at the sight of the passing trains. A group of school friends and I used to stand beside the track in Gothenburg, where the 'leave trains' went by at slow speed. We indulged in mock Nazi salutes and sundry rude gestures – our childish protest against this humiliating traffic.

After the war another breach of neutrality was disclosed. Following the German attack on the Soviet Union in June 1941, the Swedish government had allowed the transport of soldiers and military material in secret through Swedish waters to Finland. It was then at last admitted that during the years 1941-42 the Swedish navy escorted 62 German convoys through the Baltic. This was a serious deviation from the country's declared neutral stance.

The way Sweden interpreted its neutrality was thus clearly controversial. A key man at the Foreign Office in Stockholm at the time, Erik Boheman – later ambassador in London – summed up this epoch in Sweden's history as follows:

'Much that took place in Swedish politics during the war years up to 1942 – our most dangerous time – has left a bitter after-taste for many of us, also a feeling of guilt which is quite unnecessary. I do not think that Sweden was neutral in the strict sense of the word during the Second World War. In the early years we made concessions to the Germans, and during the later years we made them to the Allies. We were not in the war, but not strictly neutral either. Still, we have nothing to be ashamed of – it was our only chance of survival'.

His simple analysis was resurrected when the post-war generation began criticising the submissiveness and the concessions during the war. The reply from those responsible, then as now, is always the same: we had no choice.

Freedom from alliances in peacetime, neutrality in war, became the official Swedish line from 1945. The war demonstrated how helpless small countries are when threatened by neighbouring big powers. As a consequence, the idea of a Nordic defence alliance found proposal, however, came to nothing when Norway and Denmark joined NATO in 1949. Sweden then chose to follow its own path, partly because of concern for Finland. Swedish membership of NATO would almost certainly have meant the Iron Curtain coming down on Torne river, which marks the land frontier between Sweden and Finland. Inevitably, the Soviet position in the Baltic and beyond would have been advanced.

We now perceive the outline of a new Europe. The fall of the Berlin wall, German reunification and the dissolution of the Soviet Union have drastically changed the security picture. Old threats have faded or disappeared. This affects the Swedish neutrality concept. When the Swedes voted in November 1994 to join the European Union, the peace argument was predominant, and the Union seen as a step towards peace and liberty in Europe.

The question many have been asking recently is 'Has Swedish neutrality any *raison d'être* in the new Europe?' *Expressen*, a Stockholm evening paper with an extensive circulation, has answered 'no' and started a campaign for Sweden to join NATO.

The new Social Democrat government in Sweden is not prepared to go as far as that. It does not exclude eventual Swedish participation in a Europe-wide defence collaboration. The moderate (Conservative) party, which is Sweden's second biggest, is toying with the same idea. It is no longer fanciful to suppose that the period of Sweden's neutrality is nearing its end. In any case, it would appear that a significant change in the concept of neutrality is at hand. The process has already begun.

16 Compendium of Articles From The RUSI Journal 1945-1989

Since it was first published in 1858, the Journal of the Royal United Services Institute has been able to publish lectures and articles from contemporary leading practitioners and thinkers in military science, defence and security studies. The extracts below have been taken from Journals over the years since the end of the Second World War. So quickly has the Cold War passed into history that the fears and perspectives that characterised the period now appear remote and almost alien, especially to a generation growing to consciousness in the wake of the fall of the Berlin Wall. The selection below charts the shifting developments of allies into enemies, the spread and escalation of the arms race and growth of deterrence, and changes in strategic thought which have shaped British and Alliance policy since the end of the War. It is by no means a comprehensive selection, but aims to give a flavour of the era and the debate that took place over the years, both serious and somewhat whimsical. The framework has been taken from immediately after the War, starting with a discussion of the military government in Germany, to 1989 with the historic meeting at the RUSI of the respective heads of NATO and the Warsaw Pact, General Galvin and General Lushev. It is the road to that watershed that we have tried to recall and document here. If some of the concerns seem familiar, plus ça change...

****

Military Government in Germany
By Major-General G.W.R. Templer C.B., D.S.O., O.B.E., Director of Military Government on the Staff of Field Marshal Montgomery
28 November 1945.

...The size and complexity of the problems facing Military Government can only be properly understood in relation to their physical and mental setting, and that is why I want to start by spending a few moments in reminding you of certain salient facts about the British Zone. They are not novel but they are important. In the first place it is an area of 38 000 square miles – it may help to visualize this in relation to our readiest unit of comparison, England. This area to the best of our knowledge, without up-to-date census figures, contains a population of about twenty millions– about half a million more than the basic resident population at the outbreak of war. This increased population now finds itself at the end of the War left with vastly diminished resources in food, fuel and housing – above all, in communications, transport and very many of the amenities of normal European life.

...The basic policy was summed up in the Supreme Commander's initial Proclamation to the German people: 'We come as conquerors, but not as oppressors. We shall overthrow the Nazi rule, dissolve the Nazi Party and abolish the cruel, oppressive and discriminatory laws and institutions which the Party has created. We shall eradicate that German militarism which has so often disrupted the peace of the world. 'The plan for operation 'Eclipse', the occupation of North-West Germany, stated moreover: 'The establishment of Military Government in Germany is therefore the logical conclusion of our declaration of war on 3 September, 1939, and it will be our policy to make this clear to the German people. Germany will be treated as a defeated and not as a liberated country.'

Denazification Policy

The main difficulties are these – in the first place there is the thorough Nazi permeation of all but the lowest administrative grade; almost all German officials were more or less deeply compromised with Nazism. Then there is the corollary, the paucity of trained and acceptable German personnel. Democratic officials, dispossessed in or after 1933 and now available, are relatively few in number, and many of these are too old or rusty for responsible employment. The sincere anti-Nazis also have their shortcomings, and they too do not necessarily make good administrators.

...The whole task of denazification is one which calls for unremitting energy and a steady refusal to compromise. To those who still see persons in office or positions of influence who had strong Nazi sympathies or Party ties – and nearly every German knows of someone at whom he can point – our system appears perhaps both slow and patchy. But as the work goes steadily forward, many of these early critics are being gradually brought round to the view that 'Slow but sure' is no idle phrase where the British are concerned, and that there is indeed a wide plan in operation rather than a capricious and fitful elimination policy....

****

The Other Side of the Iron Curtain
By B. Kingsley Martin, author and journalist, 6 November 1947.

...On the whole the Germans obeyed the Hague conventions in the West. But in the East, it was a war of extermination. It is only when you understand this that you begin to realize this psychological gap that now appears between the Slavs and the western countries.

...The Partisans built up a force of 400 000 men. They actually held 25 divisions of enemy troops in Yugoslavia during the latter part of the War, and they necessarily carried out a social revolution. The upper classes there were on the whole ready to accept the Germans and their Quislings– not all of them, but very many. The people who fought this war and came through have not the slightest intention of going back to the old Serbian dictatorship. The Partisan armies were made up of Slavs, Croats, Macedonians and Serbs. For the first time those four groups, who have hated each other like poison throughout history, had fought on the same side. All four were included in Tito's new Army. All four were included in the Government. Those of you who know anything about that part of the World will understand why I emphasize the fact that I have met Serb peasants who admitted that there might be some grain of decency in Croat peasants. Some Croats actually believe that not all Serbs are their enemies. They talk in terms of a single united country of Yugoslavia, not in terms of a Serb and Croat dictatorship.

In Yugoslavia many things are happening which are bad; but some are good. Just as in Poland, you must not expect people who have come through that incredible war to be tolerant. It would be as foolish to expect the Partisans who have survived to be Gladstonian Liberals as it would be to blame people in XVIth Century England for not appreciating the toleration of the XIXth Century. I am always trying to look for a way in which to explain that point to people who are still astonished when some peasant leader, who has been hostile to the Government, leaves that part of the World, or some public man is executed, perhaps unjustly. There has never been a case in history of a country which has gone through a great revolution and then behaved tolerantly to those who have been defeated. It is not a question of saying that all the new Government do is right. Personally, I think they have been often wrong. But let us have some sense of perspective....

****

Mercenaries
By Lieut.-Colonel M. St. J. Oswald D.S.O., M.C., R.A. (1948).

In time of peace, our need is for sufficient Regular recruits to provide the garrisons of our overseas bases, to train the National Servicemen, to assist the Territorial Army and to form an Imperial reserve which can be sent to any trouble spots at short notice. During a period of high wages and full employment it is impossible to obtain sufficient good quality recruits unless we are prepared to bring their pay and prospects into line with those in civil occupations. This we apparently cannot afford to do. Like all great Empires in the past we shall, therefore, have to rely on the use of mercenaries.

...To some extent we have already accepted this principle and are only too glad to employ Gurkha troops in Malaya. Far nearer home there is a larger and, for the purposes of modern warfare, better source of mercenaries – Western Germany, already over-populated with some 40 million inhabitants. Traditionally, Germany has always been one of the greatest producers of mercenary troops, and even to-day the bulk of the French Foreign Legion is still German. The Western Zones are full of young men, most of whom have had war experience, who have little hope for the future, who are disinclined to engage in any legitimate trade and are rapidly drifting into crime, apathy and general disillusionment. At heart they are still soldiers, and as such their qualities need no emphasis.

We should therefore make up our minds to accept a limited number of German recruits into the Regular Army. That these recruits would be forthcoming is not in doubt, provided the terms of service are reasonable and are given good publicity....We should, however, take steps to retain his loyalty after discharge by seeing that he obtained good employment, possibly working for British Military Government, and that units in BAOR arranged periodic reunions for German reservists. This, combined with the average German's fear and hatred of Russia, would ensure that his services were available when required.

****

The Western Union and its Defence Organization
A Lecture to the RUSI by Field-Marshal the Viscount Montgomery of Alamein K.G., G.C.B., D.S.O., 12 October 1949.

...The organization which I have described may prove to have a great significance in the history of attempts by mankind to organize and guarantee World peace. In the past, such efforts have invariably depended upon the attempt to superimpose at the beginning a superior organization, such as the League of Nations, upon the existing Governments of Treaty Powers. In the present case, the approach to the problem is different. Activated by a common fear, the Western European Powers formed a military organization to strengthen their combined defence. The requirements of military co-operation at once involved supply and financial questions. Political co-operation at all levels inevitably followed. In this organization, therefore, there is an element of evolution, and it is by the evolutionary process that the affairs of mankind, and of nations, are most readily settled.

...Under peace conditions, nations are particularly conscious of their individual sovereignties and of their national pride. Moreover, in approaching many problems, national attitudes are affected by individuality of language, tradition and customs. These variances are not easily swept away. It has been a difficult year. But it is quite clear to me that *provided the problem is understood*, and provided nations will face up bravely and with *good intentions* to the difficulties and 'snags', *then* it is fully possible to reach agreed solutions and to make progress in building up united strength in Western Europe....

Confidence and Mutual Trust

It is essential that each nation should have faith in the sincerity, good intentions, and wholehearted co-operation of the others. Once a nation conceals things, or is not frank and open, or hesitates when it becomes necessary to take practical measures to implement agreed principles, then suspicion creeps in; and once that happen the results may be catastrophic. The only sound Allied motto is:–'One for all, and all for one.' There must be no ambiguity. We must all mean what we say, and say what we mean.

Proper Linguistic Qualifications

It has become very apparent that the members of the working staffs must have adequate linguistic qualifications to enable them to work together with sympathy and understanding. We have learnt by experience that differences of language can lead to great misunderstandings, which sometimes require considerable efforts to resolve. Two languages are used, English and French. In my view it is essential that nations should set and demand a high standard in their interpretership examinations. I am doubtful if this is done at present in all cases.

A Final Requirement

A final requirement, equal in importance to any of the others, is that we must all have a very clear realization of the truth contained in the old proverb:–'God helps those who help themselves.' It is rather well put in J. de la Veprie's *Les Proverbes Communs*, printed in Paris about the year 1498:–'Ayde toy dieu taidera.'

We must not develop a tendency to look across the Atlantic and say we cannot do this, or we cannot do that, unless America will *first* do something else. *We* must all act first and must get on with the job. Our friends will rally to our support in their own good time, and will do so with greater eagerness when they see we are taking every possible step to help ourselves.

Conclusion

In conclusion I would like to say again that I am full of hope and optimism about the future of Western Union Defence. Our triumphant cry should be:–'Strength through Unity.' And this strength can easily be obtained given an international outlook, faith in the task, and whole-hearted unselfish co-operation – all leading to Unity.

****

The Soviet Armed Forces
A lecture to the RUSI by Major-General Richard Hilton D.S.O., M.C., D.F.C., Military Attaché in Potsdam with the Soviets and then Attaché in Moscow, 26 October 1949.

Never having been a military attaché in any other Country, I cannot of course compare, from personal experience, the Soviet practice and technique in dealing with foreign attachés with that of other nations. All that I can say with certainty is that, from a military attaché's point of view, matters could hardly be worse anywhere else. General Seraev – the officer detailed to act as sole link between foreign attachés in Moscow and the High Command – once told me candidly that, in the opinion of the Soviet authorities, all foreign attachés were *ipso facto* spies. We were certainly treated accordingly!

...Whether you decide to think that the Soviet Union is concealing strength or weakness, one thing at least is certain – i.e., that things 'are not what they seem' on the surface. The whole Country is a hot-bed of propaganda. Practically nothing can be accepted safely at its face value. The control of 'Truth' is so complete that the authorities can almost make black seem white. It is specially important to treat with suspicion anything which is gratuitously offered to the public gaze of foreigners. This, I personally believe, applies particularly to the great military parades on the Red Square – the only warlike functions that foreign attachés (except of course those of the 'satellite' Countries) are ever invited to see.

...Any old soldier who is reasonably observant can see quite a lot of the true state of affairs without in any way transgressing the correct etiquette of a diplomat. The training which one gets on many a barrack-room inspection in peace-time, and the resultant skill in spotting the dust beneath the 'eye-wash', stands one in very good stead on such a job as this! On the surface these Red Square parades undoubtedly look impressive, magnificent, and impeccable. But so does many a barrack-room till you peep under the beds.

... If the impossible were to happen – if one could persuade a senior Soviet officer to define to you his conception of the fighting forces of his Country – he would not, as most of us would, speak of three distinct Services – Navy, Army and Air Force; he would, I feel sure, think of *four* distinct elements in the Soviet war-machine. These four would be:–
(a) *The Armed Forces* – regarded and used as one weapon.
(b) *The 'Rear'* – the whole nation or 'Home Front', organized as one industrial and agricultural and man-producing machine for the maintenance of the armed forces.
(c) *The M.V.D.* – the essential security police force to keep the 'Home Front' up to the mark, to prevent sabotage, fifth column activities, idleness, or any other waste or diversion of war effort.
(d) *Fifth Column* – subversive activities of all kinds abroad. These may cover anything from open civil war down to the dissemination of a defeatist or 'go slow' policy among the dupes of Communism. This includes 'Partisans' when applicable.

It is important, I think, to realize that the Soviet leaders have got this much broader conception of what constitutes a war organization. They would no more think of planning a war without giving full consideration to these four items than an air-minded soldier of to-day would start planning military operations without giving full consideration to the air. The general impression which I should like to leave with you is that of a formidable fighting machine, but one by no means free from very serious weaknesses. However good the actual fighting forces may be, their ability to sustain a long world war will depend on the economic state of the Soviet Union and on its people's enthusiasm for the war. In both these respects the Soviet Union still has a long way to go. They know this as well as anyone and they are certainly not 'marking time'.

****

The American Attitude Towards International Affairs
By Professor D.W. Brogan M.A., LL.D., 23 November 1949.

...[The] misunderstanding begins first in the belief that American policy is directed by extremely astute, Machiavellian, greedy people – and the two things are not incompatible. The picture of American policy being directed from Wall Street or other places of the same type is false. American policy at the moment is suffering, if anything, from too much goodwill. I should like to see it...directed with more 'hardboiledness' towards our problems than is being shown at the moment. If it were, in fact, directed by extremely hardboiled, astute, profit-making people, it would not have taken the form of the Marshall Plan or the present lines on which the Administration is carrying on. The assumption that all American policy is directed by selfish Wall Street interests, by extremely smart, foreseeing people who are in it for something, I consider to be totally untrue. Rightly or wrongly, wisely or unwisely, it is directed by people who have, as the Quakers say, a 'concern'.

...What are the consequences of this outlook for our own future? It means that we must, in any policy that we put up to the Americans, do two things to satisfy them. We must, and we should, show a rational, solvent accountancy in our policy. It must be realized that they are tempted by a vast number of approaches of that kind – by what would happen if they put money in India, Ceylon, South Africa, North Africa, and so on. If they are asked to choose from a great many possibilities of doing good, or of valuable investment, they will choose that which will do good to the United States and to the Countries concerned.

What should *we* put up? What we should put up is, in fact, an appeal – a legitimate appeal, to the American moral sense. It *is* more important to preserve in Europe the kind of life that the United States grew out of, than it is to raise the level of living in India or Madagascar or South Africa; that is to say, we have as Europeans, a special claim on American policy: this is where they came from, not merely physically (in fact, most Americans did come from Western Europe), but that, emotionally, the kind of life that the Americans lead comes from the kind of life that we lead. If we fail to lead it, the whole of American life would be compressed and reduced to mere mechanics instead of being the free, spiritual life that they have now.

We should approach the Americans on two lines. First of all, we must present – it is good for us as well as for them – good book-keeping accounts and show that there will be some tangible cash dividend. I should like to remind you that I grew up in a Country which invented double-entry book-keeping! But also, when you are putting to the United States any such policy, you must allow for the fact of their profound moral concern about the external World. It is not enough to put up to them something in which there is a profit; it must also be the kind of profit which, having at the moment the choice of all kinds of profits, they want to have. What they want to have is the preservation in Europe of the American way of life – which, of course, is the Western way.

...We ought to notice more what they are doing, and above all we ought to remember that the imaginative effort of the American people to understand the problems of other people is a test for them which they have met. They have a lot to learn, but since 1945 they have learned it every year, and they are now accepting reluctantly – who would not be reluctant – but freely, their responsibilities as the leaders of the English-speaking peoples, and they are ready to show, and are showing that, however painful it may be, they will take that responsibility.

All we can do is to notice the fact, to share our problems together, to forget to tell ourselves again what we did in 1940, and to remember what we have got to do in 1950, which is to share the same burdens with the Americans. They have much more power, but we have more power than we pretend to think we have; and I would rather see us over-stretching ourselves and taking more responsibilities than we have at the moment. I do not like saying, 'It is all over now, let us pass the burden to other people.' I would rather that we shared it and not, like elderly uncles, say that we have retired. I am sure we could contribute a great deal to the American solution for the World, and we must do so, because if we leave the Americans to themselves they will do extremely well, but they will lack a little in tact, and finally Europe will say, 'Of course, all this American dictation is all right, but...' If we share the burdens we shall not have to take the whole responsibility for American policy. We shall not have a bad conscience at having suddenly thrown up the sponge and said, 'We are too old, too poor, to do what we have done in the past.' Let us now give Europe a lead in the way of freedom and civilization, and also interpret the United States to Europe, which was done successfully in the past – and I think we can often do it better, if I may say so, than the Americans do for themselves.

****

The Case for Planned Mass Migration from Britain to the Dominions
By Squadron Leader W. J. Swift R.A.F. (1952).

...Other great nation and empires have existed; they have dominated their eras; but their epitaphs have been written. We must strive to avoid a verdict of history which might read:– 'Britain had her short period of power and glory. With her empire she possessed an abundance of economic and strategic resources, but she failed to make proper use of them. Her decline and fall can be traced to her refusal to face the realities of the time. In her death-throes she was magnificent, but her demise was nonetheless complete, utter, and final.'

...If we carry on as we have done during the first half of the XXth Century, not only a continual lowering of the standard of living, but complete economic collapse, is inevitable; that annihilation in war is possible; and that the only practical method of avoiding this dire fate is to embark on a scheme of planned mass migration from Britain to the Dominions.

...Britain has 50 million mouths to feed. Experts estimate that with the more advanced methods of farming, development of marginal land, and intensive use of fertilizers, only sufficient food can be home-produced to feed a maximum of 30 million people. The other 40 per cent of food requirements, together with many of the raw materials for industry, have to be imported. And they have to be paid for. However adverse the terms of trade, Britain must, therefore, export or perish.

****

Psychological Warfare
Based on two lectures to the RUSI by Mr. R.H.S. Crossman O.B.E., M.P. in February 1953 and July 1954.

...The accurate way of defining our problem is this. *What use should we make of propaganda in a period when the great Powers are pursuing* their policies by all means short of general war – including the means of small local wars? Or put it another way. How far can we use the techniques and the organization which we employed in general war, at a time when there is not a general war but only a number of small wars plus a struggle for power?

I would suggest to you that the whole idea that in such a period we could use psychological warfare is ruled out straight away for a very simple reason. There is no agreed policy between the democracies. We could not have had any psychological warfare during the war unless Britain and America had had an agreed policy. We could not have what is called a Western democratic psychological warfare offensive as long as the various nations of the West had no agreement on that at which they were aiming.

Of course, our opponents suffer under no such disadvantage! It is the definition of a totalitarian state that it behaves in periods of peace exactly as though it were at war, and it merely eschews the actual fighting for the reason that it thinks it can do better without it. The fact is that the Russian Communist State not only feels itself to be at war with the rest of the world, but its whole organization, internal and external, is that of a nation at war. Therefore, it has a simple overriding purpose – to win the war. The problem of the Western democracies is that one of their purposes at present is to avoid a war, and another one is to win a war if it comes. That means in effect not having one overriding purpose but two conflicting purposes. You cannot conduct a psychological warfare campaign if, not only between two Powers but inside one large Power, there is not a simple overriding aim but a conflict of aims.

Let me now set down my conclusions. My first is that in a cold war, as in a hot war, the major aim of our propaganda must remain to achieve credibility. Long before you try to demoralize, exdoctrinate, or indoctrinate, the first job is to be believed. It is no good having a most brilliant 'agitation' if you are not believed. That is the reason why the B.B.C. is still superior to the Voice of America; it confines itself to telling the truth as accurately as it can and thus makes itself a most valuable weapon.

(From 1954)

...So the way to carry out good propaganda is never to appear to be carrying it out at all. We discovered this in 1940, when we had nothing else to do but to tell the truth because we were being defeated so badly. I remember speaking to an American who was in Berlin in 1940 about the news which was being broadcast about the blitz. He said he turned his radio on to a British home station and heard a voice saying 'And now I will tell you about a series of talks which we shall be giving next December on the life of Charlotte Brontë'! The American told me that a little thing like that boosted morale more than all the propaganda in the world. The British BBC was planning a series of talks on the life of Charlotte Brontë when it was due to be wiped out the following week! That proved that Britain had not been defeated.

...In a cold war you also need to deduce the mood of the men who are in control on the other side. To understand their actions, taken to placate their public opinion, is of enormous value quite apart from any propaganda you may carry out. As for psychological warfare in the narrow sense, there is plenty of it to do in areas where the war is going on. Areas in which we can experiment are Malaya, Indo-China, and Korea. I hope that considerable sums of money and men of good enough calibre are being used in those areas, testing out the well-tried methods under new conditions and with new types of treatment. But let us in a period of cold war *confine psychological warfare to these areas*, and let us with regard to the remainder of our propaganda understand that unless we ourselves become totalitarian, it will be impossible to reply to Russia's psychological warfare with anything that corresponds to it. All we can do is to tell the truth, to build up credibility, to understand our purpose, and not to try the kind of technique which can only be used when actual fighting has begun.

...But one conclusion is definite. If our psychological warfare is to be effective, our Governments must know what they are trying to achieve with it, and must co-ordinate the official propaganda line with the unofficial anti-Cominform. This has now become a matter of the greatest urgency. I am sure that, as a result of the East German rising, the present *status quo* is untenable. The Germans in the Eastern Zone have been shown to be totally unreliable from a Russian point of view, and are likely to be unreliable again. Do our Governments want another East German rising, or do they not? And if one occurs unexpectedly, as the last one did, will it be possible once the West Germans have arms, to stand idly by while it is suppressed? These are the kind of awkward questions which the psychological warrior is bound to ask, and to which the Chiefs of Staff require an answer as much as they do.

****

The Council of Europe
A lecture to the RUSI by Mr. S.H.C. Woolrych O.B.E., UK Consul in Strasbourg and official lecturer for the Council of Europe, 6 October 1954.

...We now come to the question of what ought to be the attitude of the British to this Council of Europe. I can think of three good reasons for supporting it. First of all there are the political activities at Strasbourg which are bound to increase with time. If continental Prime Ministers and Foreign Ministers can go there and expound their countries' points of view, can we afford to do anything less ourselves?

Secondly, I think that Strasbourg will increasingly be an organization whose services will be looked to for settling European disputes....

Thirdly, there is the question of what will happen in the future on the continent of Europe. Sooner or later a group or *bloc* of Powers is bound to be formed, because these countries will not go on for ever dying on their feet and counting for less and less. We may, or may not, be able to join that group on account of our Commonwealth commitments, but surely it is a matter of life and death to us to be associated with it on terms of utmost co-operation and cordiality.

Then, finally, there is the matter of our European heritage, and we cannot go back on that, because in all the things that count for most in this world– the general standards of life, of education, things of the mind, and spiritual values – Europe is still supreme, and the civilization of Europe is still the civilization of the world. I think that Europe will continue to count as one of the great world factors so long as we decide to stick together. We have not found the right answer yet to European unity, but I do suggest that it is our duty to play our part, which must be a major part because we are the biggest member, in finding the right answer to this question of European unity.

****

Organization for War in Modern Times
A lecture to the RUSI by Field-Marshal The Viscount Montgomery of Alamein K.G., G.C.B., D.S.O., 12 October 1955.

...The nations of the Western Alliance are straining under defence budgets which are heavy and painful. Ahead lies a vista of ever-increasing Government expenditure and wage claims. In this Country, the battle against inflation is on. All nations are looking for ways and means of reducing defence budgets and, in the case of the bigger nations, the problem is rendered the more difficult in that they have to be prepared to fight two kinds of war, conventional and nuclear. In general, limited or small wars call for conventional weapons. But once war becomes unlimited and global, nuclear weapons would be used from the outset by both sides.

In war, offence and defence alternate. The attempt to create an adequate organization *for both* is becoming increasingly expensive. Where is the money to come from to provide all that is needed in this nuclear age?... I consider that we shall build up an adequate defence within the definite limits of economic possibilities only by making a completely new approach to the problem and by working on the principle of economy of force.

...What it amounts to is that there must be a new approach to the whole problem. But again we run head-on to a difficult problem. It is this. The keyword of the old world is tradition; the keyword of the modern world is progress. These two guiding principles are in direct opposition to each other. I hold the view that when the two meet, if a compromise cannot be found it is tradition that must give way. Only by so acting will the new approach be successful.

...I am quite certain about one thing. The more we mess about with old organizations designed for conditions that will not recur, the further we shall get from the right answer.

I now put it to you that the words 'win' or 'lose' no longer apply to contests between nations which have nuclear power of any magnitude. If attacked, our aim must be to impose our will on the enemy. But the price will be heavy.

I have been studying nuclear war for a considerable time and I have come to the conclusion that man will have it within his power in the future to destroy himself and every living thing in this planet. I do not believe this to be man's destiny. But we must face the facts *now*, or it will be.

War is not an act of God. War grows directly out of the things which individuals do or fail to do. It is, in fact, the consequence of national policies or lack of policies. Do not let us fail to do the right things now. Our aim must be to prevent war; the prospect of winning or losing is not a profitable subject. We must find another court of last resort for adjusting political differences.

****

The Alternative to the Nuclear Deterrent: Non-Violent Resistance
A lecture to the RUSI by Commander Sir Stephen King-Hall, 9 October 1957.

In August of this year, the Minister of Defence, then in Australia, made a statement about defence. He said that the Government had – I quote his words– taken 'a very bold step in deciding not to do the impossible.'

I think this is worth a moment's reflection.

Mr Sandys continued, 'We decided not to defend the whole country but to defend only our bomber bases. I must pay tribute to the people of Great Britain for the readiness with which they have accepted these harsh but inescapable facts.'

I submit that these statements could be rephrased as follows: 'There is no known method of defending the United Kingdom against H-bomb attack. We must concentrate our defences to defend our airfields, and what the public must realise is that whilst they are being incinerated – or very shortly afterwards if all goes well – a very large number of Russians will be in close pursuit to wherever your after-life may be.'

These facts are certainly harsh but are they inescapable? I daresay some of my audience came here expecting to hear a rather cranky series of proposals by someone who was possibly a moral pacifist. I respect but do not share the moral view of the pacifists. If a statement on my part that as a result of reflections about the nature of war which first took shape in about 1925 I have reached the conclusion that orthodox thinking about war, and hence defence, is radically wrong is to label myself a crank, then crank I am.

...War should not be thought of as merely military operations. But it usually is. Consequently military operations have become regarded as ends in themselves and not means to an end. Since about 1939 the idea that if there were no bangs we were 'at peace' has become so manifestly untrue that we have had to invent qualifying degrees of war, i.e. cold war, tepid war, hot war, political warfare, economic warfare. By 1965 we may be hearing something about non-violent warfare.

War is fundamentally a clash of ideas; the object of war is to change the enemy's mind and, either by persuasion or violence or a mixture of the two, cause him to abandon his ideas and accept ours. The clash of ideas now going on is between democracy and communist ideas. The object of our defence is to defend our ideas or way of life against this communist attack.

...Over and above this reinforcement of our conventional forces with tactical (so-called) nuclear weapons, we have the 'great deterrent' idea. It does not seem to be understood that with this idea we have moved military force into psychological warfare. We aim at creating a thought in the Russian mind which is that there is no point in mutual suicide. It does not matter theoretically whether we have an H-bomb or not, provided the Russians believe we have an H-bomb, and also believe that we, after they have wiped us out, can wipe them out and that even the advantage of a surprise attack on us would not save them and that their target is as vulnerable to an H-bomb as ours is. I hope and pray the Soviet leaders do believe all this. I suppose it is conceivable that they don't, or are we so infected with wishful thinking that we cannot, we dare not, admit that they can't believe it?

...The new idea which I think is worth looking into is that the United Kingdom should make an unilateral declaration that it will make no use of nuclear energy for military purposes. I have found that quite a lot of people say, 'That sounds rather attractive,' and I then discover that they have no idea of what they are letting themselves in for, Mr. Bevan, for example, who as recently as last May was, if I understood him right, in favour of the kind of idea I am suggesting being looked into, has had a peep and changed his mind rather smartly. What I am sure he has not done, and this goes for all our political leaders, is to bring himself to believe that if you look hard enough and long enough there is a new and unexpected field of defence beyond the frontiers of violence.

...Something dramatic and new has got to be done by someone to find and apply a new idea and shift the whole basis of the struggle from the dead-end of nuclear violence to the unlimited possibilities of the field of psychological operations. This new thing, this bound forward in defence thinking which I believe to be the logical next step from the fact that physical violence has reached its optimum, can only be undertaken by a nation sure of its destiny and accustomed to living up to Milton's words when he wrote: 'Let not England forget her precedence in teaching the nations how to live.'

****

Future Trends in Warfare
A lecture to the RUSI by Lieu.-General Sir John G. Cowley K.B.E., C.B., A.M., Controller of Munitions at the Ministry of Supply, 4 November 1959.

...To sum up my opinion about limited wars, I suggest that we should be able to send a force quickly to the aid of a friendly Power who invites our help. I believe that normally the British force would be a part of an Allied force. In any case, we must have the strategic mobility to arrive quickly. We should not become involved in a limited war where masses of enemy can be deployed against us. Our force should be equipped with conventional weapons, but also it should have available to it nuclear weapons, but with no intention of using them first. We should, however, have the ability to retaliate immediately with nuclear weapons once these had been used against us, realizing that from the moment these weapons were used, the whole nature of the fighting would change and our logistic system might be rapidly put out of action.

I come now to the most difficult war of all, the ultimate war between the United States and her allies on the one side and Russia and her satellites on the other. The prospect of such a war is so hideous that it must be clear to everybody that the main object is to prevent it ever happening. This leads me to the theory of the deterrent. The idea is that the Western Powers can deliver such a tremendous and immediate knock-out blow to any potential aggressor that such an aggressor is deterred from ever starting a major war. It is the old theory of the fear of the policeman deterring the criminal from committing a crime.

When considering the deterrent, one thing must be remembered. It is effective because of its existence and it ceases to be of any use to anybody once it is used; this a paradox worthy, I think, of Lewis Carroll. You will remember a delightful character represented by an old man sitting on a gate who had several provocative theories of life and who kept on being asked, 'Come tell me how you live and what it is you do?' He answered one of these questions by saying:

'I am thinking of a plan to turn my whiskers green,
and then to use so large a fan that they should not be seen.'

Another verse could be added:

'I also have a plan to spend a thousand million pounds,
To buy some guided missiles and to hide them in the ground,
And then to clearly paint on each 'these things must not be used,'
No wonder that our citizens are getting so confused.

The Deterrent and Disarmament
A lecture to the RUSI by The Hon. Alastair Buchan M.B.E., Director of the Institute for Strategic Studies, 1 February 1961.

...My purpose is to suggest that, in the modern age, any attempt to relegate the problems of strategy or national security, and the problems of disarmament or international security, to separate compartments of the mind, or departments of government, is not only misleading and potentially disastrous, but it is impossible.

...As far as the dangers of catalytic war or of escalation from limited conventional to strategic nuclear warfare are concerned, clearly the most dangerous aspect of continuous technological innovation is the steady cheapening of the processes involved in the production of nuclear weapons, and the clear danger that they will spread to other countries....Nor should this danger be considered solely in terms of nuclear weapons; chemical and biological weapons will become increasingly within the grasp of smaller countries as the years go by.

...For my part, I would like to see the Western Powers make a candid declaration to the world that, in the present state of international relations, total, or even far-reaching, measures of disarmament are incapable of fulfilment, but to couple this with a number of specific and imaginative proposals on arms stabilization. These the Soviet Union would find hard to resist, since in reality it is as deeply concerned with stabilization, and as unwilling to face the implications of a totally disarmed world, as we ourselves. But the time is past for generalizations, and unless we can rapidly apply the same kind of intellectual brilliance to the problem of stabilization that we now apply to the arms race, not only disarmament but peace itself may elude us.

****

Nuclear Deterrence after Nassau
By Marshal of the Royal Air Force Sir John Slessor G.C.B., D.S.O., M.C. Based on addresses to the NATO Defence College and published in 1963 and 1964.

...when we in NATO speak of war, we obviously mean war between two great Powers, or groups of Powers, which surely we can agree would be total and world-wide. And when we speak of war, do not let us confuse the issue by trying to break it down into nuclear or conventional war as though they were alternatives. There has lately been some recrudescence of the idea that another great war could be fought in what is described as a 'non-catastrophic' manner, by conventional forces alone.

I believe that to be a complete and dangerous fallacy. This is one of those areas where logic and statistics are no match for common sense and practical realism. I know, for instance, that Western Europe has more manpower and material resources than Russia; but that, with due respect to Mr. Dean Acheson, is really not the point. It is not a matter of what is *possible* but of what is practicable. Even if it were economically, politically, or socially practicable for the forces under SHAPE to match man for man, gun for gun, and tank for tank the Soviet-bloc forces that could be brought against them (and I do not consider that even desirable) I would still believe 'non-catastrophic' war to be a delusion. And to convince the Kremlin that they could conduct a conventional war on someone else's ground, without risk of nuclear retaliation on their own country, would be the surest way of bringing real war back into the picture.

...Actually, even if it were possible (which of course it is not) to scrap all nuclear weapons tomorrow, the progress of nuclear technology in recent years has been such that another great war, started with conventional weapons alone, could not last any appreciable time without nuclears finding their way back into the armouries of both sides. In the less unbelievable situation of a war starting with nuclear weapons on either side, even if they are limited and under strong control, I believe it still to be inconceivable that the use of anything more than short-range 'battlefield' nuclears could fail to escalate into all-out nuclear war. And I think it an important part of the deterrent policy to keep the potential aggressor convinced that that would be so.

Perhaps the most significant remark made by any statesman in the past decade was that by Khrushchev in his speech on 12 December, aimed at his Chinese friends: 'People who call imperialism a paper tiger,' he said, 'should remember that the paper tiger has nuclear teeth. It may still use them, and it should not be treated lightly.'

...The word 'independent' is another which seems to me urgently to need more precise definition. It seems that to some the independent character of a deterrent depends on whether all the hardware concerned is home-made; to others, upon the precise terms of some written agreement, which, we know from experience, does not always retain its validity in circumstances of critical emergency. To others it is a matter of national prestige. To me, the term independent nuclear deterrent – or, for that matter, European deterrent – is meaningless unless it implies that there could be circumstances in which the force could be used to strike at the heartland of an enemy (who in the European context could only be Russia) independently, by Britain or France or the two in combination, without the support and by implication even against the wishes of our allies – and particularly of the United States. I will make my position clear at once by admitting frankly that in my view such a thing is inconceivable.

Those who talk of our having to pull our nuclear force out of NATO and go it alone in some unspecified 'supreme national interest' surely overlook the fact that this idea postulates one of two assumptions. The first is that the Atlantic Alliance has already virtually disintegrated – in that event a few Polaris submarines or bomber squadrons would be neither here nor there. The second is that circumstances could arise somewhere outside Europe where we should feel it so important to undertake some military action in which the US would not support us against a consequential threat of attack by Russia, that we should feel it necessary deliberately to wreck the Alliance – because that in effect is what it would mean. Is that really a basis for a policy? The fact is that the only defence policy that can make any sense in this day and age is an Atlantic defence policy.

...The conclusions about nuclear deterrence that I personally draw from all this are two-fold. First, that what we rather misleadingly call strategic nuclear striking power must be supplemented by adequate tactical strength, on the ground and in the air, mainly but not exclusively conventional, that must be already on the spot, as in Europe, or can get there very quickly.

Secondly, that there is no such thing as nuclear independence, even for the United States. The Americans, spending as they do on their nuclear forces alone more than the total defence expenditure of all their NATO Allies put together, will inevitably always have the last word; that, whether we like it or not, is a fact of life which is merely silly to ignore. If some future Administration in Washington ever went crazy enough to force an all-out nuclear war with Russia against the express wishes of their Allies, there is nothing we could do about it; any idea that we could sit back as disinterested spectators of a nuclear battle between the two colossi going on over our heads is just plain silly. But I believe the chances of that are so remote as to be negligible; that fears of being dragged into a nuclear holocaust against our will by some 'John Birch' President are quite unrealistic.

I find it equally inconceivable that America could be dragged into nuclear war against her will by any of her European Allies. If the President of the United States refused to commit the might of America to war (and remember in the NATO context that involves the six American divisions and their powerful Tactical Air Forces in Europe) then there would be no war – again whether we like it or not. The theory that I have seen ventilated in France that the *Force de Frappe* could be used to trigger-off American nuclear power just does not make sense. On the other hand we need not be afraid of the US running out on their obligations to NATO, falling back on 'Fortress America', and leaving us to face a Russian threat by ourselves. I do not say that is inconceivable, but if it did happen it would involve for us in Europe a complete and fundamental re-orientation of our whole foreign and defence policy and stature – a few Polaris submarines or Mirage bombers would be neither here nor there. But I believe it to be in the highest degree improbable; Americans, in their enlightened self-interest, are keenly aware of the truth that the front line of their defence runs through Europe. And anyway the best means of averting that catastrophe is to make the unity and cohesion of the Alliance the first plank in the foreign policy of all of us, and not to go on telling the Americans that we do not trust them to stand by us if ever the chips go down.

...It is curious how often people seem to overlook the fact that this deterrent business is a two-way street. It may be that the Kremlin would be deterred by the threat of destruction of the western-most Russian cities and the loss of millions of Russian lives. Who can say? What does seem to me beyond any reasonable doubt is that the damage that one of us, Britain or France (or even both together), could inflict on Russia would be incomparably less than what Russia could inflict on us, on the highly concentrated, densely populated, and relatively small area of Britain and Western Europe. And I can never understand why anyone should assume that, if we are not deterred by the prospect of virtually complete obliteration, Russia would be deterred by the prospect of something far less cataclysmic.

****

Peacekeeping – A UN Commander's View
A lecture to the RUSI by Brigadier A.J. Wilson C.B.E., M.C. Formerly Acting Commander and Chief of Staff with the United Nations in Cyprus, 29 November 1967.

...In UN peacekeeping operations, as in other military operations, no situation is identical. The techniques and tactics, applicable in one area, will not necessarily prove valid elsewhere. There are, however, certain matters of principle which remain virtually unchanged wherever a peacekeeping force is deployed. In this lecture, therefore, I aim to cover some ideas which may help a senior officer going out to a UN operation for the first time, or who finds himself involved in the job of training troops for possible participation in peacekeeping.

...One of the main problems facing a UN commander is that the UN role requires qualities not normally developed by military training. This, by its nature, tends to make army officers quick to seek decisions and always to aim for firm and tidy solutions to the problems which beset them. In a peacekeeping operation, the problems which have called the force into being will seldom be susceptible to simple options. If a simple solution were possible, the UN force would never have been established in the first instance. It follows, therefore, that quite a different approach is necessary to peacekeeping problems, and the ordinary army officer involved in this sort of situation for the first time needs quickly and decisively to adjust many of his attitudes. I found in Cyprus that a Micawber-like approach to one's problems was not necessarily wrong; I also found that both the Greek and Turkish Cypriot parties to the dispute often made use of an inverted Micawber technique – waiting patiently to turn down any proposal put forward by the UN!

...The first and most immediate problem facing a senior officer in a UN force is that he will, as generally never before, find himself faced with an acute double loyalty. As a serving officer in his own country's armed forces, he will of course retain his normal loyalty towards his country of origin; at the same time, however, as member of a UN force, he will have an equal, if not overriding loyalty, to the United Nations Organization. Yet this division of loyalties is in principle little different to that facing a senior officer whose force forms part of an alliance like NATO or an allied combination of forces of the Second World War.

...Whatever its frustrations, peacekeeping is an experience not to be missed. The classically educated will be aware of the character in the Greek legend, Sisyphus. He was given the task of pushing a stone to the top of a hill, but whenever he got near the summit the perverse gods of Greek mythology used unfeelingly to direct the stone back again to the bottom of the hill. Perhaps peacekeeping is a little like this legend, but however daunting his experiences may have been, I am sure that Sisyphus's character was improved by his sufferings!

...I should perhaps end by saying a word about the United Nations Organization as a whole. It was, I think, Voltaire who said, 'If God did not exist it would be necessary to invent him'; this, I suggest, is also true of the United Nations Organization whatever its current failings. I believe the United Nations Organization will advance in skill and effectiveness as the nations of the world, and in particular the two Super powers, become more aware of the paramount need to live together in peace.

...The Secretary-General is fond of employing an analogy, first used by Adlai Stevenson, describing the UN as a mirror which accurately reflects international tensions and disagreements at any particular time. This is a good analogy and, like all good analogies, there is a lesson to be drawn from it. If, when you look in the mirror you do not like what you see, the remedy is to change the image and not to start by smashing the mirror. Whether one agrees or not, UNFICYP has surely carried out useful task by minimizing the effects of the Cyprus problem for the past four years. Those of all nations who have contributed to this partial success have, in my view, every right to be proud of their efforts.

****

NATO and Disaster Relief
By Hugh Hanning, Secretary for the International Committee of the Church of England, 1977.

...Nobody should deny that a primary need is for disaster-prone countries to organize and improve their own relief arrangements, in which context one would now like to see exercises being held as a matter of course, and preferably on an international scale. UNDRO has made a good start in holding training courses for officials of such countries. In practice, however, there is a limit to what these reforms can achieve. In general, local administration will be, by definition, in a state of shock, confusion and disarray. More bluntly, some national administrative machines are not exactly flawless even when there is no emergency.

A grouping of almost any four or five of NATO's members could revolutionise disaster relief operations providing one of them was Britain or the US, preferably both....

Aid from Atlantic Community?

The precise name and insignia of such a group would be a matter discussion. I have met hard-headed diplomats who vehemently con that it should proclaim itself loud and clear as a NATO group with N markings. Others say that this would limit its political accepta military aid may, after all, be acceptable – but what about aid military alliance? There is something in this; and perhaps the term Community should figure in the title.

But this should not be used in any apologetic sense. Th Community, up to now largely co-terminous with NATO, is very much larger concept, and one more suitable than NAT some of the challenges of the last quarter of the 20th century. Today, unlike 1949, the challenge to the West is bigger than the military threat of Russia to Europe, alarming though that threat remains. Within the rubric of *détente*, a battle of hearts and minds is now beginning between Communism and democracy; and the battleground is the Third World. The weapons may or may not include military hardware – opinions vary sharply on the wisdom of this; but they must certainly include every means of demonstrating to the developing countries the sincerity of the West's compassion and concern for their welfare. Hearts and minds is the name of the game inaugurated by *détente*; and in that context the Atlantic Community must now seek greater harmonisation of its policies in the civil as well as the military sphere. Disaster relief falls on the border-line between the two. It presents a challenge to the West to prove by its actions that its values are superior to those of Communism. We possess the capability in overwhelming measure. We now need to develop the will.

****

Limits upon Soviet Military Power
By Dr Keith A. Dunn, Strategic Studies Institute, US Army War College, 1979.

When Western analysts avoid discussing Soviet weaknesses and vulnerabilities they quite often double 'worst-case' the situation. On one hand, the Warsaw Pact is granted numerical superiority in weapons systems and personnel, which can be mobilised and introduced to the battlefield on short notice. On the other hand, Pact forces are not quantitatively or qualitatively reduced because of deficiencies while NATO forces are.

The point in this article is, however, that the Warsaw Pact does have weaknesses and vulnerabilities. NATO can exploit them, but some creative thought in this area is required. The threat analysis portion of NATO force posturing is, or should be, more than just the discreet cataloguing of an opponent's military capabilities and equipment inventories. The equation should also include Warsaw Pact shortcomings, if we want a more comprehensive assessment. To date this really has not been done.

...Why have Soviet vulnerabilities and weaknesses been neglected? While this is a difficult question to answer, it is possible to suggest three underlying assumptions which have contributed to the lack of analysis done in this area. First, the question becomes tangled in many analysts' minds with an old cliché: Intelligence can assess capabilities but not intentions and military commanders are primarily concerned with enemy capabilities because intentions can easily change. While it takes some very contorted logic to transpose vulnerabilities or weaknesses into intentions, it still occurs.

On a variety of occasions when the author was trying to obtain a grasp on the issue of Soviet military vulnerabilities and weaknesses, the point kept being raised that the US-NATO could not posture its forces on the basis of Warsaw Pact deficiencies because those problems could and would be corrected. That concept is true, but likewise Warsaw Pact capabilities, as well as NATO capabilities, change over time. The entire process is a dynamic one that is constantly changing and must continually be re-examined. The important issue, however, is that NATO should posture to nullify Warsaw Pact strengths and exploit weaknesses and vulnerabilities, not posture solely on the basis of Warsaw Pact strengths.

Second, traditionally, intelligence analysts have not been tasked to think in terms of Soviet vulnerabilities or weaknesses and how these limitations would affect Soviet capabilities to project its quantitatively awesome military power. If this area were to become an issue of prime consideration for decision makers, analysts would have to consider this topic if they had any pretensions of affecting US political-military decision making. Finally, in Western political systems, where the budgetary process and annual arguments before legislatures for defence appropriations often drive the military force structure, posture and size more than a potential adversary threat, it is extremely difficult for government bureaucrats to support the study of Soviet military vulnerabilities and weaknesses. A fear seems to exist that pointing out Soviet deficiencies will be interpreted as an attempt to describe the Soviet Union as impotent and lead to less spending of scarce NATO dollars for defence.

****

SALT II's Political Failure: The US Senate Debate
By Dr Robin Ranger, Associate Professor of Political Science, St Francis Xavier University, Nova Scotia, Canada, 1980.

The Soviet invasion of Afghanistan has apparently killed SALT II, proving, yet again, that arms control questions are, first and last, political not technical questions. This had, however, already been confirmed by the US Senate's move to reject ratification of SALT II for political reasons. These reasons need to be properly understood to appreciate the full impact of SALT II's failure and the collapse of *détente* which meant that President Carter's 28 January State of the Union Message, heralding a new Cold War, was following, not leading, the American Senate and public. The importance of the Senate's SALT II debate has been underestimated, because the surface debate on technicalities obscured the underlying political debate. For most Senators uncommitted on SALT II, the central issue was whether or not it was proper to approve this particular SALT II Treaty with a Soviet Union that was behaving the way it was – even before conquering and occupying Afghanistan.

However much the Carter Administration tried to reject this linkage argument, originated by Dr Kissinger, it would not go away. Ironically, the Administration's sincere commitment to arms control compounded this inability to answer the central questions of the propriety of dealing with the Soviet Union in the way represented by SALT II. The conventional wisdom of American arms control thinking has treated this as a self-contained, apolitical, technical exercise, whose political side effects, notably strengthening *détente*, are valuable, but still secondary. The Administration's SALT-sellers thus assumed that any objections to SALT II stemmed from a lack of understanding of the Treaty's technical merits, and so based their arguments on the logical merits of the Treaty within its four corners. Such an approach completely failed to address the gut-feelings of Senators, who were inclined to agree that, on balance, the US would be marginally better off militarily with SALT II than without it; but would be so much worse off politically that SALT II should not be approved, at least, not until the political questions it raised had been answered.

...None the less, the Senate's SALT II debate did show the way in which American policy is moving; towards a new hard-line, bipartisan, consensus, shaped by the Senate and the electorate, not by President Carter. The implications of this trend are most significant.

The effects of SALT II's demise will be profound, making arms control far more difficult to achieve in the 1980s than in the 1970s. Senate supporters of arms control and *détente* have had their basic assumptions about Soviet policies proved incorrect in the most damaging way possible, politically, whilst their critics have been proved correct, and will benefit politically. It will thus be extremely difficult to get, in the future, Senate support for arms control agreements, and probably impossible if these require Senate consent.

The Senate debate on SALT had already shown the extent to which the American body politic had been forced, by Soviet intransigence, to move towards a conservative, Hobbesian, Cold War view of American's role in the world. These trends have been dramatically reinforced by the Soviet invasion of Afghanistan. This will shape American, and Allied attitudes in the 1980s in the same way the Soviet-approved North Korean invasion of South Korea shaped attitudes in the early 1950s. The Senate Hearings on SALT II may, for future observers, mark the end of the road to *détente* and arms control that started in 1963. Above all, they should finally prove that arms control is a matter of politics, not technology. SALT II's fate was decided not by complex technicalities, but by armies marching across frontiers.

****

Defence and Security in the Nuclear Age
A lecture to the RUSI by The Rt. Hon. Sir Geoffrey Howe QC, MP, Secretary of State for Foreign and Commonwealth Affairs, 15 March 1985.

Arms control negotiations

...We warmly welcome the renewal of US Soviet talks. The joint *communiqué* agreed between them as the basis for the talks describes their aim as the prevention of an arms race in space and its termination on earth. We applaud and endorse that aim. There is no doubt however that progress will be painstaking and slow. We cannot expect sudden breakthroughs. In the words of Tolstoy's General Kutuzov, patience and time will have to be our watch words. There is no quick or easy route to success. Progress will be that much more difficult if we fail to establish a new basis for confidence and trust between the nations of East and West. This political process provides the framework within which arms control negotiations take place. If political relations are bad and mutual trust and confidence low, the possibility of making progress on arms control is reduced. All arms control agreements are based on a mixture of technical and political judgements. A broader range of contacts and a deeper understanding of either side's real concerns are an essential element in the process.

...Mr Gorbachev's recent visit to London, the Prime Minister's talks in Moscow with him earlier this week, my meetings with Mr Gromyko in 1984 and, I hope, later this year, represent part of our own contribution. We intend to continue this. In our contacts we have been frank about Soviet policies which cause us concern. But we have also made clear our understanding of Soviet security interests and concerns. We know that historical experience has inclined them towards over-insurance. But complete protection is not available to any country. The best that can be hoped for is a balance of capability matched by mutual confidence about intentions together, they should create greater stability and thus security. We are prepared to do the same. At the same time our efforts must not slacken in maintaining cohesion of the Alliance. The debate proved one thing at least. Alliance unity can not only enhance our security. It can provide a new incentive to our adversaries to meet us around the negotiating table. Geneva has shown that Russians have realised when the self-imposed policy of isolation was self-defeating.

But Allied cohesion must be sustained. We will need to continue the process of close consultation we have always enjoyed within NATO, and in bilateral meetings with our Allies, of which the Prime Minister's recent talks were an outstanding example. I know how much important our American friends attach to this process. It will be all the more important in the face of the concerted campaign we must expect from Moscow in the months to come. The Soviet leaders claim to be in earnest about arms control. The whole world must hope they are. But of one thing we can be certain. If they feel confident that they can attain their objectives without making the concessions necessary in any negotiations, they will not hesitate to see all the propaganda at their undoubted disposal. The more they are tempted to pursue their aims outside the negotiating room, the less serious they will be at the table. And if they can in the process split the Alliance, even if this means forfeiting an agreement, they may be tempted to rate this a greater prize. They tried on INF. And they failed. We can be sure they will try again. United as we have been so often in the past, the West must stand together. We cannot afford to fall divided.

****

Mikhail Gorbachev's Economic Reconstruction and Soviet Defence Policy
By Wing Commander R W Hooper, Winner of the RUSI's 1988 Trench Gascoigne Prize Essay Competition.

From Western analysts of Soviet affairs to members of the Politburo, there is wide agreement that the Soviet economy has stagnated and reached a crisis situation. Wide-ranging reforms have been called for and promoted by the Soviet President, Mikhail Gorbachev, using the slogan-like Russian words: *demokratizatsia* (democratisation), *uskoreniye* (acceleration), *glasnost* (speaking out publicly or openness) and *perestroika* (restructuring). Gorbachev is under no illusion as to the magnitude of these reforms while addressing other problems including internal unrest and his anti-alcohol and anti-corruption campaigns. There is also resistance to the reforms, fostered by a mixture of conservatism and disbelief, which can be summed up by a current Moscow jibe: 'Why is *perestroika* like a forest?', to which the answer is, 'Because at the top it is light and airy but down below all is dark and nothing moves'.

Besides this lack of credibility for the success of these reforms, there is the matter of how they are to be budgeted. Investment in the internal infrastructure will have to be paid for by economies elsewhere. Gorbachev has already curtailed Soviet foreign policy, but more particularly, to be examined here, Soviet defence policy may also be affected by the economic reconstruction....

A climate for disarmament

The future achievement of economic reconstruction in the USSR is linked very closely to the need to scale down Soviet military activity. Gorbachev has placated his military leadership, introduced the concept of reasonable sufficiency for a reduction in Soviet armed forces and placed renewed emphasis on a defensive military doctrine. On examination, there are both stated intent and precedence for unilateral and asymmetric multilateral disarmament by the Soviets to achieve reasonable sufficiency, and some unilateral cuts in troops and aircraft have been offered. Furthermore there are minor indicators that *perestroika* has begun to bite into Soviet military activity. However, while there have been aspirations for change, there has been no significant shift in actual Soviet defence policy nor an equally significant reduction in military activity.

Both Gorbachev and his Defence Minister Yazov have clearly made signs that change is possible. Furthermore, US President Bush needs to moderate his fiscal programme, particularly in defence, because of his budget deficit problems, and some European NATO nations are looking to lighten their defence burdens. The climate is therefore right for disarmament, particularly concerning conventional weapons....

The future

No one can predict how the CSCE talks will develop, but the signals from Gorbachev are unmistakable, and change in Soviet defence policy is tenable. However, Gorbachev writes in his book *Perestroika*, 'I shall not disclose any secret if I tell you that the Soviet Union is doing all that is necessary to maintain up-to-date and reliable defences'. We should take great note that he has a conflict of aims that require the maintenance of the USSR's military preparedness while introducing his *perestroika* reforms. His defence policy and *perestroika* are inextricably linked, and he needs to parallel these changes in the military with the disarmament process. As with the INF Treaty, there is a certain amount of lead from the Soviet Union on conventional disarmament through promises and a vigorous propaganda campaign. NATO should stand firm to bring about an effective and asymmetric reduction of Soviet forces by negotiation rather than by short-term reaction to unverifiable assurances. While on the one hand the prospects are exhilarating, NATO must maintain its guard during these heady days and throughout Gorbachev's skilful rhetoric.

****

The RUSI Annual Conference in 1989 'Defence and Security: Today's Challenges, Tomorrow's Responses' was staged on 18 May 1989 and was the scene of the first face to face meeting between the heads of the Warsaw Pact and NATO. The following are extracts from their presentations.

Soviet and Warsaw Pact Goals and Developments
A Lecture to the RUSI by Army General Petr G Lushev, Commander-in-Chief Joint Armed Forces of the Warsaw Pact.

I never really thought that I, as Commander-in-Chief of the Joint Armed Forces of the member states of the Warsaw Treaty Organisation, would have an opportunity to visit London – the capital city of a member country of the North Atlantic Alliance. Surely, this is evidence of the new political thinking which is beginning to reach military leaders as well. I will not conceal the fact that it is something that does not come too easily for us military men. Diplomats, scholars, scientists and political leaders find it easier to readjust more quickly. But I am confident that direct contacts between military leaders of the two alliances will ultimately become the norm.

Unfortunately, the development of political and military thinking has lagged far behind the realities of the present-day world for a long time. Admittedly, in recent years there has been a tendency for that gap to narrow. And in this an invaluable role is played by summit level dialogue between the leaders of states with different socio-political systems. General Secretary Gorbachev's meetings with Mrs Thatcher and the leaders of other Western countries are creating the political conditions necessary for shaping a new model of security – one which is mutual and indivisible, one which is based on lowering the level of military confrontation. We see emerging before our very eyes a new political reality – a turnaround from the principle of superarmament towards the principle of defence sufficiency. It should be said that the role of taking the initiative in this process should not belong to the socialist states alone. But the advance of the new political thinking and its first practical results, in our view, are not due to pressure exerted on other countries, nor to concessions of one kind or another, but to the fact that the new thinking is based on realities; it matches realities and draws the strength of its arguments from realities.

...The activities of the Warsaw Treaty member countries in the field of defence are based on the principles of the new political thinking. It should be emphasised that the new political thinking involves not only profound theoretical conclusions about present-day realities, but also serves as guidance for practical actions. Above all, mention should be made of the new concept of security which has determined the main areas of the development of the Warsaw Treaty Organization's defence policy. Underlying this concept is the idea that security can only be equal and indivisible and that any attempts to create a unilateral 'margin of safety' lead only to an increase in the level of armaments and the threat of war. And, there is a second conclusion that stems from this – namely that security in today's world can be ensured not by stepping up military confrontation but only by lowering it.

...What is new and most important here is the fact that whereas military doctrine was previously defined as a system of views on preparing for a possible war and on how to fight it, the key point in the definition now is the prevention of war. The task of preventing war is becoming the highest goal, the nucleus of our military doctrine and the main function of our states and their joint Armed Forces....

NATO's nuclear argument

Today NATO is trying to justify the need for keeping nuclear weapons in its arsenals by invoking Warsaw Pact superiority in conventional weapons. However, these arguments are taken care of by the unilateral reductions of the Warsaw Pact armed forces, and by their willingness to negotiate the elimination of imbalances. In the not too distant future the problem of tactical nuclear systems may act as a major constraint on the Vienna talks unless it is resolved now.

It is clear that with deep cutbacks in conventional armed forces, the threat posed by tactical nuclear weapons will grow. It is well-known that NATO envisages the possibility of early use of nuclear weapons, and the level at which a decision to that effect may be taken in a crisis situation may be substantially lowered. As a result, any mistake, ambiguous situation or tension, is fraught with the danger of nuclear catastrophe.

Unquestionably, the present level of military equilibrium of the two sides is much too high. A further increase in it will lead only to a greater danger of war and not to its prevention. It is becoming increasingly obvious that in present-day conditions true security can be ensured only by political means, on the basis of equality and reciprocity, openness and *glasnost* in the military field, on the basis of both sides using the principle of reasonable sufficiency for defence and of lowering the threshold of military confrontation to the greatest extent possible. To that end, it is in our view essential to broaden the East-West dialogue in every possible way, to negotiate, to break down the barriers of prejudice and stereotypes and to find mutual understanding.

...In closing, I would like to say once again that peaceful coexistence of states with different social systems in present-day conditions, and a transition to openness in political and military affairs, is the only possible path leading to confidence-building and, accordingly, to ensuring security for our nations and peoples. We must find in ourselves the resolve to proceed further along this path.

A Strategy for the Future
A Lecture to the RUSI by General John Galvin, Supreme Allied Commander Europe, North Atlantic Treaty Organization.

All day long I have been adjusting my speech. It now bears little resemblance to what I was planning to say. I'm going to try to mix the questions of strategy and arms control because, at this moment, I think that strategy is inextricably linked with arms control. I want to use a technique that I have not used in the past. I would like to frame my talk and concentrate on issues that, if General Lushev and I had an official working session, I would have discussed or tried to discuss with him. In that sense, the subtitle for my presentation might be 'Areas of Questions and Concern', for, despite all the progress that has been made in East-West relations over the past year or two, I do have some concerns.

...Reducing the overall capability for offensive war may be the best way to approach 'defensive defence'. I have seen a dozen versions of this concept, but I still don't understand what it is. I don't understand what it means. If it means no more mobility, I'm not sure that is any defence. I think we might be able to approach it from a different point. Let's think about what is 'offensive offence', and eliminate that; then maybe we'll end up with defensive defence.

...The questions I would ask General Lushev follow from these concerns. Can we remove or reduce the operational manoeuvre groups? And some of the *Spetznaz*? And some of the airborne forces? Can we actually slow or stop the production of armament; especially the ground-gaining armament? If so, can we see some kind of schedule? You would have thought President Gorbachev could have said – two or three years ago – 'Why do we really need to produce 3000 tanks a year? Why don't we produce 2000? How about 1500? The other side produces less than 1000. What are we doing making 3000?'. That seems to me, at least, a logical question to ask. Maybe there's a good logical answer also.

Can we remove some of the forward based supplies? Can we dismantle some command and control and logistical infrastructure? Can we get a better chance to observe even unilateral reductions when they take place right now? Tanks are moving eastward but new tanks are also being produced and moving westward. Does this simply mean that T-72s and T-80s will continue to be manufactured while the reductions that take place will be T-54s and T-55s? In the end, after three of four years, or by 1997, will the whole Soviet force be T-80s and T-72s? Would you be willing to recognize these problems I have of geographical disparity? Could we talk about how to deal with that? Could we discuss, some more, this question of overall modernization? You have said that we should not modernize the missile – the Follow-on to Lance. Does it mean in the end we should not modernize anything? Thirty years from now should we still have the same equipment that we have now? Or should we say that under the reductions, modernization should go ahead? Frankly, we think that the capability to continue with technological progress is vitally important to us not only in the military sense but in all senses.

I would also be willing to listen to the same kind of questions from you, General Lushev. I know that you have concerns which have to be as deep as mine and things that worry you. I'm saying this to you symbolically, of course, because I think this meeting today in which you and I have come together is something of a symbol. I hope that we will continue to push toward parity – a true parity of capabilities. We should recognize that numbers are only numbers and that the so called 'bean count' is a superficial way of looking at the military balance. I also recognize that in the end something has to be reduced and that it has to be counted. But in the meantime, there are many other considerations.

Conclusion

Let me end by saying that NATO is more than a coalition for collective security. It is a sharing of the same values of democracy, liberty, justice, human rights, self-determination and all the principles that we stand for and have enjoyed together. Let me also say a word about my counterpart. I have admired, General, the way that you have come for the first time to London – not only wondering what your counterpart might be like but also wondering what the press conference would be like, and from all that we can see that you handled all that very very well. It shows, again, your patience and fortitude. I think it was good that we had this opportunity to get together. I would also close by thanking the Institute for setting all of this up. I believe that it has been something very significant and very special.

Index

Abyssinia 61
Adenauer, Konrad 2, 18, 38, 129
Adjustment of Alliance Structures and Procedures 83, 86–8
Afghanistan 19, 232–3
Africa 19, 62–4, 100, 123, 131, 137, 212
Algeria 100
Alphand, Hervè 189
arms control 6, 81, 83, 85–6, 93, 100, 112–13, 232–5, 240
Asia 137, 143, 166
Atlantic Alliance 7, 39, 97, 190, 225
  see also NATO
Atlantic Charter xii
Auriol, Vincent 185, 189
Australia 52, 62
Austria 27, 50, 61

Balkans 74, 93, 100, 102, 105, 108, 124–5, 136, 140
  see also Yugoslavia
Baltic States 160, 173
Beck, General 178–9
Belgium 62, 78
Benelux countries 9, 190, 192
  see also specific countries
Berlin crisis 6, 18, 78, 97, 108, 110, 190
Berlin Wall 6, 72, 73, 130
  fall of 7, 25, 95–6, 99, 113, 129, 135, 203, 204
Bevan, Aneurin 221
Bevin, Ernest 18, 108–9
Bidault, Georges 184, 185, 191, 192
Blum, Leon 184

Bonaparte, Napoleon 53, 54, 55, 62, 69, 107, 125
Borneo 111
Bosnia 102, 114, 115, 116
Bousquet, René 183
Brezhnev, Leonid 21
Briand, Aristide 187
Britain xviii, 2–3, 4, 21, 107, 183, 214, 215
  and Council of Europe 217–18
  and European Union 26, 117
  and Sweden 194–5, 201
  armed services 28, 108, 111–14, 115, 128, 207–8
  British zone in Germany 204–5
  in WWII 61–7, 126–7, 158, 167, 181, 188, 216
  maritime heritage xv, 43–57, 67–9
  WWI 57–60
  WWII 61–7
  nuclear weapons 122, 124, 155,156, 157, 159, 161, 219–22, 225
  relationship with France 9, 44, 46–55, 61, 109, 121, 127–8
  relationship with Soviet Union 17, 78–9, 147–8, 152, 153, 163–4, 165–6, 188, 220–1
  relationship with USA 21, 51–2, 56
Brooke, Sir Alan xii, xix, 154
Brussels Treaty (1948) 78–9, 109, 128, 190, 191
Bulgaria 109
Burma 64
Bush, George 18, 236
Byrnes, James F. 38

242

Index

Callaghan, James 18
Cambodia 115
Canada 49, 50, 62, 79, 92, 93, 190
Carter, President Jimmy 232–3
Ceausescu, Nicolae xvii, 138, 144
Central Europe xiv, xvii, 13, 14, 25, 70, 74, 76, 78, 100
   and European Union 131, 136
   and NATO xvi, 80, 82, 83–5, 92, 94, 101, 104, 131, 136
   see also specific countries
Ceylon 212
Charlemagne xiv, 2
Chechenya xiv–xv, 10, 100, 168
China 24, 28, 56, 57, 166
Christopher, Warren 103
Churchill, Winston xii, xviii, xix, 2, 16, 34, 66, 67, 96, 109, 112, 146, 166, 183
   and united Europe 98, 191
   iron curtain speech xii, 153, 187
Claes, Willy 89
CMEA (Comecon) 73
Cold War xiv, 21, 67, 108–9, 151–3, 187, 204, 214, 216, 233
   Europe and 5–8, 12, 116, 189
   NATO and xvi, 79–80, 109, 113, 114
Combined Joint Task Forces (CJTF) 86–7, 92, 100, 104–5, 116
Cominform, the 189, 216
Common Agricultural Policy 13
communism 2, 106, 166, 230
   fall of 7, 96, 99, 105, 143
   in East Germany 113, 129–30
   in Eastern Europe xvii, 18, 134, 136, 137, 138, 142–4, 188–9, 211
   in France 183–4
   in Soviet Union 78, 97, 172, 187
Conference on International Organization xii
Conference on Security and Cooperation in Europe (CSCE) 23, 76, 93, 236
   see also Organization for Security and Cooperation in Europe (OSCE)
Conventional Forces in Europe Treaty 13, 93
Council of Europe xvi, 70, 72, 75, 191–2, 217–18
Countering Proliferation of Weapons of Mass Destruction 83, 85–6, 100
Crete 62–3
Cuba 165
Cyprus 227–9
Czech Republic 24, 136, 142
Czechoslovakia 6, 19, 61, 70, 78, 97, 133, 138, 177, 187

Daladier, Edouard 184
de Gaulle, General xviii, 2–3, 9, 10, 18, 79, 129, 182, 183–5
Denmark 26, 79, 164, 187, 192, 202
deterrence xii–xiii, 6, 68, 79–80, 81, 88, 103, 105, 106, 112, 122, 123, 219–21, 222–7
disarmament 20, 61, 75, 141, 223, 236–7
Dunkirk Treaty 109, 190
Duverger, Maurice 192–3

East Germany 95, 130, 138, 216–17
Eastern Europe xiv, xvi, 10, 36, 39, 70, 74, 76, 78, 100, 119, 127, 145
   and defence xv, 13, 14, 23, 24, 80, 82, 83–5, 89, 92, 94, 100, 104, 131, 134, 140–1
   and European Union 26–7, 131, 134, 136–7
   communism in xvii, 18, 134, 136, 137, 138, 142–4, 188–9, 211
   Soviet Union and 5, 9, 18–19, 35, 133, 138–9, 153, 160–1, 162, 188–9
   see also specific countries

Ebert, Friedrich 173
European Free Trade Organization
    (EFTA) 27
Egypt 54, 57, 58, 62, 63, 68
Eisenhower, Dwight 18
Elser, Georg 175
environmental degradation 11–12, 75
Ethiopia 61
ethnic conflict 3, 100, 126, 139–40
EURATOM 3
European Coal and Steel Community
    xiv, 2, 3–4, 7, 8, 192–3
European Community xv, 12, 13,
    19, 39, 128
European Defence Community 8, 11
European Economic Community
    3–4, 7, 9
European Federalists' Union 188
European Recovery Programme
    189–90
European Security and Defence
    Identity (ESDI) 92, 104
European Union 11, 116–17, 120,
    121, 203
  and Eastern Europe 26–7, 131,
    134, 136–7
  future of 25–8

Falklands War 69
Far East 4, 53, 64, 111, 164, 166
Fedorov, Colonel P. 161
Finland 27, 131, 199–200, 202
France xviii, 2–3, 4, 10, 68, 78,
    107, 113, 123, 125, 131
  and NATO 20–1, 79, 98
  communism in 183–4
  devastated state after war xviii,
    3, 182
  in WWII 62, 128, 176, 182, 185–6
  nationalization 182–3
  nuclear weapons 122, 124
  relationship with Britain 9, 44,
    46–55, 61, 109, 121, 127–8
  relationship with Germany 8–9,
    11, 13, 25, 26, 38, 57–8,
    127–9, 181, 185–6, 192
  relationship with Soviet Union
    21, 188–9
  Resistance 183, 185, 187–8

Germans 16–17, 29–30, 36–42,
    74, 126, 172
  and genocide of Jews xv, 30–3,
    39, 174, 176
  see also Germany
Germany 1, 2–3, 10, 99, 117,
    192
  and the Jews 30–3, 39, 174, 176
  division after WWII 110–11,
    113, 127, 204–6, 207
  in WWI 58–60, 109, 172
  in WWII 17, 34–6, 61–7, 109,
    126–8, 148–9, 154, 158,
    159, 161, 166, 167, 176–7,
    180, 194, 196, 201–2, 206
  power of a united xiv, 4, 11, 25,
    26, 73–4, 108, 132
  re-armament 8, 128, 175
  relationship with France 8–9,
    11, 13, 25, 26, 38, 57–8,
    127–9, 181, 185–6, 192
  relationship with Soviet Union
    40, 130, 152, 153, 177, 208
  relationship with Sweden in
    WWII 194–202
  resistance xviii, 175–81, 187
  reunification 21, 73–4, 113,
    129–31, 135
  Soviet occupation forces in 160,
    161, 162
  Weimar Republic 172–4
  see also Germans
Gibraltar 48
glasnost 161, 235
Goebbels, Joseph 197
Goerdeler, Carl 178, 181

Index

Gorbachev, Mikhail 7, 40, 234, 235–7, 240
Grant, General Ulysses S. 114
Greece 35, 56, 62, 78, 79, 97, 98, 131
Gromyko, Andrei 234
Gulf War 13, 21, 22, 69, 123
Günther, Christian 197

Haiti 22
Hansson, Per Albin 196
Harriman, William Averell 146
Healey, Denis 115
Heath, Edward 18
Hempel, Bishop 40
Herriot, Édouard 184
Hindenburg, Field Marshal von 173, 174
Hitler, Adolf 34, 35, 61, 62–3, 69, 110, 133, 172, 173–81, 194, 199
  assassination attempts 175, 176, 179–80
  hatred of Jews 32, 42, 174
Holland 3, 46–8, 53, 54, 62, 78, 103, 132, 187
Honecker, Eric 130
Howard, Sir Michael 127–8, 129
human rights 11, 71, 72, 78, 93, 135, 137, 192, 241
Hungary 6, 19, 70, 136, 138

Iceland 79
India 46, 51, 53, 54, 56, 62, 152, 165–6, 212
INF Treaty 113, 235, 236
International Committee for the Coordination of Movements for European Unity 191
Ireland 47, 54, 191, 194
Iron Curtain xii, 71, 80, 99, 153, 187, 202, 206–7
Israel 37, 39, 68, 133
Italy 79, 123, 187, 191, 192, 199
  in WWII 61–4

Japan 24, 166
  in WWII 64–5, 67, 126, 127, 154–7
Jews, genocide of xv, 30–3, 39, 174, 176
John Paul II, Pope xvi, 76–7

Kapitsa, Peter 155
Kennedy, John F. 6
Khrushchev, Nikita 224
Kissinger, Henry 232
Kohl, Helmut 25
Korean War 5, 68, 108, 110, 166, 216
Korolev, Sergei 160

Laval, Pierre 183
League of Nations 61, 109, 120, 187, 208
Lenin, Vladimir Ilyich 172
Libya 123
living standards 75, 135, 136, 137, 212
Lushev, General 239–41
Luxembourg 78

Maastricht Treaty 10, 12, 26–7, 83, 119, 121, 123–4
Macmillan, Harold 2, 18
Malaya 64, 207, 216
Malenkov, Georgiy 163
Malraux, André 184
Malta 63–4
Mao Tse-Tung 166
Marshall, General George C. 97, 99–100, 189
Marshall Aid 5, 7, 97, 189, 212
Martel, Lieutenant General Sir Giffard 147
Middle East 39, 165
Mitterand, President François 18, 120, 122
Moldova xiv–xv, 10
Molotov, Vyacheslav Mikhailovich 109, 155, 164, 189
Monnet, Jean 3, 25, 38, 142
Movement for a United Europe 188
Mussolini, Benito 61, 62, 199

Nasser, President 68
National People's Army (NVA) 129–30
nationalism xiv–xv, 8–10, 34, 120, 125, 139, 187
Nazis 17, 30, 35, 73, 127, 133, 174, 177, 178, 187, 188, 205–6
New International Teams 188
New Zealand 52, 56, 62
North Atlantic Cooperation Council 14, 82, 86, 94
North Atlantic Treaty (1949) 79, 81, 85, 86–7, 91–2, 105, 109–10
North Atlantic Treaty Organization (NATO)
   and Soviet Union 6, 20–1
   and Yugoslavia 82, 86, 88–90, 92, 101–2, 106, 131, 134
   Britain and 9
   Central Europe and xvi, 82, 83–5, 92, 94, 101, 104, 131, 136
   conception of xii, 5, 18–19, 97–8, 109–11, 162
   disaster relief 229–30
   Eastern Europe and xv, 24, 82, 83–5, 89, 92, 94, 100, 104, 131, 134
   France and 20–1, 79, 98
   future of 11–14, 23–4, 90–3, 105–6, 117, 120–1, 125, 236–7, 239–41
   Germany joins 8
   in the Cold War xvi, 79–80, 109, 113, 114
   new peacekeeping role 81–2, 87–90, 101, 116
   nuclear strategy 19–20, 24, 79–80, 83, 85–6, 98, 101, 223, 225–6, 238–9
   specific initiatives from Brussels summit (1994) 83–8, 100, 103–5
   strategic concept 80–1, 82, 90, 100
   Sweden and 202–3
   USA and 14, 79, 92, 93, 95–101, 104–6, 109–11, 114, 116, 128, 225–6, 229–31, 234

Norway 27, 45, 62, 78, 79, 187, 192, 196, 199, 200, 202
nuclear war 18–19, 146, 218–19, 223–4, 226
nuclear weapons xvii, 5–6, 100, 112–13, 120, 122, 134, 149
   and NATO 19–20, 24, 79–80, 83, 85–6, 98, 101, 223, 225–6, 238–9
   Britain 122, 124, 155, 156, 157, 159, 161, 219–22, 225
   France 122, 124
   Soviet Union xvii, 19–20, 100, 146, 149, 153–60, 161, 162, 163, 167, 190, 224, 226–7
   USA 6, 19, 24, 79, 122, 124, 154, 156–8, 159, 161, 163, 225–6

Organization for Economic Cooperation and Development (OECD) 190
Organization for European Economic Cooperation (OEEC) 7, 189–90
Organization for Security and Co-operation in Europe (OSCE) 11, 13, 14, 83, 86, 93, 116, 120, 121, 136
   see also Conference on Security and Cooperation in Europe (CSCE)

Pakistan 165–6
Partnership for Peace 14, 24, 83–5, 100, 103–5
perestroika 235, 236
Perry, William 98
Pétain, Henri 183
Philip, André 188
Philippines 51, 64
Pleven, René 185
Pokrovskiy, Major-General G. 158
Poland 138, 144, 160, 206
   and NATO 24, 103, 133, 136
   in WWII 31, 37, 187

Index

invaded by Germany 34, 61, 109, 194
joins Council of Europe xvi, 70–7
Portugal 4, 44–5, 55, 79, 194
Potsdam 154, 183
Prussia 50, 58

Ramadier, Paul 189
Riou, Gaston 187
Romania xvii, 109, 133, 136–9, 141–5, 188
Roosevelt, President Franklin D. xii, xix
Russia 11, 14, 22, 23–4, 28, 50, 55, 56–7, 58, 100–1, 107, 134, 148
and NATO 103, 104, 131
Rwanda 115

Saddam Hussein 21, 69
SALT 11 232–3
Sandys, Duncan 219
Schmidt, Helmut 18
Scholl, Hans 176
Scholl, Sophie 176
Schuman, Robert xiv, 3–4, 38, 192
Security Council 22, 88, 101–2, 109, 114, 156
security structures xv, 4, 8, 9, 11–14, 18, 79–83, 119–21, 136, 140
four pillars of 121–5
see also NATO
Seraev, General 210
Sicily 63, 64
Singapore 65
Slovak Republic 136
Socialist Movement for a United States of Europe 188–9
Sokolovskiy, Marshal 161
Solzhenitsyn, Aleksandr 168
Somalia 22
Soustelle, Jacques 184
South Africa 57, 62, 212
sovereignty 9, 78, 191

Soviet Union
and Eastern Europe 5, 9, 18–19, 35, 133, 138–9, 153, 160–1, 162, 188–9
builds up navy 67–8, 162, 163–5
conventional forces 160–3, 210–11
defence policy 223, 230–1, 235–7
dissolution of xiv, xv, xvii–xviii, 7, 8, 19–21, 23, 25, 27–8, 31, 74, 80, 135, 136, 203
economic reconstruction 235–7
expansionist policies xvii, 5, 18, 78, 97, 128, 152–3, 164–6, 187, 232–3
in WWII xvii, 3, 66–7, 126, 146–51, 154, 157, 159, 161, 166–8, 176
nuclear weapons xvii, 19–20, 100, 146, 149, 153–60, 161, 162, 163, 167, 190, 224, 226–7
relationship with Britain 17, 78–9, 147–8, 152, 153, 163–4, 165–6, 188, 220–1
relationship with France 21, 188–9
relationship with Germany 34, 40, 130, 152, 153, 177, 208
relationship with USA 5–7, 11, 17, 19, 110, 112–13, 147, 151–3, 161, 165, 166, 233–5
Spain 44–6, 47–9, 51, 53, 54, 55, 79, 99, 194
Stalin, Joseph xii, 5, 7, 17–18, 110, 138, 146, 149, 151, 162, 166, 172
and the atomic bomb 153–4, 157, 160, 163
Stauffenberg, Count von 176, 179–80
Strategic Defence Initiative 7
Suez Canal 61, 63, 68, 69, 98
Suez crisis 6, 68, 98
Svechin, Aleksandr 146–7
Sweden xviii, 27, 192
and Britian 194–5, 201
neutrality in WWII 194–202
after war 202–3
Switzerland 194

Tatarchenko, Major-General E. 156, 157
Thatcher, Margaret 234, 237
Third World 143, 230
Thomsen, Dr. Hans 199
Thorez, Maurice 183
Tito, Marshal 21, 206
totalitarianism 71, 97, 98, 108, 215
transatlantic relationship xv, 96–9, 106, 116, 117
  see also NATO
Treaty of Rome 3–4, 10
Treaty of Versailles xviii, 61, 172, 173
Truman, President Harry 5, 97, 100, 108, 110, 154, 189
Truman Doctrine 1947/8 5, 108
Turkey 52, 54, 56–7, 58–9, 78, 79, 97, 98, 119, 131, 165, 194

United Nations xii, 28, 68, 69, 78, 79, 81, 104, 116, 120, 126, 152
  and Yugoslavia 22, 86, 89, 101–2
  peacekeeping operations 227–9
  Security Council 22, 88, 101–2, 109, 114, 156
United States of America
  aid from xviii, 5, 7, 38, 97, 117, 147, 182, 189, 212
  and Europe 1, 7–8, 12, 14, 20–5, 34, 95–100, 116, 122, 128–9, 131–2, 136, 140, 162, 190, 209, 212–14, 226
  and NATO 14, 79, 92, 93, 95–101, 104–6, 109–11, 114, 116, 128, 225–6, 229–31, 234
  and SALT II 232–3
  in WWI 60, 96, 108
  in WWII xii, 3, 64–5, 67, 96, 98, 108, 167, 181, 188, 216
  Korean War 68

nuclear weapons 6, 19, 24, 79, 122, 124, 154, 156–8, 159, 161, 163, 225–6
  relationship with Britain 21, 51–2, 56
  relationship with Soviet Union 5–7, 11, 17, 19, 110, 112–13, 147, 151–3, 161, 165, 166, 233–5
Urquhart, Sir Brian 22

Vandenberg, Arthur 110
Vietnam War 111–12, 115

Warsaw Pact 6, 80, 93, 104, 110, 113, 230–1, 237–9
Wavell, General 62, 63
Wellington, Duke of 55–6, 68
West Germany 8, 35, 38–9, 79, 95, 192, 207, 217
Western European Union (WEU) 8, 11, 13, 14, 83, 86, 88, 92, 102, 104, 105, 119, 120–1, 125, 190, 191, 208–10
Wied, Prinz von 197
World War I, 18, 34, 115, 117, 128
  and Britain's maritime heritage 57–60
  Germany in 58–60, 109, 172
  USA in 60, 96, 108

Yalta xii, xvi, 70, 71, 126, 127, 130, 131, 188
Yeltsin, Boris 116
Yugoslavia
  break up of 21, 140
  in WWII 187, 206–7
  nationalism xiv–xv, 10
  NATO and 82, 86, 88–90, 92, 101–2, 106, 131, 134
  OSCE and 13
  UN and 22, 86, 88, 89, 101–2